Hacking Hybrid Media

Oxford Studies in Digital Politics

Founder and Series Editor: Andrew Chadwick, Professor of Political Communication and Director of the Online Civic Culture Centre (O3C) in the Department of Communication and Media, Loughborough University

Apostles of Certainty: Data Journalism and the Politics of Doubt
C. W. Anderson

Using Technology, Building Democracy: Digital Campaigning and the Construction of Citizenship
Jessica Baldwin-Philippi

Expect Us: Online Communities and Political Mobilization
Jessica L. Beyer

If . . . Then: Algorithmic Power and Politics
Taina Bucher

The Hybrid Media System: Politics and Power
Andrew Chadwick

News and Democratic Citizens in the Mobile Era
Johanna Dunaway and Kathleen Searles

The Fifth Estate: The Power Shift of the Digital Age
William H. Dutton

The Only Constant Is Change: Technology, Political Communication, and Innovation over Time
Ben Epstein

Designing for Democracy: How to Build Community in Digital Environments
Jennifer Forestal

Directed Digital Dissidence in Autocracies: How China Wins Online
Jason Gainous, Rongbin Han, Andrew W. MacDonald, and Kevin M. Wagner

Tweeting to Power: The Social Media Revolution in American Politics
Jason Gainous and Kevin M. Wagner

When the Nerds Go Marching In: How Digital Technology Moved from the Margins to the Mainstream of Political Campaigns
Rachel K. Gibson

The Politics of Platform Regulation: How Governments Shape Online Content Moderation
Robert Gorwa

Trolling Ourselves to Death: Democracy in the Age of Social Media
Jason Hannan

Risk and Hyperconnectivity: Media and Memories of Neoliberalism
Andrew Hoskins and John Tulloch

Democracy's Fourth Wave? Digital Media and the Arab Spring
Philip N. Howard and Muzammil M. Hussain

The Digital Origins of Dictatorship and Democracy: Information Technology and Political Islam
Philip N. Howard

Analytic Activism: Digital Listening and the New Political Strategy
David Karpf

The MoveOn Effect: The Unexpected Transformation of American Political Advocacy
David Karpf

News Nerds: Institutional Change in Journalism
Allie Kosterich

Prototype Politics: Technology-Intensive Campaigning and the Data of Democracy
Daniel Kreiss

Taking Our Country Back: The Crafting of Networked Politics from Howard Dean to Barack Obama
Daniel Kreiss

Media and Protest Logics in the Digital Era: The Umbrella Movement in Hong Kong
Francis L. F. Lee and Joseph M. Chan

Bits and Atoms: Information and Communication Technology in Areas of Limited Statehood
Steven Livingston and Gregor Walter-Drop

Digital Feminist Activism: Girls and Women Fight Back against Rape Culture
Kaitlynn Mendes, Jessica Ringrose, and Jessalynn Keller

Digital Cities: The Internet and the Geography of Opportunity
Karen Mossberger, Caroline J. Tolbert, and William W. Franko

The Power of Platforms: Shaping Media and Society
Rasmus Kleis Nielsen and Sarah Anne Ganter

Revolution Stalled: The Political Limits of the Internet in the Post-Soviet Sphere
Sarah Oates

Disruptive Power: The Crisis of the State in the Digital Age
Taylor Owen

Affective Publics: Sentiment, Technology, and Politics
Zizi Papacharissi

Money Code Space: Hidden Power in Bitcoin, Blockchain, and Decentralisation
Jack Parkin

The Citizen Marketer: Promoting Political Opinion in the Social Media Age
Joel Penney

Tweeting Is Leading: How Senators Communicate and Represent in the Age of Twitter
Annelise Russell

The Ubiquitous Presidency: Presidential Communication and Digital Democracy in Tumultuous Times
Joshua M. Scacco and Kevin Coe

China's Digital Nationalism
Florian Schneider

Networked Collective Actions: The Making of an Impeachment
Hyunjin Seo

Credible Threat: Attacks against Women Online and the Future of Democracy
Sarah Sobieraj

Presidential Campaigning in the Internet Age
Jennifer Stromer-Galley

News on the Internet: Information and Citizenship in the 21st Century
David Tewksbury and Jason Rittenberg

Outside the Bubble: Social Media and Political Participation in Western Democracies
Cristian Vaccari and Augusto Valeriani

The Internet and Political Protest in Autocracies
Nils B. Weidmann and Espen Geelmuyden Rød

The Civic Organization and the Digital Citizen: Communicating Engagement in a Networked Age
Chris Wells

Computational Proaganda: Political Parties, Politicians, and Political Manipulation on Social Media
Samuel Woolley and Philip N. Howard

Networked Publics and Digital Contention: The Politics of Everyday Life in Tunisia
Mohamed Zayani

The Digital Double Bind: Change and Stasis in the Middle East
Mohamed Zayani and Joe F. Khalil

Hacking Hybrid Media

POWER AND PRACTICE IN AN
AGE OF MANIPULATION

STEPHEN R. BARNARD

OXFORD
UNIVERSITY PRESS

Oxford University Press is a department of the University of Oxford. It furthers
the University's objective of excellence in research, scholarship, and education
by publishing worldwide. Oxford is a registered trade mark of Oxford University
Press in the UK and certain other countries.

Published in the United States of America by Oxford University Press
198 Madison Avenue, New York, NY 10016, United States of America.

© Stephen R. Barnard 2024

All rights reserved. No part of this publication may be reproduced, stored in
a retrieval system, or transmitted, in any form or by any means, without the
prior permission in writing of Oxford University Press, or as expressly permitted
by law, by license, or under terms agreed with the appropriate reproduction
rights organization. Inquiries concerning reproduction outside the scope of the
above should be sent to the Rights Department, Oxford University Press, at the
address above.

You must not circulate this work in any other form
and you must impose this same condition on any acquirer.

CIP data is on file at the Library of Congress

ISBN 978–0–19–757028–9 (pbk.)
ISBN 978–0–19–757027–2 (hbk.)

DOI: 10.1093/oso/9780197570272.001.0001

For my parents, Robert Barnard and Julia Heath, and for all who strive to make media serve the public good

Contents

Preface xi
Acknowledgments xvii

1. Introduction: The Mediatized Politics of Manipulation   1

2. Power and Problematic Information in an Era of Hybrid Media   15

3. Channels of Distortion: The End of the Fairness Doctrine and the Resurgence of (Domestic) Information Warfare   33

4. What Are Platforms For? Profit, Persuasion, and (Dis)Information   51

5. Hacking Meaning and Influence in the (Dis)Information Age: The Acosta "Assault" Case   77

6. We Are Trump's Digital Army! Capital and Practices of Manipulation on The_Donald   98

7. Trouble with Power, Practice, and Information in the Hybrid Media System   134

Notes   161
References   165
Index   189

Preface

The belief that contemporary social life is increasingly shaped by media appears to grow more widely accepted with each passing year. And for good reason. The profound shifts in the media landscape that began taking shape at the start of the 21st century led many media scholars and practitioners to call attention to the potentially transformative power of information and communication technologies in general, and social media in particular. Many observed how platforms such as Twitter could function as something like a public sphere, facilitating the sharing of information as well as public deliberation about it. While such observations remain relevant, recent events have forced many to reconsider the role media plays in the political field.

One glaring example is billionaire Elon Musk's purchase of Twitter in late 2022. The rapid succession of events that occurred in the days and weeks following Musk's takeover, such as suspending journalists' accounts, undoing the protective mechanisms to limit the spread of problematic information, and inviting serial offenders back on the platform (cf. Ghaffary, 2022), have forced many to reckon even more intensely with an uncomfortable but increasingly important truth. That is, if technologies can be constructed and leveraged to facilitate democratic communication, they can also be used to undermine it. Some of the most pressing questions in this vein are not about *whether* communication technologies are being used to manipulate public discourse but rather *how* such manipulation manifests in practice, *how* sociotechnical structures enable and constrain manipulative practices, and *what* consequences might follow. These are questions that I have been grappling with, in one way or another, for the better part of a decade.

Back in the fall of 2014, I spent countless hours glued to my Twitter feed searching for the right time to officially start collecting data on #Ferguson and hoping to better understand the debate as it unfolded. It was hard to miss the stark polarization. On one side, there were #BlackLivesMatter supporters who also used other episodic hashtags like #Ferguson, #MichaelBrown, #HandsUpDontShoot, #WalterScott, #FreddieGray, and more to spread relevant news and views. On the other side, there were discussions happening on right-wing hashtags—namely, #AllLivesMatter, #BlueLivesMatter, #PantsUpDontLoot, and #tcot, a formerly prominent hashtag that stands for "top conservatives on Twitter." The views aired in these spaces painted the issues of racial profiling and police violence in a very different light. While some conservatives were using left-leaning hashtags like #BlackLivesMatter to make their messages of disagreement more visible, progressive actors appeared much less likely to intentionally address conservative audiences.

As I poured over the sea of tweets flowing through many of these hashtags, waiting for news about the grand jury's decision in the Michael Brown case, which eventually decided not to indict Darren Wilson, the police officer who killed Brown, I noticed something strange. Whereas many accounts appeared to be run by real people—with names, locations, and profile photos that seemed legitimate—there were also a lot that looked less than authentic. I came across thousands of accounts with generic usernames, profile photos of eagles or American flags, and biographies that were chock full of cliché keywords such as "patriot," "guns," "faith," and "bible." Likewise, rather than seeming like genuine public discourse, posts from these accounts were often outrageous, highly inflammatory, and at times overtly racist.

Having studied the history of racism in America as well as the ebbs and flows of online political debates, I was under no delusions about how toxic the debate could turn or how deeply entrenched certain views may be. Nevertheless, I found myself repeatedly shocked by how ignorant and extreme many users appeared to be. Rather than present themselves as authentic and independent thinkers, many users were predictable caricatures parroting relatively well-known, albeit outrageous political talking points. It appeared that something was awry.

I began to suspect that many of these accounts were what internet researchers call *sock puppets*—that is, fictitious online identities created by users to mimic or manipulate perceptions and who often speak with or about their (clandestine) creator. But all I had were suspicions. The tools designed to detect automated bots were still rudimentary and, more important, were available to only a small cadre of researchers (to which I did not belong). In addition, we were still years away from learning about the attempts by Russia's Internet Research Agency to use social media to sow confusion in the American public sphere. At that time, it was difficult to imagine a coordinated effort, yet too noticeable to chalk it up to coincidence.

I started talking with my students about what to make of such discursive trends and what validity, if any, they could be ascribed. We also grappled with the affective implications and emotional labor required to read thousands of such tweets, all seemingly the same and from similar sources, with extremely racist valence. However genuine, many of these accounts appeared focused on drowning out or at least muddying the waters of Twitter discourse about racial injustice and calls for reform.

I was conflicted as a researcher and grew increasingly skeptical about treating such discourse as authentic. The prominence of these accounts raised serious questions about the basic assumptions many users—including journalists, politicians, and social scientists—were making about Twitter content in particular and social media in general. But I had to shift my focus elsewhere because I lacked the means to test my theories at the time. As a citizen, though, I was alarmed by the apparent rise of extremism and irrationality, and I grew more disillusioned about the health of the American public sphere. Such disillusionment, I later learned, is an intentional tactic of disinformation campaigns.

Following the election of Donald Trump as the 45th president of the United States, social media platforms like Facebook, Twitter, and YouTube have increasingly been put in the limelight for their role in amplifying fake news and fueling extremism. One issue of great concern is the power that tech companies have over the information marketplace and, by extension, over democracy. A related concern has to do with the lack of public knowledge or corporate transparency about how content reaches consumers' news feeds or how companies make decisions about which content should be removed or "down-ranked." Beyond companies' lack of transparency, there is a deeper issue pertaining to their business models, which compels them to profit from virtually all kinds of content, including disinformation and political manipulation, no matter its origin or potential effects. While social media platforms continue to amplify problematic information, many have also made a measure of progress on the issue, as evidenced by extremists' migration to other, less mainstream sites.

In late 2018, after a user of Gab—a social media app popular with the far right—posted anti-Semitic rhetoric, he entered a synagogue in Pittsburgh, Pennsylvania, with an assault rifle, killing 11 and injuring at least six more (Van Sant, 2018). A few days after the shooting, a synagogue in Brooklyn, New York, was defaced with anti-Semitic phrases (Jamieson, 2018). By the next morning, Twitter users in New York may have seen "Kill all Jews" among their local "trending topics." Although the specific reasons why this (or any) topic appears to trend on the platform are unclear, it seems to have been the result of a number of erroneous online reports (i.e., misinformation) shared on Twitter which led the phrase to trend despite its being in violation of the company's terms of service (Notopoulos & Mac, 2018). This is because, like much of social media, Twitter trends were, at least at that time, driven largely by algorithms rather than moderated in real time.

As tragic as it is, the shooting in Pittsburgh provides a clear, albeit extreme illustration of the real-world consequences that can follow from problematic information being shared online. What is at stake is more than just a realization that words matter; it is a reminder that the entities and media channels that deliver them wield remarkable power in modern societies—a kind of power that we still struggle to understand. Indeed, in the age of mediatization, where information flows increasingly rapidly between networked users, the bases of power—that is, the ability to establish legitimacy, to construct meaning and knowledge, to shape public awareness, and to set political agendas—have been fractured by entities seeking to manipulate them according to their own agendas.

One of the main conclusions of my first book, *Citizens at the Gates: Twitter, Networked Publics, and the Transformation of American Journalism* (Barnard, 2018a), was that cadres of networked outsiders occasionally wielded outsized influence in the political and journalistic fields. However, those instances were the exception, not the rule. In most cases, it was more typical that thought leaders were able to harness the power of the hybrid media system to help them wield greater symbolic power. At the time, my focus centered on the contestations of power in the media fields from activists on the left—a focus that was easily justified by the nature of digital politics in the Obama era. Nevertheless, the developments outlined above, many of which began to unfold as I finished writing that first book, have raised a number of pressing questions that still loom large today: How can the digital public sphere function effectively when trust in democratic institutions is eroding, and when many are grossly misinformed—at times, intentionally—about issues of social importance? What if the structures and practices of the contemporary media system are being hacked to increase attention in the name of politics and profit? How do the tools of propaganda and "organized persuasive communication" (Bakir et al., 2019) work in an era of social media saturation, and what are the implications for the flow of media power?

This book picks up where my first one left off by critically examining some of the greatest and most prescient challenges to deliberative democracy—those posed by the growing prominence of problematic information and media manipulation. While the platform revolution may have created a new frontier for manipulation, the opportunities are in many respects hardly new. For decades, conservative media activists have used sensationalism and dog-whistle politics to rally and grow their base. Whether it is through the promotion of lazy, hyperpartisan thinking or an appetite for propaganda—which further contributes to such thinking—would-be agenda-setters have long sought to cultivate an agreeable and ultimately fundamentalist mindset among (a subset of) the American people.

In today's "information age," when the market for people's attention is extremely saturated, communicators must be highly skilled in order to wield such influence. Beyond possessing a "capacity to produce and transmit symbolic forms" within a highly networked social space, as I previously argued (Barnard, 2018a, p. 44; cf. Thompson, 1995), those who are successful must also possess an adeptness in the art of hybrid media that enables them to create and disseminate information in ways that can effectively command and shape attention. I have come to refer to this latter capacity as "networked media capital."

Accordingly, I have written this book to develop a greater understanding of the workings of contemporary media power. While some readers may find that the arguments and analyses presented here contradict some of the conclusions reached in my previous work, I am more inclined to see them as complementary, or at least as evolving based on shifting media landscapes. While *Citizens at the Gates* sought to reveal the democratic potentials of digital media, *Hacking Hybrid Media* examines their antidemocratic influence, with an emphasis on the transformative power of hybrid media and an eye toward the linkages to more traditional media structures and political communication practices. With that in mind, I hope reading this book proves helpful in discerning the enduring power of media in a time that is defined by remarkable change. I know writing it has.

Acknowledgments

I have often reflected on what it means to be a member of a scholarly community, thinking at times that if only I could make more time to attend conferences, join writing groups, participate in workshops, and the like, I would feel more connected and also find greater value in my social capital. But like many others, the COVID-19 pandemic has forced me to rethink how I approach so many things, including scholarly networking. While the structures of my day-to-day life have afforded me with greater opportunities to strengthen the ties I have to people with whom I work every day, they have also allowed me to develop a greater appreciation for those I see less often but who have had no less an impact on who I am and on the scholarship I produce. It is with this mindset that I acknowledge the vast array of scholars and activists whose work has inspired and strengthened my own.

I am grateful to the Eastern Sociological Society, the North Central Sociological Association, and the American Sociological Association (ASA) for providing me space to present portions of this work, and especially to my fellow members who offered words of encouragement and criticism as I sought to refine my thinking on these endlessly complex issues. More to the point, I am especially thankful for my Communications, Information Technology, and Media Sociology ASA section colleagues for creating a community of scholars that I am proud to work alongside and for whom I write. Jenny Davis, Tim Recuber, Jeff Lane, Sarah Sobieraj, and Deana Rohlinger, among many others, have done much to inspire me over the years, and I do not take them or their collegiality for granted. I am also exceedingly grateful to my comrade and collaborator, Andrew Lindner. His comments on early drafts of this work helped me hone my arguments and prose in ways that made an immeasurable difference in how the project took shape in later stages. Additionally, Joan Donovan, Nick Couldry, Adrienne Russell, and Rodney Benson have each inspired my work in uniquely remarkable ways, and I am humbled to follow in their footsteps.

Francesca Tripodi, Leslie Jones, Rachel Durso, and my other friends from the Digital Sociology Collective have provided valuable inspiration and comradery over the years. I look forward to strengthening those ties in the years ahead.

My sincere thanks go out to Andrew Chadwick, Angela Chnapko, Alexcee Bechthold, and the production team at Oxford University Press. As editor of the Oxford Studies in Digital Politics series, Andy expressed an interest in this project before it even existed, and he proved to be a continuous source of inspiration and support as it evolved. Not only did his work inspire my own in immeasurable ways, but he championed the project in its early stages and provided tremendously valuable feedback on the manuscript in its later stages. Angela Chnapko has also proved to be a steady source of support. Despite the delays this project underwent thanks in part to the COVID-19 pandemic and my decision to take on the responsibility of chairing a department at a new (to me) institution, Angela did not waver, remaining committed to this project and to helping me complete it. I am also grateful to the anonymous reviewers and the OUP production team for their efforts to improve and produce this book.

This work has been immeasurably strengthened by the prior opportunities I have had to write, speak, and teach about these topics. I am thankful to all who have played a part in that process, especially the editors and reviewers. Portions of chapters 2 and 6 have appeared in article form in *Information, Communication & Society*.

Over the years, I have been fortunate to work with many extraordinary colleagues. At St. Lawrence University (SLU), I had the privilege of working and teaching alongside John Collins. In addition to being a talented and endlessly critical media scholar, John is also a true friend and comrade. Our conversations over a coffee or beer not only helped me discover many of the insights underlying this book but also inspired me to keep pushing for a media climate worthy of an open, inclusive, democratically oriented society—and vice versa. Damon Berry is another SLU colleague whose important work on the religious and cultural roots of White supremacism has inspired me to continue seeking answers to questions about the role media environments play in enabling the spread of such troubling ideologies. With John and Damon, I was also fortunate to meet and work with Somdeep Sen (and many other fellow Laurentians) on an edited volume about the power of discourse in an increasingly troubled global society. Through our work together, Som, John, and Damon helped me hone my thinking about the discursive power of so-called fake news—ideas that have shaped my thinking and writing throughout this work. In addition to my colleagues, I am grateful to the countless SLU students, but especially those in my seminars on media and power, fake news, and information activism who helped explore various portions of the terrain covered in this book.

I am also deeply indebted to my friends, colleagues, and students at Butler University, whom I have had the good fortune of working with since 2021. I am especially grateful to my colleagues in the Department of Sociology and Criminology for welcoming me and helping me carve out space to complete this book. Thanks especially to my longtime friend and colleague Jesse Van Gerven for being a constant source of support. Whether we were sharing a meal, offering words of encouragement, or exchanging looks of exhaustion, it was truly fulfilling to feel so accepted and understood. I am also grateful to Stuart Glennan and the rest of Butler's Science, Technology, and Environmental Studies program for encouraging me to explore the power of communication technologies in the classroom. Thanks to them and my sociology and criminology colleagues, I have had the opportunity to work with some extraordinary students, who themselves serve as a source of support and encouragement, who push me to hone my analyses, and who inspire me to strive for an ever-greater understanding of—let alone a more just approach to—the relationship between media, power, and politics. I am indebted to Jay Howard and Kate Novak for providing useful feedback on early portions of chapters 2 and 5, as well as to Josh Petrusa and the Irwin Library staff for providing me the space and support to finalize this manuscript.

I owe many thanks to my family and friends as well. Some provided feedback or served as a sounding board while I brainstormed ideas. Others offered me solace and permission to temporarily step away from the work. Still others encouraged me to keep going as I too grappled with the challenges of living, working, and writing amid a global pandemic. My wife, Anna, played all these roles (and many more) these past few years, stepping up to the plate in countless ways so that I could carve out the time in my calendar and space in my head to complete this book. She and our children, through their sheer presence and love, provide constant reminders of what is important in life and encourage me to arrange my schedule accordingly. Without them, none of this means anything. I am grateful to my father for following the news about disinformation and platforms so ardently and for sharing relevant occurrences with me just to make sure I did not miss anything. My mother, stepfather, sister, mother-in-law, grandparents, aunts, uncles, and so many other family members offered support and encouragement, each in their own way, that collectively helped me push through to the finish line. I am grateful to my dear friends Anna Sorenson, Desiree Lebouf-Davis, Karen and Dan Foster, and their respective families for welcoming us into their lives. You all have taught me so much about what unconditional love looks like, and I hope to give as good as I get in the years ahead.

As long as this list of acknowledgments is, there are surely some I failed to mention. I hope you'll forgive me and remind me (in no particular order) so that I can make it up to you somehow. Any errors or limitations that remain in this book are, of course, my sole responsibility.

Chapter 1

Introduction

The Mediatized Politics of Manipulation

> To each and every one of you, I say: Thank you very much, on behalf of a nation. Thank you very much. It's very important what you're doing. You're getting the—you're getting, in many cases, the honest word out—not in all cases, but in many cases.... [W]ith amazing creativity and determination, you're bypassing the corrupt establishment—and it is corrupt—and you're bypassing the very, very corrupt media—which not all of it, but much of it is far greater percentages than anyone would understand.
>
> To all of the social media influencers here today—a lot of—you have a lot of power and you have a lot of strength. And, you know, you have to use it wisely. Many of you do, but you have to.... I want to thank you once again for being here. You're very special people. You're very brilliant people, in so many cases. I look around the room—I mean, I see people that really have almost found a new life over the last short period of time with this new technology. But this new technology is so powerful and so important, and it has to be used fairly. It has to be used fairly.
>
> —Remarks by Donald Trump at the presidential social media summit (Trump, *2019*)

On July 11, 2019, President Donald Trump hosted a social media summit at the White House. The occasion had all the trappings of an official White House event: a tightly restricted guest list, a speech from the president, a press conference, and even an after-party at a Trump-owned hotel. But this was no ordinary event. Rather than inviting a large cohort of Washington insiders, media professionals, and leaders from tech companies like Google, Facebook, and Twitter, whose platforms were being scrutinized, the guest list catered to online influencers—many of them self-professed "trolls"—along with right-wing media personalities. Guests at the summit included political meme makers

@mad_liberals and @CarpeDonktum; James O'Keefe, the founder of gotcha journalism organization Project Veritas; Benny Johnson, a reporter fired from multiple publications for plagiarism and current executive at the right-wing organization Turning Point USA; along with activists, politicians, and media personalities from a host of other organizations on the right.

The strategy behind the summit was to bring together conservatives with a particular kind of capital—media influence—in order to solidify their commitment to the Trump brand and to help Trump sell it for the 2020 general election. The event was described by *New York Times* White House correspondent Katie Rogers (2019) as a "lovefest between Mr. Trump and 200 of his most passionate online followers" and as "the closest thing to a campaign rally that [they] have seen inside the White House" (Martin, 2019). Trump's hour-long public speech focused less on tech companies' alleged discrimination against conservatives than on other issues on the president's political agenda. Such topics included Trump's (2019) frustrations with China, Democrats, socialism, and even house flies. Considering the added emphasis on Republican triumphs in recent elections, including specific shout-outs to elected officials attending the summit, the event aimed to bolster the confidence of those in attendance and to galvanize their support.

The event was also designed to elicit coverage from establishment media outlets and to ramp up pressure on social media companies at a time when they were facing increased scrutiny from across the political spectrum. The scrutiny coming out of the summit, however, was far different compared to other political circles. Whereas many Americans are concerned about the use of social media by foreign entities to spread propaganda and sow confusion among the electorate, Trump and his attendees rallied instead behind charges of digital platforms' purported "liberal bias." Even though evidence demonstrating systematic discrimination against any particular group is lacking—with the exception of those disseminating hate speech or otherwise violating platforms' policies for conduct and abuse, behavior which appears to be increasingly common on the political right—Trump and a slew of his guests shared stories of suspected censorship. There was plenty of talk of platforms allegedly "shadow banning" conservatives, which the White House defined as "the subjective hiding or demotion of a social media user's visibility, typically in search results" (Romm, 2019).

Despite the numerous criticisms of digital media platforms, Trump was also inclined to boast about his use of these media. For example, speaking about his use of Twitter, Trump (2019) exclaimed, "Boom. I press it and, within two seconds, 'We have breaking news.' . . . But if I put that out in a press release, I'm telling you . . . people don't pick it up. . . . If I put it out on social media, it's like an explosion." Of course, social media and digital or even establishment media are not mutually exclusive. As I have found previously (Barnard, 2018a), Trump has used social media to both attract attention from and circumvent establishment media gatekeepers. As Andrew Chadwick (2017) put it, Trump's strategy "was not disintermediation, but intermediation" (p. 283). We should expect nothing less of those who possess the capital necessary to work the hybrid media system to their benefit.

After the event, the Trump administration held a press briefing in the White House Rose Garden. The briefing was yet another indication that it was anything but politics as usual. Instead of professional journalists being granted full access to the standard press area, as reporters typically are, they were situated outside the ropes. On the inside were Trump's summit guests, many of whom had made their names in part by lambasting establishment news outlets for what they deemed to be unfair or unfavorable coverage.[1] This role reversal sent a not-so-subtle message to the Washington press corps and the American public about who the administration saw as its allies—partisan acolytes and culture warriors—and who it saw as its enemy: the press.

Setting aside for a moment its undeniable success in galvanizing support from Trump's volunteer army of social media warriors, the summit was, like much of what occurs in the age of hybrid media, a textbook "pseudo-event." Coined by political historian Daniel Boorstin (1962/2012), the concept describes a spectacular event, often held in person, the primary function of which is to attract and shape media attention. In this case, Trump and his team were seeking to draw attention to the alleged problem of digital platforms' political bias, which in their view was not receiving the news coverage it deserved. The added attention, it stands to reason, would not only increase public awareness of (Trump's framing of) the issue—which could make the audience more likely to question future media messages that strayed from their chosen narratives—but would also heighten public pressure on the platforms themselves.

There is substantial evidence that this pressure campaign has worked. Meta CEO Mark Zuckerberg and former Twitter CEO Jack Dorsey both sent clear signals that they took these concerns seriously. In fact, they went out of their way to avoid such criticisms. For example, in October 2019, Facebook announced its curated news service, Facebook News, which would include content from a small number of "trusted" news sources, including the far-right website Breitbart (Robertson, 2019). Twitter was hesitant to enforce some of its policies regarding abuse because they would disproportionately affect influential conservatives, including Trump himself (Newton, 2019a). Of course, much has changed in recent years, and Twitter's new owner, Elon Musk, appears to have taken the claims of liberal bias seriously enough to make implementing countermeasures a core part of his leadership agenda. This and other such shifts in public opinion should be credited in part to the effectiveness of such message campaigns to travel swiftly throughout much of the hybrid media system.

In the days leading up to and following the summit, the leading right-wing media outlet Fox News published over a dozen stories about the event. One segment on the morning talk show *Fox & Friends* introduced the summit as providing an opportunity for "those who have made claims of censorship against tech giants to talk about the challenges of the online platforms." The segment featured an interview with Talking Points USA founder Charlie Kirk, who accused tech companies like Google, Facebook, and Twitter of "engaging in suppression of conservative ideas." "If these tech companies are going to be acting in ways that are misrepresenting true information," Kirk said, "then you might have people actually acting based on false information from these tech companies" ("White House Hosting," 2019). While other stories from conservative media may have framed the issue in a slightly different manner, the message was essentially the same.

The irony of Fox News contributors warning the public about "tech giants" intentionally spreading false or misleading information that could weaken American democracy should not be overlooked. The network's reputation for systematically misinforming its audience has been decades in the making (Kull et al., 2003). Today, Fox News plays a leading role in what Yochai Benkler, Robert Farris, and Hal Roberts (2018) describe as the right-wing "propaganda feedback loop" (p. 79). Like the slurs of "fake news" hurled by summit attendees to professional reporters covering the White House, Fox News alleging that other media companies are applying political bias might be seen as peak hypocrisy—or at least as Orwellian doublespeak (Orwell, 1982).

Fox News is undeniably one of the largest and most influential channels through which the American political right wages information warfare. It has long been recognized as America's most popular cable news channel, and its website ranks as the 60th most popular in the United States ("Foxnews.com Traffic," n.d.). Nevertheless, it is far from the only source of American-made distortion. While television and radio remain highly influential sources for much of the public, more and more Americans are turning to the internet and social media for their news (Shearer, 2018). Considering this along with the increasingly hybrid structure of contemporary media (Chadwick, 2017), this book is about much more than one media outlet's attempts to deceive. It is about the myriad ways political and pseudo-journalistic actors use media to subvert the narratives of democratic institutions and, more generally, to manipulate public awareness by amassing and wielding media power. Further, its focus is both broad and specific, accounting for institutional-level dynamics as well as for the ways individual actors work within the ever-evolving media system to share their account of the world.

In the case of the social media summit, the Trump administration used a variety of techniques to attract and shape attention from the news media. First, they leveraged the agenda-setting power of the White House. In addition to taking advantage of their formal communication channels, the use of official spaces such as the East Room and the Rose Garden lent an air of formality to the event and therefore helped boost its claims to legitimacy. Second, the administration drew upon Trump's brand of media spectacle. Trump and his team used their own social media channels to generate sensational imagery and soundbites made for virality in the age of hybrid media, playing up Trump's reputation as a savvy rhetorician and media personality. Third, by inviting an army of conservative online influencers to the White House, the administration sought to harness the collective power of Trump's most vocal supporters. Being included on the guest list gave many a boost in legitimacy and propelled them to reach wider audiences—whether online or through more traditional media. Fourth, the administration organized the press conference following the summit so that it would do double duty. In addition to serving as a spectacular victory lap for the president and summit attendees, Trump used his public address to announce his signing of an executive order to add a controversial citizenship question to the 2020 census, effectively guaranteeing widespread press coverage of the occasion.

While onlookers might assume the event had already reached peak media spectacle by the time the attendees took their places in the seats typically reserved for the professional press corps, who were both literally and symbolically situated as outsiders for the day, there was even more drama in store. The Twitter platform was ironically down for much of the day, plagued by outages due to an "internal figuration change." But it was back up in time for onlookers to capture a conflict between Sebastian Gorka, a talk radio host and former Trump administration staffer, and reporter Brian Karem (Rogers, 2019). Still in the spotlight following Trump's address, the two minced words and even hinted at a physical altercation. Although Gorka walked away after shouting at Karem, "You're not a journalist, you're a punk," the spectacle continued to unfold with jeers from the crowd. Eager for her place in the limelight, singer/songwriter Joy Villa—wearing a red, white, and blue gown with the word "freedom" pasted at her feet—stood alone in front of the press corps to announce her fellow attendees' status as "citizen journalists" and to insist the professionals "stop reporting fake news" (Schwartz, 2019).

On the whole, the social media summit proved to be a spectacular springboard to garner attention within the hybrid media system. The pseudo-event provided ample opportunities to generate imagery and soundbites well suited for cable news and talk radio, as well as for the broader digital media system—both professional and not. According to Lexis Nexis, there were 1,646 English-language news stories mentioning the "social media summit" published during the month of July 2019.[2]

Certainly, what has been described thus far paints a narrow and incomplete picture of the strategies and tactics used by political communicators. That is, while this brief reflection on the social media summit's mediated history offers a window into many important strategies in contemporary political communication, it does not speak to the ways that carefully crafted rhetoric, search engine optimization, targeted advertising, automated bots, sock puppets, and other forms of media manipulation are used to attract and shape attention. Such is the nature of this book. It does not aim to provide an exhaustive account of all the ways contemporary media are used to persuade or manipulate. Many others have made and continue to make important contributions toward such ends, and I believe we all stand to benefit by leaving it to them. Rather, this book seeks to examine some of the nuances of hybrid media structures and practices and to excavate these materials to unearth a more thorough understanding of the practical and theoretical implications for the relations of media power. This chapter offers a brief characterization of the concerns driving the study—namely, the changing dynamics of media power, practice, and propaganda—and situates the phenomena within the context of the hybrid media system. The next sections introduce some of the book's central claims and concepts before providing a brief overview of the chapters that follow.

Spectacle and the Mediatization of Political Communication

The story of the social media summit is not just a dramatic anecdote. Like many of the cases examined here, it provides a useful illustration of many of this book's central concerns. It not only asks us to consider how communicative structures and practices recursively shape one another, but also encourages us to grapple with broader questions about how various forms of capital combine to enable expressions of power. In doing so, we are led to consider the roles status and spectacle play in attracting attention, how changes in the media environment are reshaping relations between publics and the press, and, ultimately, how power works in a time of mediatization.

At the center of any inquiry pertaining to media and political communication lies the question of their effects. News media have long been regarded for the role they play in shaping public attitudes (Cohen, 1963). While many conceptualize this influence as persuasion (Jowett & O'Donnell, 2014), framing (Entman, 1993; Scheufele, 1999), or agenda setting (McCombs & Shaw, 1972), others emphasize media's "minimal effects" due to audience members' preexisting beliefs as well as their propensity for selective exposure (Lazarsfeld et al., 1948). More recently, scholars have found that news media's coverage of particular issues can increase their significance for topics of discussion among members of the networked public (King et al., 2017). This may explain why so many willingly engage in extreme acts to garner greater media attention.

Media spectacle is one of the most common, tried-and-true formulas for generating attention. As has been previously argued, spectacle "occurs when events are presented in a sensational manner, maximizing the likelihood for audience interest—and thus, media attention" (Barnard, 2018a, p. 129; cf. Kellner, 2009). Within the field of politics, outrage is often the most prominent and effective form of spectacle. According to Jeffrey Berry and Sarah Sobieraj (2014):

> Outrage discourse involves efforts to provoke emotional responses (e.g. anger, fear, moral indignation) from the audience through the use of overgeneralizations, sensationalism, misleading or patently inaccurate information, ad hominem attacks, and belittling ridicule of opponents. Outrage sidesteps the messy nuances of complex political issues in favor of melodrama, misrepresentative exaggeration, mockery, and hyperbolic forecasts of impending doom. (p. 7)

When used in this way, outrage can serve the dual functions of contemporary mediation: generating revenue and spreading the mediator's messages. But it comes at a cost. Indeed, as Berry and Sobieraj argue, "Outrage discourse and programming may be effective at increasing advertising revenues and political support, but . . . the mainstreaming of outrage in American political culture undermines some practices vital to healthy democratic life" (p. 6). While media professionals may be best situated to engage in media spectacle, the social media summit saga illustrates that anyone with a desire for attention—to gain profit, ideological influence, or both—may be drawn to its allure. Furthermore, thanks to the ongoing transformations in the hybrid media environment, the ability to produce and disseminate media messages is increasingly distributed across a broad array of networked publics. These developments provide greater opportunity to create and spread media spectacle (Mihailidis & Viotty, 2017).

The assertion that the evolution of the contemporary media environment has fundamentally altered other sociological dynamics is reliant on an acknowledgment that the social world has been *mediatized*, or "changed in its dynamics and structure by the role that media continuously (indeed recursively) play in its construction" (Couldry & Hepp, 2017, p. 13). Theorizing about *mediatization* asserts that

> "the media" has conquered every corner of social life. The media is not just differentiated sectors, industries, technologies, and/or information and entertainment platforms situated externally to everything else—a

> field or institution with discrete boundaries, mission, and performance. It is... an all-dominant zeitgeist that impregnates absolutely everything. Every aspect of life is mediated—work, sociability, transportation, consumerism, education, politics, and religion. The media connect divided worlds, catalyze unprecedented social transformations, and force social institutions to adjust to a different logic. (Waisbord, 2016, p. 1175)

Such a bold claim calls us to better understand and explain the structures and practices of networked media, as well as how they undergo and facilitate change throughout society.

Given the rapid proliferation of media's importance across all spheres of social life, it should be clear by now that what we are witnessing—on television, online, and in public discourse writ large—is a revolution in the relations of media power. This realization raises numerous questions of interest for the lines of inquiry pursued in this book. Considering the focus on communicative strategies found on the American political right, we might ask: What media-related practices were employed to facilitate the spread of pro-Trump messaging, and to what extent were these efforts successful? What forms of capital were required to effectively wield power in the hybrid media system? In what ways were capital-building opportunities being shared with (potential) members of Trump's "digital army"? And what implications does this have for our understanding of how media power operates in an age of mediatization?

While these questions (and many others) will be addressed in detail in future chapters, I want to call our attention to the question of capital. According to a Bourdieusian conception of capital (Bourdieu, 1993) there are four distinct types of resources that actors draw on when engaging in social action: economic, social, cultural, and symbolic. Certainly, these four forms each contribute to the media practices discussed in this chapter and beyond, as do more recent conceptions like Couldry's (2014b) media(-related) capital.[3] Indeed, actors must have the requisite resources to effectively navigate the political, journalistic, and technological fields, and they increasingly stand to benefit from sophisticated uses of media. Nevertheless, considering the extent to which these fields are *mediatized*, prior theories of capital fail to capture the complex ways that power operates in a hybrid media system.

There are a variety of resources actors may draw from when waging campaigns of manipulation or deception (Benkler et al., 2018; Chadwick & Stanyer, 2022; Federov & Leviskaya, 2020; Giglietto et al., 2020; Marwick & Lewis, 2017). Given the hybridity of the contemporary media system, where previously disparate structures, actors, and practices are increasingly intertwined (Chadwick, 2017) as well as the deepening of mediatization where everyday life is increasingly defined by media (Couldry & Hepp, 2017), there is extraordinary potential for well-resourced actors to wield power through deceptive communication. Each tactic is part of the growing repertoire of communicative practices that actors may draw upon. But in order to deploy these practices successfully, one must not only have access to the aforementioned forms of capital. Due to mediatization and hybridization, actors must also possess networked media capital, an emerging form of power that enables its possessor to utilize media in enterprising ways to disseminate information.

If media hold power, they do so in part because of their immersion in everyday life, as well as because of the public's trust in the individuals and institutions who have access to the means of communicative production. Yet adequately capturing how media power operates requires careful consideration of a variety of factors as well as analyses that operate on multiple levels (micro, meso, and macro). Hence, this book offers a critical assessment of the structures and practices that enable problematic information to flow through the hybrid media system. Before we dive in further, let us first take a moment to consider the significance of the work before glancing ahead to see what is to come.

The Book

Hacking Hybrid Media dissects the ways in which media and communication technologies combine with practices in social contexts to reshape the public sphere, with an emphasis on the role publishers, platforms, propagandists, and publics play in the transmission of information, manipulation of meaning, and commanding of attention. More specifically, the book examines some of the nuances of hybrid media structures and practices and excavates these materials to unearth a more thorough understanding of the practical and theoretical implications for the dynamics of media power. The book's primary contribution is to update and advance our understanding of power, propaganda, and manipulation given the changing realities of the contemporary media environment. Central to this advancement is the theoretical construct of "networked media capital," which is a conceptual tool that helps explain and contextualize how media power works in the contemporary hybrid media system.

The book argues that actors and organizations develop and implement enterprising approaches to political communication by drawing on their trans-field powers of media (meta)capital. Building on Nick Couldry's (2014b) theorizing of "media meta-capital," I use the term "networked media capital" to refer to the facility with which actors use the tools of the hybrid media system to create and disseminate information. The concept does the sense-making work of disparate but interconnected empirical phenomena that have largely been documented elsewhere yet remain inadequately understood. Given the changing logics of contemporary media (Barnard, 2018a; Chadwick, 2017), influence no longer requires the kinds of power and position that generated success in the era of mass media. While such traditional forms of influence remain significant, the structure and culture of digital media allow, and often require, new kinds of capital to achieve virality. Indeed, many of today's political influencers have developed remarkable abilities to hack systems of political information, thus wielding extraordinary and often clandestine influence within various parts of the public sphere. In a time of increasing media hybridity and complexity, many manifestations of this capital can be classified as *problematic*—that is, misleading, manipulative, or otherwise deceptive. Like more traditional "hackers," today's media manipulators have the knowledge and skills necessary to identify vulnerabilities in a system and to exploit them by leveraging numerous forms of capital. This emerging form of media power is present among many case studies examined for this research.

By tracing transformations of media power corresponding with evolutions in media cultures, technologies, and norms around political messaging, this book provides a revealing analysis of the digital media landscape while remaining attuned to the continued significance of broadcast media. It situates experienced publishers' use of power and position to deceive audiences alongside digital activists' attempts to achieve similar ends through their own (seemingly) grassroots efforts. Furthermore, through a critical examination of some of the greatest and most pressing challenges to journalism and deliberative democracy, this book contributes to ongoing conversations about the dynamics of media power in an age of professional crisis and (dis)information overload. In striking a balance between theoreticism and empiricism, it shows how the emergent structures and practices of the contemporary media system shape how information flows, how meaning is made, and, ultimately, how networked social influence works. Grounding its analysis of recent developments in the production and dissemination of organized persuasive communication within a historical context of the American media system, and using data and illustrative examples from recent history, the book weaves together original insights with those synthesized from relevant research to uncover the inner workings of the ever-changing field of media power.

Since this introductory chapter has thus far offered a broad overview of the terrain ahead, it is only appropriate to now provide a more detailed appraisal and sketch out a path forward. Accordingly, chapter 2 further establishes the book's theoretical, conceptual, and practical foundations. This includes introducing issues central to debates surrounding media power, propaganda, and organized persuasive communication, and further contextualizing these issues within the emergent realities of the 21st-century media environment. The chapter begins with a brief recollection of Edward Herman and Noam Chomsky's (1988/

2002) theorizing about mass media to demonstrate their power and to illustrate just how much has changed in the decades following its initial publication. Next, the chapter lays some groundwork regarding the exchange of power in a hybrid media system before considering its structural and practical manifestations. Following an introduction to affordance theory, it then delves deeper into the relevant theorizing on capital, identifying strengths and limitations of prior work, situating it within the context of media manipulation, and making the case for greater conceptual innovation (hence, networked media capital). The chapter reflects on the continued value of scholarship on propaganda, problematic information, and other related phenomena, and makes the case for a closer consideration of how emergent forms of capital facilitate their proliferation. It then draws from social movement studies to situate practices of manipulation within the context of political actors' broader repertoires and, through the construction of a typology, calls for a consideration of how various practices serve generative, amplifying, and legitimating functions. The chapter concludes with a brief reflection on some of the core assumptions that guide the work, as well as a broad overview of how the core insights from chapter 2 relate to other aspects of the study.

Chapter 3 digs deeper into the transformation of the mediated public sphere, starting with the proliferation of conservative talk radio in the late 1980s and cable television in the 1990s, and continuing into the rise of social media from the late 2000s until today. After offering a brief history of the partisan press in the United States and examining shifts in the structures of legacy media institutions as well as the practices of the people who run them, it traces common threads across both eras to theorize the fundamental elements of media power in the age of mediatization. The chapter asks questions such as: In what ways have the structures and practices of the late 20th century paved the way for contemporary dynamics of media power? How has propaganda evolved along with changes in media structures and practices? What role do media—including organizations, professionals, producers, and technologies—play in the formation of media power, as well as in the production and dissemination of problematic information? By tracing the lineages of persuasion and political information consumption between the broadcast and networked eras, the chapter argues that their emergent logics and practices have helped to grow a polarized public sphere and to cultivate a taste for propaganda and other problematic information. Furthermore, by examining the role of political rhetoric, celebrity, and media-savvy practices, the chapter outlines the formation of media-related capital at key moments in the mediatization of the public sphere. In doing so, the chapter draws on illustrative cases from popular talk radio and cable TV pundits such as Rush Limbaugh and Bill O'Reilly, as well as media celebrities turned politicians, such as Donald Trump.

Chapter 4 more closely examines the structures that make up today's hybrid media system and considers how these structures shape communicative action. Against the backdrop of the January 6, 2021, storming of the U.S. Capitol, much of which was organized on social media, the chapter asks what values and logics shape the design and governance of digital platforms as well as how those decisions affect media-related practices. By emphasizing the intersecting influence of political, economic, and technological factors, the chapter offers a critical examination of how platforms structure mediated communication, the uses they afford, and the consequences following their entry into media fields previously controlled by traditional publishers. Using platforms' disjointed approach to moderating Trump's social media accounts as an example, the chapter demonstrates how the democratic potential of these media is undermined by political-economic pressures. Additionally, by drawing on relevant literature and examples from recent political messaging campaigns, the chapter considers how social media platforms allow and at times encourage manipulative media practices. In doing so, it situates these practices within relevant structures and demonstrates how structural shifts in the hybrid media system enable and require a new form of power, networked media capital, for many to wield the kind of influence they desire.

Chapter 5 focuses on strategies of persuasion and attention-hacking in the hybrid media system, with an emphasis on the efforts of digital news sites. Through a multimethod analysis of information flows pertaining to the alleged assault of a White House intern by CNN reporter Jim Acosta in November 2017, this chapter asks: What patterns emerged in the most prominent content produced about the incident? What role did publishers, pundits, platforms, and publics play in spreading and responding to the messages? And what are the broader implications for dynamics of media power? By considering factors such as actors' field position, promotional practices, audience participation, and the political leanings of publishers, among others, this chapter sheds light on where problematic information was most likely to flow online, and how. The chapter finds that while stories from top-performing sites on both the right and the left were framed in ways that generally conformed to the journalistic norm of objectivity, others stretched that convention or abandoned it altogether in favor of more sensational coverage. Moreover, while mainstream sites typically drove the most traffic, others were able to attract a disproportionate amount of attention by using a variety of ordinary and innovative methods. Based on these findings, the chapter considers how various political and economic forces bear upon the production and distribution of digital news. Finally, it unpacks the tactics used for content promotion and, in congruence with other forms of capital, theorizes their existence as an emergent form of networked media capital that provides greater opportunities for manipulation.

Chapter 6 dives deeper into the sea of factors shaping the formation and application of networked media capital. Focusing on The_Donald, an alternative platform popular with members of Trump's "digital army," it uncovers some of the ways activists discuss and deploy practices of manipulation to attract and shape attention in the hybrid media system. Following an introduction to the forum and a brief discussion of relevant scholarship on networked activism, the chapter considers some of the agenda-setting tactics popularized by alt-right activists, especially through the use of alternative media. After summarizing the case study's methodological approach, the remainder of the chapter presents findings from a detailed analysis of online discourse spanning two years (August 2020 to 2022). In addition to addressing how the structure and culture of The_Donald afford manipulative practices, the analysis shows how the content generated and shared on the forum exudes a variety of problematic themes and practices discussed in previous chapters. Most notably, the chapter concludes by demonstrating and reflecting on how users leverage the affordances of The_Donald and other media to generate and exert networked media capital to spread deceptive information, while also grappling with critical questions about what these findings mean for our understanding of power and practice in a hybrid media system.

The final chapter reviews the key conclusions reached throughout the book and synthesizes them to decipher some of the most notable challenges facing democratic societies in the years ahead. In considering the extent to which the work of networked publics is challenged by the structural realities of the (dis)information age—run increasingly by agnostic platforms and profit-hungry publishers—the chapter offers a glimpse at how the potential of the networked public sphere is being thwarted by the actors, practices, and systems that manipulate communicative processes for their own benefit. While such jostling for power and political influence is far from new, the chapter explains how new and long-standing features of the media system have led to the growth of problematic information as well as diminishing trust in journalism and other democratic institutions—in the United States and beyond. In addition to emphasizing the practical elements that animate these challenges, the concluding chapter also considers how networked media capital and practices of manipulation work within and beyond the political and journalistic fields. The final sections weigh the potential costs of a mutually reinforcing cycle—referred to as the "dialectics of (dis)information"—that intensify as the scale of problematic information increases. They also reflect on how challenges may evolve in the years ahead and consider some potential solutions.

Overall, my aim for this book is not just to expand and sharpen our understanding of right-wing media manipulation. It is also to provide a broad assessment of how power operates in the contemporary hybrid media system, to offer a close consideration of the role structures and practices play, and to develop the conceptual tools necessary to make good sense of deceptive media. Given media's extraordinary social and political significance and the extent to which problematic information threatens our public sphere, few issues are as deserving of our attention.

Chapter 2

Power and Problematic Information in an Era of Hybrid Media

Media have long been regarded as powerful enough to help shape public consciousness. As such, media organizations, professionals, and the broader institution they form (i.e., "the media") have been the subject of considerable scrutiny. While many worthwhile critiques have been waged, few have been as piercing or influential as Edward Herman and Noam Chomsky's (1988/2002) *Manufacturing Consent*. Herman and Chomsky offer a detailed indictment of the political economy of the news media establishment and the power it exercises over the public sphere. Through their famous "propaganda model" the authors assert that establishment media's profit-driven ownership, dependence on advertising and elite sources, sensitivity to public criticism, and fear of ideologies seen as un-American serve as "filters" that severely limit media's discursive products. The result is not "all the news that's fit to print," as the famous slogan of the *New York Times* portends, but a narrower subset of news and views that is often more akin to elite-sanctioned propaganda.

While controversial, Herman and Chomsky's critique inspired a broad array of scholarship about the power of media in democratically oriented societies (Bagdikian, 2014; Fuchs, 2018; McChesney, 2000, 2004, 2013; Noam, 2009; Rossman, 2012). Many of those debates persist thanks to the privileged position establishment media maintain as gatekeepers and agenda-setters. Nevertheless, the burgeoning of digital platforms and subsequent rise of networked publics have fundamentally transformed the relationship between media and society, challenging the elite hold on media power. Although traditional forms of capital remain valuable, it is now quite common for less well positioned actors to generate extraordinary attention through enterprising uses of media. Such a shift calls for a fundamental rethinking of our understanding of media power in an era of increasing hybridity. Additionally, beyond the theoretical questions about media and power lie another slate of thorny issues about information and communication.

There may be no greater threat to the institutions of journalism and democracy than the proliferation of propaganda, disinformation, and other types of mediated deception. Despite the recent moral panic over "fake news," the challenges posed by problematic information are hardly new. The combined force of contemporary media—both broadcast and targeted, institutionalized and autonomous, analog and digital—serves as a means through which motivated actors can spread increasingly radical and manipulative rhetoric, exacerbating political affiliations and divides that were decades in the making. Whether by using dishonest or sensational frames that take advantage of widely accepted journalistic norms to attract a specific audience—from dedicated partisans, persuadables, or news professionals—or by leveraging the power of social media platforms to boost a message's reach, the methods of political communication appear to have grown in complexity and consequence. Such practices have contributed significantly to the proliferation of problematic information, the fracturing of public discourse, and the erosion of deliberative democracy.[1]

This chapter lays out some of the core foundations on which the remainder of the book rests. It offers an overview of media's role in relations of power, arguing that grasping the complexity of contemporary media power requires consideration of social, political, journalistic, and technological structures as well as how those structures inform media-related capital and practices. After a brief review of literature pertaining to the hybrid media system, the chapter introduces relevant theories of media and power. It makes the case for studying media practice before situating such practice against a backdrop of social and technological affordances. Next, the chapter reviews literature on media-related forms of capital and sketches a path for theoretical advancement through the development of new conceptual tools. Then it presents some foundational knowledge on propaganda, disinformation, and other forms of problematic information, calling attention to what is known about the work of media manipulation as well as what areas of study remain underdeveloped. The chapter makes the case for closer examinations of "repertoires of manipulation" by acknowledging lessons learned from related fields such as social movement studies. It also presents a typology of manipulative media practices before concluding with a brief reflection on the dual significance of structural and practical manifestations of media power as well as a nod to how the lessons learned in this chapter shape the book's focus going forward.

An Introduction to Hybrid Media (Power)

Despite the notability of distinctions between different types of media (print, broadcast, and online) as well as between the role media institutions play (platforms versus publishers) and the kinds of content they produce (news, opinion, entertainment), these boundaries have grown increasingly blurry. Accordingly, it is necessary to view these phenomena against the backdrop of a *hybrid media system*, an integration of newer and older media where "newer media practices in the interpenetrated fields of media and politics adapt and integrate the logics of older media practices in those fields," and vice versa (Chadwick, 2017, p. 288). This increasing hybridization, Chadwick argues, has "partially reconfigure[d] social, economic, political, spatial, and temporal relationships among existing media elites, political elites, and publics . . . by providing different normative contexts and terms of engagements for the interactions among these groups" (p. 29). Publishers and political communicators may lament the fact that the rules of this game are ever-changing, but it is this constantly evolving climate that prompted them to adapt their enterprising techniques to help them cut through the noise, attract the attention of their audience, and (hopefully) bring about their desired outcome: profit, persuasion, or both.

To exercise power in the hybrid media system, communicators must design their approach to create and disseminate messages across media platforms (Chadwick, 2017). In other words, they must adapt their practices to work within media's hybrid structures. Whereas older media logics have long rewarded those who can savvily craft rhetoric and circulate it by drawing on their social, economic, cultural, and symbolic capital (Bourdieu, 1993), the hybridizing of the media system requires actors to develop new strategies for creating and disseminating messages. Thus, as illustrated by the variety of examples considered throughout this book, contemporary media manipulators must cultivate and draw upon a diverse array of media-related skills and practices in order to wield power in an increasingly diverse and convergent media system. As media's affordances continue to evolve, it becomes increasingly clear that they present notable opportunities and challenges for the contestation of power.

The rise of the participatory web has brought about wave after wave of political contention from members of the networked public and, with it, a litany of scholarship on the democratic potential of digital media. Although much of this work has focused on uses of digital media by progressive political actors and social movement organizations (Earl & Kimport, 2011; Mattoni, 2013; Stephansen & Treré, 2019), others have recently argued that the evolving system of information communication technologies favors conservatives—in large part due to their organizational structures and resourcefulness (Schradie, 2019). At the same time, scholars in and around the field of political communication have studied how digital media have been mobilized to spread more traditional forms of political persuasion as well as various forms of problematic information (Bakir et al., 2019; Ball & Maxmen, 2020; Egelhofer & Lecheler, 2019; Woolley & Howard, 2018). While this scholarship has led to numerous advancements in the collective understanding of the dynamics shaping political participation in an age of hybrid media, many gaps remain, especially regarding the rapidly evolving tactics enabling political actors to engage in manipulation (Benkler et al., 2018; Bradshaw & Howard, 2017; Donovan & Friedberg, 2019; Marwick & Lewis, 2017; Nadler et al., 2018) or other forms of organized persuasive communication (Bakir et al., 2019). With these concerns in mind, this book carves out a space within the study of information, communication, and society to further develop theories of practice in order to better understand the practices of manipulation and to better theorize the dynamics of media power.

Additionally, this inquiry is deeply rooted in enduring debates from multiple schools of social theory, including work by Pierre Bourdieu (1993), Nick Couldry (2003), and Charles Tilly (2008). Although Bourdieu, Couldry, and Tilly each had distinct intellectual projects, they shared an interest—like many others in and around the field of sociology—in developing rich understandings of the relationship between structure, practice, and power. While the argument advanced here leans notably on theoretical and conceptual foundations built by Bourdieu, Tilly, and indeed many others, it builds most notably on Couldry's formulations of media power.

The Power of Media

Debates about the flow and locatedness of power have persisted for decades (Bourdieu, 1991; Domhoff, 2001; Foucault, 1995; Lukes, 2005; Mills, 1956; Weber, 1958). Nevertheless, social scientists, following Lukes (2005), have come to understand *power* as having three dimensions. Whereas the first dimension of power has to do with active and intentional forms of domination exhibited through behavior, and the second dimension is exhibited in ways that are not necessarily active or intentional, the third dimension of power describes the control (active or not) over what comes up in public discourse. In other words, it is "the capacity to secure compliance to domination through the shaping of beliefs and desires, by imposing internal constraints under historically changing circumstances" (Lukes, 2005, pp. 143–144). Although examinations of power frequently consider (with varying intentionality) more than one dimension, this book will place its emphasis primarily on the third. More specifically, it will focus on the more or less active manifestations of power expressed in and through media. Media's role in active contestations of power appears to have grown over time, and consequently, so has scholarly interest in the subject. Whereas some have argued that the power of media derives largely from other areas—that is, media are little more than a means through which political and economic power is exercised—others see media as holding unique, power-generating potential

(Couldry & Curran, 2003). As the media system has grown more hybrid it has become increasingly clear that media are more than expressions of power—they are also a means through which it is further amassed. Given that power can be made most visible through practice, it also takes on many forms and is expressed in a multitude of ways (Freedman, 2014; Lukes, 2005). Similarly, Chadwick (2017) puts it thus:

> Power in the hybrid media system is exercised by those who are successfully able to create, tap, or steer information flows in ways that suit their goals and in ways that modify, enable, or disable the agency of others, across and between a range of older and newer media settings. (p. 285)

One notable current running across these perspectives is that regardless of how one conceives of power, it is clear that media play an important role in its expression.

Against the backdrop of a hybrid media system, where practices and power dynamics fluctuate as systems evolve, it may be tempting to conclude, however paradoxically, that continued technological disruption is helping to balance equilibriums—between old and new, native and interloper, constancy and change. But power rarely operates in such a linear, dichotomous fashion. Instead, the era of hybrid media has given rise to new means through which motivated actors can generate attention and manipulate meaning. Before we examine these manifestations of media power, it is necessary to consider the ways media structures shape relations of practice.

Theorizing Media Power through (Structured) Practice

Power cannot be conceived as either wholly structural or wholly practical, nor as being fixed within a single entity, position, or institution. Rather, to understand the actuality of social relations one must contend with the dual significance of structure and practice (Fayard & Weeks, 2014). By conceiving of practice as inherently embedded in structure (Benson, 2014; Bourdieu, 1990; Davis, 2020; Shove et al., 2012), it is possible to develop nuanced understandings of power through practice-oriented analyses (Couldry, 2004; Stephansen & Treré, 2019).

The practical turn in social theory (Schatzki et al., 2001) has given rise to an abundance of scholarship focusing on the actions of citizens situated in a variety of fields. More specifically, the proliferation of media across social fields has led many to call for more detailed considerations of media-related practices

(Couldry, 2004; Rodriguez, 2001; Stephansen & Treré, 2019). This is in part due to the methodological advantages posed by analyzing practices at the micro level, which can then be connected to larger forces operating at the meso and macro levels (Stephansen & Treré, 2019).

Drawing on practice theory (Bourdieu, 1977, 1990; Shove et al., 2012), I see cultural systems and practices, of which media are a part, as both a manifestation of power and a possible generator of it. Thus, while examinations of practice may not reveal the full nature of power relations—also exhibited through deeply embedded structures as well as matters of inaction—practices provide a novel window into more or less active expressions of power. Thus, practice-oriented approaches lead researchers to pose questions like: "[W]hat types of things do people *do* in relation to media? And what types of things do people *say* (think, believe) in relation to media?" (Couldry, 2012, p. 40). Furthermore, because practice is inevitably rooted in structures—whether political, technological, cultural, economic, or otherwise—examinations of practice necessarily require that attention also be paid to its origins. Accordingly, the analyses presented in this book focus primarily on the elements of media-related practices, while keeping them situated within social, cultural, political, economic, and technological systems.

Similar applications of social theory have led to advancements in the collective understanding of media-related practices as well as their implications for dynamics of media power (Barnard, 2018a; Couldry, 2014b, 2016). But we would be remiss to examine the nature of media-related practice without first acknowledging the role social and technical structures play in shaping it. To accomplish this, we draw some important insights from the literature on affordances.

The Power of Affordances

In order to understand how power manifests through practice, it is necessary to consider the role social and technical structures play in shaping social action. Focusing on media-related practices, we can see how the affordances available to users make certain practices appear more normal and desirable, and others less so (Fayard & Weeks, 2014; cf. Davis, 2020; Liu, 2020). Thus, the affordances embedded in various structures shape the dispositions and practices of actors as they vie for power (Liu, 2020). Such dynamics are particularly visible through media.

Although institutional structures and their complex interrelations notably shape how power flows through media, so too do technological structures—and indeed, the cultures and practices that stem from them. Accordingly, thinking about how power is exercised through media necessarily entails considerations of the technologies that make up the hybrid media system and, ultimately, how those technologies shape practice. Scholarship in this vein has taken a particular interest in technological *affordances*, "the type of action[s] or... characteristic[s] of actions that a technology enables through its design" (Earl & Kimport, 2011, p. 10). A slightly more practice-oriented conception views affordances as "possibilities and opportunities for action that emerge from agents engaging with a certain property of technology in a specific context" (Liu, 2020, p. 53).

The concept of affordances has proven useful in studies of media and communication technologies because of its ability to highlight the significance of technological structures in a nuanced way (Davis, 2020). That is, rather than viewing technologies as either neutral or deterministic, it is important to recognize the varying "mechanisms of affordance" where technologies "request, demand, encourage, discourage... refuse," and "allow" particular practices through their design (Davis & Chouinard, 2016, p. 244; cf. Davis, 2020). For example, consider how the differences between more traditional media—broadcast and newspapers—and hybrid media structures shaped the flow of trustworthy information and, as a result, the relative functioning of the public sphere. The structure of the media system that evolved throughout much of the 20th century restricted access to the means of mass communication to such a degree that it *demanded* elite status. This technosocial system *encouraged* the amplification of voices from corporations and government officials while *discouraging* or *refusing* access to those without such power (Herman & Chomsky, 1988/2002). For one's voice to be amplified through mass media, one either had to be a gatekeeper oneself (Shoemaker & Vos, 2009), or at least had to be in possession of the capital that would help one gain gatekeepers' approval. As such, disseminating information via mass media, whether journalistic or propagandistic, was an inherently elite practice.

By contrast, the contemporary hybrid media landscape affords opportunities for billions of people to create and disseminate information. Although traditional media gatekeepers have retained their power over establishment channels, digital platforms like Facebook, Twitter, YouTube, and Google *allow* new actors of all sorts to circumvent traditional media, or "gatecrash," and speak directly to audiences (Barnard, 2018a; Bruns, 2014). These media platforms rarely *refuse* access, but they do place many *demands* on actors—namely, their ability to draw on various forms of capital—to communicate effectively. The hierarchical structure of contemporary media/society also *encourages* creative, sensational, and even manipulative forms of communication in order to reach mass audiences.

We will draw upon some of this knowledge about affordances in future chapters—including in chapter 3's examination of the expression of media power in the late 20th-century broadcast era and in chapter 4's discussion of social media's propensity to aid in the spread of problematic information. But we must first devote more of our attention to the literature on media-related practice and expressions of power through capital. There are a number of conceptual tools that can help explain and contextualize the dynamics of communicative practice in a hybrid media landscape. However, most fall short of accounting for the enterprising capability of some actors and collectivities to combine their knowledge and experiences in ways that allow them to hack the hybrid media system for personal or professional gain. Accordingly, the following section introduces some of the most notable literature before demonstrating its relevance to the practices of media manipulation.

Hacking Media (with Media-Related Capital)

If one's capacity to act is shaped by these structured positions and dispositions, the nature and success of these actions are also determined in part by the *capital* actors possess. For Bourdieu (1993), capital consists of four types: *economic* (monetary), *social* (networks), *cultural* (class-related capacities), and *symbolic* (status and reputation). In addition to serving as conceptual tools to explain how their possessors build and maintain transferable forms of influence, such notions of capital, alongside habitus—individuals' disposition toward (in) action based on their field position and prior experience (Bourdieu, 1990)—capture the ways power manifests at the micro level. This characterization also demonstrates that capital and habitus are structurally situated yet also discernable through practice.

Recent shifts in the mediated social order have led scholars to grapple with the implications of Bourdieu's theorizing (Couldry, 2003, 2014a, 2014b; Maares & Hanusch, 2020;) and, more important, for the dynamics of power and practice. Media's growing salience within and ubiquity across a variety of social fields has led scholars to develop new concepts that build on preexisting theories of practice. For example, my own research focusing on Twitter as a site of intersection between the journalistic and political fields found evidence of an emergent "networked habitus" that reflects actors' "growing acceptance of digital, interactive values and practices throughout much of the field" (Barnard, 2018a, p. 74; also see Barnard, 2016). Additionally, the idea of *celebrity capital* (Couldry, 2016) builds on Bourdieu's typology of capital by emphasizing how cultural influencers can shape public discourse within and beyond their field of influence (cf. Driessens, 2013). More important, the concept of *media meta-capital* describes one's ability to "exercise power over other forms of capital" (Couldry, 2014b, pp. 59–60; see also Couldry, 2003). In other words, "media meta-capital is an emergent form of networked capital that, due in large part to the growing ubiquity and symbolic power of media, can fundamentally alter relations of power and competition in other fields" (Barnard, 2018a, p. 44).

Despite the utility of these concepts in explaining how some aspects of practice and power work in a mediatized society, there are still parts missing from our shared toolkit. Indeed, due to their extraordinary social, cultural, and political salience, digital media not only "broaden the stage on which politics is played out" (Couldry, 2012, p. 146) but also *transform* the nature of relations within and across fields. While the concept of media meta-capital has been useful in explaining media's broad reach across other forms of capital, shaping how actors amass social ties, knowledge, status, and wealth, it cannot—nor was it intended to—explain the increasingly enterprising nature in which actors use media to disseminate information, manipulate meaning, and otherwise exercise power through the hybrid media system. Thus, I contend that actors and organizations develop and implement enterprising approaches to (political) communication by drawing on their transfield powers, but they do so in ways that go beyond what can be explained by prior notions of capital.

We can find some refuge in the notion of *media-related capital*, which describes how "media skills and media capacity (of some sort) produce 'capital' within the political field" (Couldry, 2014b, p. 63). The concept has already been fruitfully deployed by scholars seeking to explain media's growing influence in other spheres of social action (Couldry, 2012, 2014a; Kristensen & From, 2015). Nevertheless, the concept thus far remains underdeveloped. That is, in addition to needing a more thorough explication of its composition, we are also in need of a greater understanding of how media-related capital manifests in practice, as well as how to apply the concept in empirically grounded scholarship. This book takes up this charge by examining in detail how actors rely on media-related capital and practices to create and disseminate political messages. I argue that by drawing on diverse aspects of media-related capital from across the hybrid media system, political actors are able to *hack the media system* to garner greater attention and more salient influence.

Accordingly, I use the term *networked media capital* to refer to the facility with which actors use the tools of the hybrid media system to create and disseminate information. Networked media capital takes on individual and collective forms and operates within and across media formats and fields; hence, it is a uniquely *hybrid* form of capital. Whereas distinct media personalities undoubtedly possess the capacity to shape the flow and valence of attention, standing out in the contemporary media environment often requires a coordinated effort. Whether through organizations like marketing teams and political campaigns or loosely coordinated participatory networks such as fan communities and political constituencies, actors adopt a hacker-like mindset, creatively mixing their knowledge of media, culture, and politics to mobilize social and technical forces that will help spread their myriad messages far and wide. As such, deployments of networked media capital serve as a means through which actors and institutions shape public awareness and generate political capital for themselves.

The concept extends Couldry's (2014b) theorizing about the potential for *media capital*—"a super-ordinate [form of] capital based on media influence and not bound to particular fields" (Barnard, 2018a, p. 51)—to more explicitly account for the intermixing of practices from various sources of knowledge, and situates it within an increasingly hybrid media system. By signaling the importance of drawing on multiple types of capital rooted in various field contexts while centering the role played by digital media, the concept brings explanatory power to the study of media-related practices and encourages consideration of intersecting field positions, embodied dispositions, and creative communicative practices. Furthermore, the notion of networked media capital is especially (but not solely) useful when grappling with the creation and dissemination of problematic information. Because the hybrid channels through which information typically flows are recursively structured to guard against certain techniques of manipulation—whether the gates are guarded by publishers' editorial practices or platforms' rules for content moderation—those wishing to artificially boost their visibility and reach may resort to enterprising techniques of communication. In doing so, they draw on multiple forms of (networked) capital.

In *Journalism as Activism*, Adrienne Russell (2016) uses a practice-oriented approach to understand the changing dynamics of media power. By focusing on "sensibilities," or "the flow of perspectives and the ethos that inform media practices," Russell makes the case that vanguard journalists' enterprising disposition toward investigation, analysis, and agenda-setting are best understood as "hacktivist sensibilities" (p. 25). By applying their own skills, and borrowing others from the repertoires of hackers and activists, many actors operating at the margins of the journalistic and political fields were able to use logics of the media system, which included relying on publics and media professionals to amplify their messages, to generate information and attention in novel ways.[2] Expanding her focus to other modes of practice, Russell (2018) later demonstrates how climate justice activists also employ hacktivist sensibilities. By engaging in enterprising practices grounded in technical skills and shared values, she argues that activists can work together to "exploit the malleability of mainstream and alternative or niche technologies" in order to "bring new narratives into the mainstream" (Russell, 2018, pp. 273, 277). Yet, while the changing logics of hybrid media afford some advances in democratic discourse, they also provide opportunities for manipulation.

Journalist Matthew Yglesias (2018) has written similarly about the "hack gap"—the phrase he uses to describe the disproportionate number of "organized, systematic propaganda broadcasters" (para. 30) found on the American political right. Whereas the enterprising journalists Russell describes employ their sensibilities in relatively isolated ways to produce and distribute better journalism, Yglesias contends that entire media operations have been designed with the principal goal of spreading conservative viewpoints. Although there are numerous examples touched on throughout the book, this tendency is most clearly illustrated by former Fox News CEO Roger Ailes. Ailes had a long history as a strategist and media consultant for many Republican presidents, including Richard Nixon, Ronald Reagan, George H. W. Bush, and, after Ailes's departure from Fox News in 2016 due to numerous sexual assault allegations, Donald Trump. Certainly, for any group to accomplish its agenda-setting goals, it needs a collective and sustained effort from numerous entities with varying styles and audiences.

While such practical applications of capital may contribute to shifts in discursive space, they also have broader societal implications. As Chadwick (2017) aptly points out, the interdependencies and hybrid configurations of "older and newer media logics may contribute to the erosion of democratic norms" (p. 271; cf. Russell, 2020). This acknowledgment calls attention to the potential of media to negate the power of others. To speak of power as potentially negative is not simply to describe a binary relationship where one party benefits at another's expense. Rather, it is a means of capturing the erosive power—from undermining individuals' placement of trust to negating the very possibility of truth (i.e., post-truth)—that can result from enterprising yet destructive applications of hybrid media (Stanley, 2016). Indeed, in recent years, we have seen a dearth of examples demonstrating that such hybridization of logics, along with their respective practices, pose new communicative challenges, especially for democratic societies. Accordingly, we now turn our attention to some of these dysfunctional systems and practices.

Problematic Information and Media Manipulation

A defining aspect of the hybrid media system is the blurring of boundaries, and one of the most notable illustrations of this blurring is the eroding distinction between informative communication and manipulation. In the context of media and politics, the latter phenomenon has most prominently been associated with propaganda. While the practice of propaganda dates back to the 1600s, masters of media have been honing this art of influence since the early 20th century (Carey, 1996; Jensen, 2013). Although there is considerable disagreement about what counts as *propaganda* and what effects it may have, the term is typically used to describe "the deliberate, systematic attempt to shape perceptions, manipulate cognitions, and direct behavior to achieve a response that furthers the desired intent of the propagandist" (Jowett & O'Donnell, 2014, p. 7).

Scholars and pundits have long acknowledged the fuzziness of this definition, given that most forms of political communication could arguably fit the bill (Jensen, 2013). Thus, Jowett and O'Donnell (2014) explain how propaganda differs from "informative communication," which is based on the accurate presentation of indisputable facts to promote mutual understanding (p. 31). Similarly, Jensen (2013) distinguishes between "democratic persuasion" that presents an argument but makes considerable effort to facilitate honest, equal, and informed dialogue, and "undemocratic propaganda." The latter, by contrast, involves the "falsification of accounts of the world to support one's interests . . . attempts to ignore or bury accounts of the world that conflict with one's interests; and/or . . . diversion of discussion away from questions that would produce accounts of the world that conflict with one's interests" (p. 76). While not exhaustive, the properties underlying the distinction between democratic persuasion and undemocratic propaganda help to clarify and contextualize the varying efforts at persuasion.

Given the increased creativity with which some actors seek to channel attention and manipulate public perception, researchers have paid greater attention to the creation and dissemination of *problematic information*, or information that is "inaccurate, misleading, inappropriately attributed, or altogether fabricated" (Jack, 2017, p. 1). Problematic information is a broad categorization that includes various forms, such as misinformation, disinformation, propaganda, and fake news. Furthermore, Wardle (2017) defines misinformation as "the inadvertent sharing of false information," and disinformation as "the deliberate creation and sharing of information known to be false" (p. 1). As these definitions suggest, the two primary attributes that differentiate misinformation from disinformation are (1) intent and (2) duration. Whereas acts of misinformation tend to be accidental and episodic, disinformation entails a deliberate and likely sustained effort to sway or sow confusion among the public by mixing facts with falsehoods and manipulating context in support of a preferred conclusion (Jack, 2017; Jackson, 2017). On top of the growing literature on problematic information, there are related bodies of work on "organized persuasive communication" (Bakir, 2020; Bakir et al., 2019; Robinson, 2019), "media manipulation" (Bradshaw & Howard, 2017; Donovan & Friedberg, 2019; Federov & Levitskaya, 2020; Ferrara et al., 2020; Giglietto et al., 2020; Krafft & Donovan, 2020; Marwick & Lewis, 2017), and "deception" (Chadwick & Stanyer, 2022). In response to the growing consensus that hybrid media are enabling the spread of problematic information, which has important implications for journalism and democracy, scholarship in media and political sociology, political communication, media and journalism studies, and other related fields has sought to contribute to this shared understanding. This book adds to this ongoing conversation.

Emerging out of the scholarship on propaganda, disinformation, and other forms of problematic information, organized persuasive communication (OPC) provides a conceptual toolkit for understanding the complexities of problematic information as advanced in a coordinated (but not necessarily manipulative) fashion. According to Bakir et al. (2019), manipulative or non-consensual OPC frequently involves deception, whether through lies, omissions, distortions, or misdirection. While other forms of manipulation occur by force (coercion) or encouragement (incentivization), this book is most concerned with those aspects of manipulation that are exercised through media. Similarly, scholars have also studied acts of *deception*, "when an identifiable actor's prior intention to mislead results in attitudinal or behavioral outcomes that correspond with the prior intention" (Chadwick & Stanyer, 2022, p. 2). By focusing our attention on the media-related practices that facilitate deceptive messaging, we can develop a greater understanding of the logics that shape such practices while also remaining attuned to the implications they hold for the public sphere.

Whereas the scholarship on propaganda, OPC, deception, and disinformation is quite expansive, the literature on media manipulation has focused more narrowly on the uses of media to garner public attention and influence public discourse by means of deception. Thanks to this literature, for example, we know that purveyors of problematic information use carefully selected keywords (Donovan & Friedberg, 2019; cf. Tripodi, 2018) and coordinated link sharing ("Ants in a Web," 2021; Giglietto et al., 2020) to maximize visibility of their messages on search engines and social media; evidence collages to increase the shareability and apparent legitimacy of problematic information (Krafft & Donovan, 2020), as well as state-run campaigns (Bradshaw & Howard 2017) and other automated accounts (Ferrara et al., 2020) to spread propaganda or other deceptive messages. Often, the goal is to reach members of the public directly through popular social media channels, while at other times media manipulation campaigns focus on attracting the attention of news professionals who can translate their messages for wider consumption by mass audiences (Donovan & Friedberg, 2019). This process, sometimes described as "trading up the chain" (Holiday, 2013, p. 18), involves capitalizing on journalistic biases to garner attention from smaller media outlets that may fail to properly vet the information, and using that publicity to generate coverage from larger media channels (Marwick and Lewis, 2017; cf. Krafft and Donovan, 2020; Phillips, 2018). Of course, such efforts to hack the media system to increase the spread of information are not mutually exclusive, since it is often the apparent popularity of an account or message, which may be artificially inflated by bots or other coordinated inauthentic behavior, that lends it legitimacy or boosts its visibility through algorithmic amplification.

In order to succeed at media manipulation, one must possess various kinds of knowledge and power, or *capital*. Beyond requiring significant knowledge of the political and journalistic fields as well as an ability to navigate them, media manipulators must also creatively use hybrid media tools to generate and disseminate messages that will ultimately garner the attention they desire. In doing so, successful purveyors of problematic information hack the hybrid media system, developing and drawing on practices—and, indeed, entire repertoires—of manipulation.

Repertoires of Manipulation

Thanks to the growing accessibility of digital media platforms as well as the ever-evolving repertoires political communicators have at their disposal (Mattoni, 2013), the practices pertaining to the creation and distribution of problematic information have grown increasingly complex. While much is already known about uses of media for propaganda and manipulation (Benkler et al., 2018; Chadwick & Stanyer, 2022; Jowett & O'Donnell, 2014; Soules, 2015; Stanley, 2016; Woolley & Howard, 2018), there is still plenty to learn about the dynamics of media power in general, and what role problematic information practices play in particular (Robinson, 2019; Zollmann, 2017). More specifically, in addition to needing a more detailed grasp of the evolving methods of deception and media manipulation, there is a need for more advanced theoretical and conceptual understandings of how media power works in practice.

One body of literature that has produced relevant knowledge is the interdisciplinary field of social movement studies. According to Alice Mattoni (2013), political activists draw upon "repertoires of communication," which she defines as "the entire set of activist media practices that social movement actors might conceive as possible and then develop in both the latent and visible stages of mobilization, to reach social actors positioned both within and beyond the social movement milieu" (p. 37). Building on Charles Tilly and Sidney Tarrow's (2006) work on "repertoires of contention" within the realm of social movements, Mattoni asserts a need for greater understanding of the communicative practices that shape political action. Similarly, Jun Liu (2020) has made the case for more research on the relationship between technological affordances, repertoires of contention, and communicative practices. Such calls have only increased in recent years as media's role in political communication and mobilization grows even more prominent (Stephansen & Treré, 2019).

As the prior discussion of media manipulation makes clear, contemporary political communicators have no shortage of options for creating and disseminating problematic information. Indeed, rather than relying on a set of fixed practices, political communicators have diverse repertoires to draw from in their quest for profit and political influence (Hersh, 2015; Karpf, 2012; Soules, 2015). Thus, building on Mattoni (2013) and Tilly and Tarrow (2006), I consider *repertoires of manipulation* to be the set of deceptive practices political actors and organizations may deploy in their pursuit of power.[3] While many such practices are not altogether new, the tools of manipulation are constantly growing and evolving due to changes in media structures, user behavior, and political context.

Practices of manipulation can serve a variety of functions. From those that assist in the *generation* of problematic information to tools that enable *amplification*, and even strategies that aid in *legitimation*, these practices afford communicators the means to attract public attention via media in order to further their political-economic causes (see Figure 2.1). While it is tempting to closely examine these differing functions and to use them as points of distinction in evaluating which practices may be combined to maximize their effect, these functions are not mutually exclusive. Thus, while a communicator might seek to create a viral meme, the meme format and, inevitably, the message it conveys, are also integral to how widely a message is spread through user shares and algorithmic amplification. By remaining attuned to the functions served by practices of

	Functions of Manipulation		
	Generation	**Amplification**	**Legitimation**
Practices of Manipulation	Kernels of truth	Viral campaigns (i.e., shares, algorithmic amplification)	Pseudo-journalistic presentation (e.g., fake news)
	Distortion or fabrication	Paid promotion (e.g., dark advertisements)	Identity confirmation
	Impersonation (e.g., trolling, sock puppets)	Coordination (i.e., soliciting shares by other groups/accounts)	Appeal to emotion (e.g., #SaveOurChildren, #stopthesteal, #MAGA)
	Memes	Search engine optimization	Association
	Populism or "othering" (e.g., racism, sexism, xenophobia)	Bootstrapping (e.g., bots, self replies)	Dissociation
	Sensationalism (i.e., selection of topics or frames to generate outrage and attention)	Hash targeting	Appeal to logic

Figure 2.1 Practices of Manipulation.

manipulation, we can better understand *how* such strategies manifest in practice as well as *what* they help accomplish.

While the typology in Figure 2.1 is not exhaustive, it is inclusive of the range of media manipulation practices found in this book. By considering these practices alongside the techniques discussed above, we can approximate the repertoires of manipulation from which purveyors of problematic information may draw, although these will inevitably vary depending on one's position and disposition. Studying these practices, including their distinguishing characteristics as well as the properties that link them together, will help us develop a more thorough understanding of the dynamics of contemporary media power. Whereas research on practices of manipulation provides an important overview of the evolving tools of organized persuasive communication and the kinds of capital required to successfully engage in it, studying repertoires of manipulation will provide a closer look at the broader toolkits used by political communicators and can also help reveal the core elements and values connecting various practices. This is precisely what the remainder of this book sets out to do.

Looking for Power and Practice in U.S. Hybrid Media

The American public sphere is rife with problematic information, and while the nation's history and political cultures play a leading role, so too do our media. A core problem with media's tendency to facilitate the spread of problematic information is a matter not merely of biased, inflexible, or irrational structures, but also of a deceptive set of actors and practices adapted to flourish in a time of mediatization, algorithmic amplification, and informational abundance. Despite some measured steps taken by companies like Google, Meta, and Twitter to slow their spread, propaganda and other forms of problematic information flow in abundance through channels small and large. The boom of research on these issues following the 2016 U.S. presidential election has led to significant advances in our knowledge about the nature of the problem in general, and about how power flows through media in particular. Certainly, critical analyses of how the structures of contemporary communications systems shape information flows are integral to building greater understanding (Christin, 2018; Davis, 2020; Noble, 2018; Tufekci, 2017a). Nevertheless, if we are to develop a more complete picture of the ways media power has evolved along with recent advancements, there remains a need for greater attention to the individual and collective expressions of media power, and to media-related practices more broadly (Couldry, 2004; Stephansen & Treré, 2019).

This book begins with the assumption that the structures and cultures prominent in U.S. hybrid media form a mutually shaping, multidirectional relationship with practices. It also assumes, for better or worse, that despite its fuzziness there are meaningful ways to distinguish between democratically aligned political communication and deception, and that certain iterations (i.e., from the political right) are more prominent and problematic than others. Additionally, while I have already addressed some of the long history of media's role in facilitating (anti)democratic discourse, I begin this inquiry with the premise that the problem has grown worse, and the deceptive practices more sophisticated, in recent years. This shift has not only contributed to the erosion of the public's trust in democratic institutions (Stanley, 2016) but continues to transform the networked publics' relationship with media, and with each other.

Given the deepening of mediatization and the growing prominence of problematic information in the contemporary public sphere (Couldry & Hepp, 2017; Jack, 2017), these conditions constitute the basis on which new forms of power and practice emerge. To better understand these dynamics, I take an analytical approach that centers the ways structures and practices converge. We begin with systems-level views of how American mass media (chapter 3) and digital media (chapter 4) facilitate the development of networked media capital and, consequently, the spread of problematic information. With this foundation in place, we examine two case studies (chapters 5 and 6) that illustrate how actors with varying positions develop and deploy practices of manipulation in hybrid media contexts to spread problematic information. Rather than focus significant attention on the effects resulting from attempts at deception (cf. Chadwick & Stanyer, 2022), I home in on the media-related practices of problematic informers as well as the ways sociotechnical structures afford these practices. By focusing on the ways messages and practices are intermediated, and by remaining attuned to the many theoretical questions underlying such an inquiry, we gain a greater understanding of how power and problematic information operate in the hybrid media system.

It is worth noting what significance these analyses hold for the study of media power in an increasingly hybrid, global society. Certainly, political and geographical contexts matter in shaping the conclusions reached. I do not contend that all structures, practices, and relations visible among American networked publics will be applicable to other political cultures found across the globe. Nevertheless, I trust that much of what is presented here will be helpful in better understanding how these factors combine to shape power relations in other networked societies. Indeed, as the upcoming chapters will illustrate, American political actors—like their counterparts in other political contexts—have grown increasingly skilled at taking advantage of the various social, cultural, political, and technological configurations available in the hybrid media system to engage in deception or otherwise spread problematic information. These efforts rely largely on actors' ability to leverage traditional and media-related forms of capital, which afford them a plethora of manipulative practices. In order to grasp the full scope of media power and its (ongoing) transformation, it is necessary to develop a greater understanding of how the structures and practices facilitating problematic information have evolved over time. Thus, in the next chapter, we examine how these combinations of capital worked for masters of the late 20th-century media system before shifting our attention to the structures and practices of contemporary media.

Chapter 3

Channels of Distortion

The End of the Fairness Doctrine and the Resurgence of (Domestic) Information Warfare

In the early 1980s, before cable brought a broad spectrum of television programming to households across the United States, Bill O'Reilly worked as a journalist and television news anchor. Starting out as a reporter for local affiliate stations, he later became a correspondent for nationally broadcast programs on *CBS News* and *ABC News*. As the rise of cable and the fall of regulations created growth opportunities for broadcast media companies, they also generated openings for on-air personalities like O'Reilly. In 1989, O'Reilly made the switch to tabloid-style television, serving as the anchor for the newsmagazine *Inside Edition*, where he worked until 1995. O'Reilly's biggest break came in 1996, when he was invited to join the new cable start-up Fox News as the host of *The O'Reilly Factor*.

Like its host, the program became known for its populist brand of conservatism, which was cleverly disguised by the promise that those who tuned in were entering O'Reilly's trademarked "No Spin Zone." Over time, the show became a smashing success, enjoying the title of the top-rated cable news show for 15 years (Concha, 2020). O'Reilly's show was so successful that in 2002 he created a nationally syndicated FM spinoff, *The Radio Factor*, which he recorded at the Fox News headquarters (Wemple, 2019). Although the radio program surely benefited from the synergies it shared with *The O'Reilly Factor*, often covering many of the same issues as those discussed on the nightly television program, it topped out at number 2 in nationally aired talk shows, just behind *The Rush Limbaugh Show*. Citing a heavy workload and inability to break Limbaugh's hold over the conservative talk radio audience, O'Reilly stopped production of his radio program in 2009 but continued as host of *The O'Reilly Factor* until he was fired from Fox News in 2017 due to a slew of sexual harassment allegations (Muto, 2013; Wemple, 2019).

While O'Reilly was stripped of his largest platform, both he and Limbaugh maintained multimodal distribution structures, using radio, online video, social media, and their personal websites to share their content. In doing so, they displayed formidable media-related capital (Couldry, 2014b) based on decades of broadcast media success.[1] Drawing on such a diverse array of delivery methods is innovative in and of itself, but the commentators' ability to combine that approach with enterprising promotional strategies and carefully crafted rhetoric helped them reach the pinnacle of 20th-century media influence. Although we will return to discussions of media hybridity later in the book, the focus of this chapter is to further contextualize the structures and practices that were essential to establishing footholds of media power in a time when mediatization was on the rise. In addition to acknowledging some of the most notable precursors to the struggles for power through contemporary hybrid media, this chapter demonstrates how the masters of the broadcast era were able to attract and direct audience attention using the capital and practices at their disposal. By focusing on the political—and, to some extent, economic—frameworks underlying the success of broadcast media personalities, the chapter sheds light on the practices that drove media influence in the 20th century and beyond.

Accordingly, this chapter begins by considering the history of partisan news media in the United States before addressing the features and potential consequences of echo chambers. The chapter grapples with the shifts in audience behavior and recounts the rise of conservative talk radio beginning in the late 1980s, reflecting on some of the strategies employed and their implications for public trust in media. The chapter then addresses the role of Fox News in confirming the beliefs of a captive and politically homogeneous audience, and considers how journalists and the public form interpretive communities. The chapter concludes with an assessment of how conservative mass media wields and generates power using various forms of capital as well as numerous practices of manipulation.

A Brief History of the Partisan Press

In the United States, news and politics have long had a mutually reliant relationship. While more than 8 out of 10 American adults believe that news media "are critical or very important to our democracy," their relationship with media differ drastically depending on their political leanings ("American Views," 2018, para. 7). Whereas 54% of Democrats have a favorable view of news media, 68% of Republicans view it unfavorably ("American Views," 2018). In today's hyperpartisan political climate, where cries of "Fake news!" are common responses to information and interpretation with which one may disagree, it is tempting to romantically reflect on—even fetishize—a time when the American public was better informed and less divided.

While there have been times in America's history when this was the case, the fact is, news media have long been at the center of political divisions. As Richard Kaplan (2002) wrote of the late 19th-century press:

> In the face of . . . rigorous competition, newspapers were forced to segment the market. They refined their sales appeal in order to capture a select share of the available readers. Differences in class, ethnicity, and especially party allegiances defined these slices of the market. Competition and the consequent division of the market along the lines of popular political preferences ensured a lively partisan press. (p. 55)

One would be hard-pressed not to see both parallels and contradictions with the American press-public today. Even during times when the news industry was notably partisan and hypercompetitive, "American newspapers carried news that helped their readers to act as competent citizens and enabled them to organize for political purposes" (Starr, 2004, p. 150). In other words, news media play an integral role in fostering a vibrant (read: functional) public sphere (Habermas, 1989; Starr, 2004). While it is clear, as Habermas suggested, that reading is an important component of an informed and engaged public sphere, this assertion itself assumes that the *content* being read by the public is also facilitative of rational-critical debate.

What, then, are we to make of the burgeoning of media that shirk or undermine democratic norms? There are at least a few important factors to consider. First, Habermas, Kaplan, and Starr were all writing of a time when the news industry had much greater technoeconomic limitations—namely, the exclusionary cost of creating and distributing content. Second, the field of journalism was not yet fully formed, and the norm of objectivity was still emerging (Kaplan, 2002; Starr, 2004). Third, the 19th and early 20th centuries contained *much* less sophisticated forms of deceptive media.

Today the art of persuasion is a fully professional endeavor, with shared ties to (corporate) advertising and (political) propaganda. Furthermore, the means of producing and distributing such content are widely available, as illustrated by the team of Macedonian teenagers who, thanks to the help of social media, were credited with producing some of the most prominent "fake news" of 2016 (Subramanian, 2017). In other words, as the previous chapter made clear, while many of the classical techniques for producing and distributing propaganda persist, the form and function have changed remarkably in the new media environment. Because of these and other factors, the ongoing democratization of news production has at times contributed to the de-democratization of the public sphere.

Despite these political and economic constraints, news media have been said to serve a fundamentally democratic purpose (Strömbäck, 2005). Indeed, journalists' original function as members of the "Fourth Estate" (Hampton, 2009) or as "custodians of conscience" (Ettema & Glasser, 1998) requires that they act as a watchdog by exposing wrongdoing. While some have argued that journalists should even engage in spectacle in order to "call attention to matters requiring urgent attention" (Zaller, 2003, p. 122), others insist that the public is better served when news media provide "independent, reliable, accurate, and comprehensive information" (Kovach & Rosenstiel, 2007, p. 3). This is especially true in the context of deliberative democracy, where journalism is expected to foster inclusive and well-informed public discourse (Strömbäck, 2005). While much of the journalistic field has strived to live up to this expectation, some have rightly criticized the profession for its role in disseminating propaganda (Herman & Chomsky, 1988/2002; Lewis et al., 2008). In this sense, the journo-pundits discussed in this chapter have parlayed their media capital in ways that have helped them increase the visibility and cultural salience of their message, thus manipulating audiences while generating additional capital for themselves and their related brands. These efforts were initially enabled by the affordances of the late 20th-century media (and political) system, and they persist today in new, ever-evolving ways.

Whereas the print and broadcast eras were defined by relative scarcity, there is no longer a shortage of news organizations. In fact, one study estimates that in 2014 there were 468 native digital news sites in addition to the plethora of outlets that publish in print or broadcast as well as on the web (Jurkowitz, 2014). This is not to suggest that the news industry has grown stronger in this era. In fact, there is much evidence to suggest it is weaker, although the cause likely has little to do with the perspectives included in the news. Rather, the crisis of American journalism is largely attributed to a structural shift that occurred following a steep decline in newspaper advertising, coinciding with the rise of web-based publishing, which was exacerbated by publishers' own market strategies, including conglomerates' overinvestment in local newspapers along with a reluctance to adapt business models to the digital age (Littau, 2019). While many questions remain about how to create sustainable mechanisms to finance the work of journalism in the 21st century, there is little question that information can be produced, consumed, and shared at greater scale than ever before.

Another factor to consider in the changing media landscape is the tone and tenor Americans can expect to find in their news. The norm of objectivity, which Michael Schudson (1978) has described as "a faith in 'facts,' a distrust of 'values,' and a commitment to their segregation" (p. 6) may be seen as mythology. But it is a working ideal that has defined and distinguished professional journalism for over a century. However, the past quarter-century has seen sensationalism slowly begin to rival objectivity as the (unstated) value shaping the production of news. Whether for profit (i.e., clickbait), politics (i.e., propaganda), or both, much of what counts as news appears to be driven less by what the public needs to know to do the work of democracy and more by what it can do for its creator(s).

Changing Media Ecosystems, Echo Chambers, and Attentional Divides

In the past few decades, the American media ecosystem has undergone a profound transformation. Beginning with the rise of U.S. hyperpartisan talk radio and cable television ushered in by the end of the Fairness Doctrine in 1987, agenda-driven media masters began honing their craft of manipulation using enterprising approaches of available media to reach mass audiences. Two decades later, the combination of revolutions in internet, mobile, and network technologies once again fundamentally transformed the media system, including many citizens' relationship to it and to each other (Rainie & Wellman, 2012). These shifts in the structures of media power, including the ability of various entities to reach and persuade audiences, fundamentally changed the press-public relationship.

Up until the early 1980s, Americans' choices for news largely consisted of local and national newspapers, a few broadcast television stations, radio, and a smattering of small, alternative media. The rise of conservative talk radio in the 1980s and cable news in the 1990s meant that Americans were exposed to more news and views than ever before. While on the surface this may seem like a recipe for a more robust public sphere, the shift also paved the way for increased partisanship in news consumption—often involving programming that featured more extreme perspectives.

One consequence of this proliferation of news choices was the rise of audience fragmentation. Concerns about media-fueled echo chambers, or what might more accurately be called "epistemic bubbles" (Nguyen, 2018)—those corners of the public sphere occupied only by like-minded audiences being fed news and views that largely confirm and conform to their own worldviews—grew to be quite common (Jamieson & Cappella, 2008). Yet empirical support for the audience fragmentation thesis is mixed. On the one hand, there is little doubt that more opinion-driven news attracts audiences with like-minded perspectives. An analysis of survey data from 2008 found that while Republicans and Democrats often had distinct media preferences, audiences rarely went as far as to avoid disagreeable information (Weeks et al., 2016). But in the 21st-century media ecosystem, where news is increasingly accessed via online platforms that help generate epistemic bubbles, users do not have to intentionally avoid news and views they may disagree with—the algorithms and their largely homophilous friend networks do it for them (Pariser, 2012). Furthermore, the increasing political polarization is often said to be both a cause and a consequence of Americans living in different information ecosystems. This environment, not to mention the combative rhetoric aimed at competing news networks with different political perspectives, is likely to erode public trust in journalism. Studies from previous decades have shown that Fox News viewers are more likely to be skeptical of other establishment media, and that they often have different perceptions of political issues when compared to those who watch other television news (Morris, 2007). Other analyses of conservative media have reached similar conclusions (Bennett, 2016; Jamieson & Cappella, 2008).

On the other hand, more recent studies appear to offer empirical challenges to the audience fragmentation thesis. In response to the concerns raised about editorially and algorithmically fueled epistemic bubbles, scholars have begun diversifying the methods they use to understand Americans' news habits. One study, which used web analytic data and network analysis to track how much time users from different political demographics spent on various news websites, found that "ideologically mixed audiences ... are spending comparable amounts of time" on the same political news sites (Nelson & Webster, 2017, p. 10). In another international comparative study, news audiences in the United States and Spain were found to be less fragmented than those in the United Kingdom and Denmark (Fletcher & Nielsen, 2017). Although these findings complicate our understanding of polarization, others have raised important questions about the validity of many approaches to the study of audience fragmentation and integration in the digital age (Mukerjee et al., 2018).

Whatever the problem looks like on the ground, the public sphere is also limited by "deep disagreements" that hinge not only on disagreements about individual facts or values but about "how to gather and assess evidence in proper ways" (Kappel, 2018, para. 2). There have long been efforts to cultivate deep disagreements—or ultimately, to convert the public to a different way of thinking—by "flood[ing] the zone with shit," as Steve Bannon, the former Trump administration official and former head of Breitbart News, put it (quoted in Lewis, 2018). Strategies that spread disinformation and sow confusion can undermine the public's trust in transpartisan institutions and, as a result, disrupt their ability to help the public arrive at well-reasoned conclusions. Although new media technologies provide troubling opportunities to spread propaganda and sow discord amongst the public (Pomerantzev, 2019), neither the problem nor the political strategy is new.

Regardless of the medium, gatekeepers have the power to provide audiences with a diverse array of viewpoints and to encourage independent thinking, or to narrow the audience's epistemic universe, making some conclusions appear more sensible than others. While the former set of criteria may describe the actions of media seeking to foster deliberative democracy, the latter are more akin to ideologically constrained echo chambers. But according to C. Thi Nguyen (2018), the problem with echo chambers is greater than the exclusion of differing viewpoints. Importantly, they also entail a discrediting of other perspectives so as to inoculate their audience from being influenced by sources that complicate or contradict the propagandists' preferred narrative. Success in such endeavors requires substantial capital, and while this power worked differently in the 20th century compared to today, we can draw many important insights from the era of mass media.

The Rise of (Conservative) Talk Radio

> All things being equal, the advantage in framing goes to the side of an exchange whose message receives more exposure. (Jamieson & Cappella, 2008, p. 143).

For nearly four decades, the Fairness Doctrine required U.S. radio and television broadcasters to provide their audiences with news about issues of public interest and to attempt political balance by airing contrasting views. Although controversial, the Fairness Doctrine provided an important framework for the functioning of the public sphere in a time when news and political information were much harder to come by compared to today. However, following a landmark legal case (*Red Lion Broadcasting Co. v. FCC*, 1969) the Supreme Court ruled that the Federal Communications Commission (FCC) was no longer required to enforce the Fairness Doctrine because access to the broadcast spectrum was no longer as "scarce" as it once was. Then, on August 22, 1987, the FCC, led by Reagan administration appointees, voted to repeal it.

Nearly a year later, on August 1, 1988, the conservative firebrand Rush Limbaugh began his tenure as a nationally syndicated radio host (Rosenwald, 2019). Although he was far from the first conservative talk show host (Hemmer, 2016; Pickard, 2014), Limbaugh was a talk radio trailblazer, and the success of his program was enabled by the loosening of restrictions on political content thanks to the repeal of the Fairness Doctrine. By mixing political news with conservative views and sensationalism designed to simultaneously entertain and outrage his primarily conservative audience (Berry & Sobieraj, 2014; Jamieson & Cappella, 2008), Limbaugh helped create a market that was both profitable and politically powerful (Rosenwald, 2019).

In the early 1990s, the *Rush Limbaugh Show* and a variety of other talk radio programs were credited with bolstering conservative wins at the federal level

(Bennett, 2016). In addition to helping hold moderate and liberal politicians accountable to conservative ideals (Rosenwald, 2019), conservative talk radio was found to generate "significant change in voting decisions" among listeners from varying backgrounds and political leanings. Limbaugh's success demonstrates "how opinion leaders and media elites may prime audience cognitive schemata to base voting decisions on one set of criteria rather than another," even if there are unquestionable limits to their effects (Barker, 1999, p. 536). This finding is in line with other scholarship on agenda-setting (Shehata & Strömbäck, 2013), and Limbaugh's political and commercial achievements speak to the success of "infotainment" and "outrage" styles in political media, which grew substantially during this period (Berry & Sobieraj, 2011).

By 1996, talk radio's influence and popularity appeared to be waning slightly (Bennett, 2002), even if its politically motivated audiences were more ardent than ever. Nevertheless, another key regulatory shift was in the works that would drastically change the American media landscape. Although the stated intent of the Telecommunications Act of 1996 (2013) was to increase competition and to "let anyone enter any communications business" (para. 1), in reality it opened the floodgates to ownership concentration and the creation of what Ben Bagdikian (2014) has contentiously called "media monopolies." Whereas America's 10 largest radio companies owned 290 stations prior to the passing of the act, by 2005 that number had increased more than eightfold to 2,504 stations (Lindner & Barnard, 2020; Rossman, 2012). Most of these stations were focused on music rather than news or political talk programming, but as many music stations grew less profitable due in part to the rise of satellite radio and online streaming services, many radio executives began converting stations to talk radio in an attempt to increase advertising revenues (Berry & Sobieraj, 2011). Indeed, if talk radio hosts could attract audiences with their political musings, they could do so in ways that would keep audiences listening more actively, for longer periods, and in ways that reflected a substantial level of trust in the hosts' words. These audience characteristics were, and still are, highly attractive to advertisers, posing extraordinary opportunities for station owners to profit (Berry & Sobieraj, 2011).

This illustrates one important aspect of media personalities' power: their ability to convert media-related capital into economic capital, and vice versa. Certainly, media celebrities' ability to attract audience attention remains a significant marker of power in media fields, and the profit-driven logic of many gatekeepers has helped celebrity pundits wield power in the political field as well. But rather than viewing talk radio's right-leaning slant as a marker of owners' personal biases or as proof that only right-wing pundits can possess extraordinary amounts of media-related capital, we might better conceptualize the slant as, on the whole, reflecting the bias of advertisers and talk radio listeners. Regardless of its origins, political conservatives' dominance of the talk radio airwaves is undeniable.

According to a 2007 analysis of political talk radio conducted by the Center for American Progress and Free Press, conservative perspectives dominated the format—amounting to 10 times the share of progressive talk among those stations owned by the five largest radio conglomerates, and three times among all news/talk stations in the 10 largest U.S. radio markets (Halpin et al., 2007). A similar assessment using 2010 data found that 11 of the top 14 most popular talk radio hosts were politically conservative, while just two were moderate or independent—none was classified as liberal or progressive. Limbaugh was at the top of the 2010 charts with 15 million weekly listeners, just ahead of Sean Hannity's 14 million (Pew Research Center, 2010; cited in Berry & Sobieraj, 2011). By 2019, Limbaugh had dropped to number 2 behind Hannity (Lipsky, 2019), who inevitably received a boost from his hit show on Fox News, which featured frequent appearances by Hannity's friend and political ally Donald Trump.

During his February 2020 State of the Union Address, Trump awarded Limbaugh the Presidential Medal of Freedom, the country's highest civilian honor, in recognition of "the millions of people a day that [he] speak[s] to and that [he] inspire[s]" ("Full Transcript," 2020). Limbaugh, who was in attendance that night, appeared to be as shocked as many Americans were by this announcement. According to Google Trends data, searches for "Presidential Medal of Freedom" were at their highest in February 2020, perhaps due to the publicity the announcement received—it was made during a national address that was broadcast live by at least seven television networks (Kelly, 2020)—as well as the controversy surrounding the recipient. In fact, although Limbaugh may have been revered by friends and foes for his knack for radio, his entertaining style, and his political prowess (Rosenwald, 2019), he had a long history of political incorrectness and incivility. Like Trump and many other media manipulators discussed in this book, Limbaugh on many occasions used racist and misogynistic rhetoric (Maloy, 2012; Perlman, 2012) to shock audiences, attract attention, and further his political-economic objectives. In doing so, Limbaugh deployed a number of the manipulative practices discussed in chapter 2, including kernels of truth, populist or racist appeals, and pseudo-journalistic presentation—strategies that were extraordinarily potent considering his substantial media capital as a nationally syndicated radio host. A related outcome of Limbaugh's skilled attempts at media manipulation is illustrated by his undeniable success in helping galvanize conservative public opinion and erode trust in American institutions—most notably, the "liberal media."

CULTIVATING (DIS)TRUST

Limbaugh may be among the most popular and influential media figures in modern American history, but he did not work alone. Rather, he operated alongside an organized effort to spread right-wing ideology and mold future generations into outspoken conservative political activists (DiBranco, 2020). To accomplish these goals, Limbaugh and his contemporaries not only needed to share conservative political views and to increase audience commitment to conservative causes through creative, outrageous framing. They also needed to insulate the listening public from influence by alternative frames produced by other, more mainstream sources.

A pathbreaking 2008 analysis of American political talk radio by Kathleen Hall Jamieson and Joseph Cappella found that "conservative outlets marginalize mainstream media and minimize their effects" (p. 4). In order to wield such influence in an already competitive media industry, pundits like Limbaugh first had to attract an audience. In addition to the creativity of mixing political opinion and infotainment, another important factor in a program's success was its accessibility. Much like their successors on cable TV news and other digital media, talk radio programming was becoming widely available to audiences, and some programs, like the *Rush Limbaugh Show*, aired for three hours each day. This extended format afforded ample opportunities for hosts to build connections with the audience and, over time, to reshape what political issues they focused on, and how.

One of the most effective ways communicators can shift how audience members think about a political issue is by offering compelling frames. If *framing* is the ability of media creators to decide which aspects of a story to emphasize and what context to place them in, then such selection will inevitably make some issues more salient than others (Entman, 1993). Framing is unavoidable, although the frames audiences encounter often differ drastically depending on where they source information and which standards media makers apply in the production process. For example, while established news outlets are likely to frame coverage in ways that adhere to the journalism profession's norms of objectivity, political talk programs on talk radio, cable television news, and the web are more likely to approach issues from more discernable political positions (Peters, 2010). Given the relative absence of recognizable conservative frames in the majority of news programs and the long-standing efforts to erode public trust in establishment news by claiming "liberal bias" (Hemmer, 2016; Lane, 2020), right-leaning consumers are often primed to believe they are being misled by journalists. Pundits like Limbaugh take full advantage of this situation, often making it the primary focus of their programming.

In order to undermine public belief in the existence of objective journalism, to position themselves as more trustworthy, and to provide counterframes of common issues covered by news media, conservative media makers commonly practice gatewatching. As I have written previously, *gatewatching* "entails observation, amplification, and criticism of professional media work with an emphasis on holding publishers accountable to the public" (Barnard, 2018a, p. 55). Although previous work has addressed this phenomenon in the context of good-faith efforts to improve the products and processes of reporting through increased citizen involvement (Bruns, 2014), there is a need to consider more thoroughly what function gatewatching serves within professional, opinion-driven media. This includes considering fair criticisms of one's competition as well as dishonest or propagandistic appeals to authority, such as by suggesting that establishment media are colluding to mislead the American public, advance a liberal agenda, and silence conservative voices, as media figures on the right often claim (Lyons, 2020; Meeks, 2020). As we will see, gatewatching is key to conservative media efforts to differentiate themselves and build credibility with their audience.

Like many other conservative media personalities, Limbaugh characterized his programming as antithetical to what listeners would encounter in the purportedly liberal mainstream media. According to one analysis of conservative talk radio leading up to the 1996 presidential election, nearly 60% of Limbaugh's references to mainstream news media were either "reframings" or "attacks" (Jamieson & Cappella, 2008, p. 169). By making a concerted effort to criticize the news media while also citing them when coverage benefited conservatives, Limbaugh's framings underscore journalists' supposedly liberal biases. They also situate conservative pundits as fair-minded for acknowledging that not all reporting from establishment sources is untrustworthy—a practice of manipulation described in chapter 2 as dissociation. Once these frames have been established, not only can they be reinforced when examples present themselves, but their hanging presence helps insulate listeners from influence by alternative frames (Jamieson & Cappella, 2008). Thus, the rhetorical strategies displayed by Limbaugh and others are integral to conservative media causes because they serve dual functions: first, eroding public trust in established media, and second, inserting themselves as the legitimate alternative. This approach has also been adopted, with great success, by America's most influential cable news outlet.

The Birth of Fox News

The link between Fox News and political talk radio should hardly come as a surprise. Both frequently rely on a similar bombastic style and consistently conservative tilt to capture audiences. They have also shared some of their most successful personalities, including Bill O'Reilly, Sean Hannity, and Glenn Beck. But the linkages date back even further, to the founding of the network.

When Rupert Murdoch hired Roger Ailes to run Fox News, he realized the network had the potential to be exceptionally profitable as well as politically influential. In addition to serving as a media advisor to Richard Nixon and George H. W. Bush and working as a producer at NBC as well as the *Rush Limbaugh Show*, Ailes had already tried his hand at launching a conservative television news network (Sherman, 2014). While some of his efforts were more successful than others, Ailes clearly possessed substantial media-related capital, having already made a career of straddling the media and political spheres. Building Fox News was his ultimate achievement. Although the network was slow to start following its launch in 1996, disadvantaged in part by its limited adoption by cable television carriers, Fox soon found its stride covering sensational issues conservatives could coalesce around (Project for Excellence in Journalism, 2004). These included the 1998 impeachment hearings of Bill Clinton, the battle over recounting ballots in the 2000 presidential election, and the events following the September 11, 2001, terrorist attacks (Sherman, 2014). By 2002, Fox had established itself as the highest rated cable television news network—a lead it has consistently held, with the exception of a short period following the 2020 presidential election (O'Connell, 2014; Peters, 2022).

The fact that Ailes was tapped to run a news organization was undeniably consequential. Although Fox initially claimed its mission was to be an outlet for objective journalism, it soon became clear that the network was more interested in differentiating itself by producing sensational content and, eventually, right-wing propaganda that would attract conservative audiences (Bard, 2017; Winner, 2013). By the start of the U.S. invasion of Iraq in 2003, Fox News had less than a third of the staff compared to its primary competitor, CNN, and less than half the number of press bureaus (Project for Excellence in Journalism, 2004). Whether a testament to its cost-saving ethos, its political agenda, or both, the network maintained a relatively narrow focus for a 24-hour news station, covering fewer stories than its competitors but devoting greater attention to its chosen issues.

Over the years, Fox News has maintained its selective focus while doubling-down on its conservative bias, earning broad recognition as an agenda-setter for the Republican Party and its voters. According to a 2018 analysis of Fox's news and opinion programming, when compared to its competitors CNN and MSNBC, the network devoted more attention to issues such as media bias, immigration, Hillary Clinton, and the Second Amendment, while devoting less attention to issues that did not play as well to its primarily Republican audience (Chang, 2018). While issue selection does provide a notable indication of a network's priorities, the way issues are covered is also deeply consequential. Although Fox's news programs still regularly produce accurate reporting that generally adheres to the norms of objectivity, its most influential, opinion-based programs form an echo chamber that push their hosts' preferred narratives with varying truthfulness while "shielding the audience from opposing facts and points of view and by discrediting opposing claims and the individuals making them" (Bard, 2017, p. 108).

Such consistent manipulation and misrepresentation of reality is bound to have consequences. Some studies have found that Fox News viewers are more likely to be misinformed compared with viewers of other programs (Kull et al., 2003), while others have shown that exposure to Fox News is predictive of decreased support for Mexican immigration—a finding that holds true for conservatives as well as liberals (Gil de Zúñiga et al., 2012). Similar research has also shown that Fox News viewership is associated with moderate increases in Republican vote shares (Martin & Yurukoglu, 2017; Schroeder & Stone, 2015), as well as lower levels of trust in scientists (Hmielowski et al., 2014). More recently, scholarship has shown that those who relied on right-wing media like Fox News and Limbaugh for news about the COVID-19 pandemic were more likely to be misinformed about the virus's origin and the threat it poses (Jamieson & Albarracín, 2020; Motta et al., 2020), and therefore less likely to act in accordance with public health guidelines (Bursztyn et al., 2020; Simonov et al., 2020).

Interpretive Communities: Media Professionals and the "People Formerly Known as the Audience"

To be clear, I am not arguing that media have "magic bullet–like" effects on members of the public (Marwick, 2018, p. 485; cf. Arceneaux & Johnson, 2013). Rather, this book considers media messages to be one part of a more complex interpretive process whereby people from various social locations, and with somewhat unique political identities and media consumption habits, interact with information from sources that affirm or, to a lesser extent, challenge their worldview. While the mediator has arguably become as important as the medium and the message, considering how much trust is contingent on *who* the perceived mediator is (Turcotte et al., 2015), the interpretive process has inevitably grown more complex in the age of hybrid media. Furthermore, as Benkler et al. (2018) demonstrate, it is not just prominent political actors (i.e., media institutions) that shape the flow of problematic information. Indeed, "the people formerly known as the audience" (Rosen, 2006) also have an important role to play.

The process of meaning-making in media is said to occur via two distinct phases of interpretation. First, there are *interpretive communities*—social groups that "share interpretive strategies not for reading but for writing texts, for constituting their properties" (Fish, 1980, p. 14). In other words, interpretive communities are those with the power to make and transmit meaning for broader publics. Accordingly, journalists have been characterized as such because they "are subconsciously members of interpretive communities that share meanings, work norms, and a 'common-sense' vision that guides them in creating the news products they produce each day" (Berkowitz, 2018, p. 1; see also Zelizer, 1993). Such a conceptualization resonates strongly with Bourdieu's (1990) view of journalists as operating in a professional field with their own "feel for the game" (pp. 66).

After a message is encoded, receivers inevitably interpret (or decode) it according to their own systems of meaning and interpretation. In a time of mediatization, this process of collective interpretation frequently occurs in digital spaces (Bruns & Burgess, 2015; Gerbaudo, 2022). While publics are rarely as organized as professional producers, they frequently engage in patterned actions that serve to construct common, shared meanings. One way this occurs is through shared identity and ideology. For example, in her study of the news consumption practices of Christian conservatives, Francesca Tripodi (2018) found that members of this social group used common methods of searching for and reading news which inadvertently led them to reach similar (and often false or highly misleading) conclusions about various political issues. This method of close reading, or "scriptural inference"—which Tripodi's subjects adapted from their approach to religious scripture, and with the encouragement of their pastor—gave preference to individuals' own interpretation of texts rather than relying on the characterization offered by reporters. By paying special attention to specific details, such as a falsely reported dollar amount, and using those details to guide their Google queries, the search platform was likely to return bias-confirming information even though the claims had been fact-checked, debunked, and widely reported elsewhere (Tripodi, 2018).

Such findings fall in line with other studies that have demonstrated how contemporary media consumption is likely to reinforce rather than challenge existing beliefs (Pariser, 2012). In their highly detailed analysis of the flow of networked propaganda around the 2016 U.S. presidential election, Benkler et al. (2018) demonstrate how various actors and media outlets—especially those occupying the right wing of the American political sphere—can work in a coordinated manner to form a "propaganda feedback loop" (cf. Guess et al., 2018). Whereas publics have traditionally relied on journalists to serve as arbiters of truth, Benkler and colleagues found that right-wing media served "identity-confirming" functions. Thus, combining the inevitability of conservative perspectives with the "fair and balanced" promise became a defining feature of the Fox News brand (Peters, 2010).

In addition to benefiting from the partisan bias of many outlets, some quirks of journalists' interpretive community led establishment media outlets to unintentionally report false or misleading information (Benkler et al., 2018, p. 213). All too often, journalists' feel for the game—in this case, the pressure to remain objective coupled with the lure of sensationalism in a highly competitive, market-driven environment—created an opening that actors in the political sphere could exploit. By providing reporters with primary source documents related to the Clinton Foundation, Trump's 2016 presidential campaign was able to manipulate media coverage and, consequently, to help set the agenda for the public. These examples illustrate how the two stages of interpretation discussed above, creation and reception, can combine to great effect.

When viewed against the backdrop of minimal effects research, which emphasizes a "two-step flow" of influence—from media to thought leaders and thought leaders to the public (Katz & Lazarsfeld, 1955)—this suggests that while the messages matter, so too does the mediator, and indeed the medium. Hence, the primary strategy of the "propaganda pipeline" (Benkler et al., 2018) is to seek coverage from specific outlets to gain visibility and, ultimately, legitimacy once a false or highly misleading claim is shared by establishment media outlets. This was the case with the Uranium One and Seth Rich conspiracy theories that played out in the lead-up to the 2016 U.S. presidential election, and it was Fox News that took the false, sensationalistic clickbait and helped push it into the mainstream (Benkler et al., 2018). As the analyses in this book will show, there were similar processes at play in drawing media attention to countless other issues and events, and it was actors' ability to combine and convert various forms of capital that proved essential to their efforts.

In a highly mediatized environment where social network ties increasingly take on digital forms, and where significant portions of the public—especially those on the political margins—receive the bulk of their news from identity-confirming sources (Mitchell et al., 2021b), it may be no surprise that today's pundits can play the role of both mediator and thought leader. In other words, they offer the potential to streamline the two-step flow. This is one development that has created new opportunities for political communicators to manipulate the agenda-setting process. Recognizing some of the enterprising ways media can be leveraged by actors from varying positions for the purposes of agenda-setting is essential to understanding how practices of manipulation and, by extension, networked media capital work. But how do media actors generate and wield such influence? What characteristics do they have in common? What practical approaches did they develop using the media of the 20th century? Addressing these questions is the focus of the chapter's final section.

Leveraging Mass Media: Assessing Pundits' Media Capital and Practices of Manipulation

As the previous chapter made clear, media afford political communicators with important tools for attracting public attention and shaping public consciousness. Like other social and technological structures, the broadcast media of the late 20th century provided a means through which communicators could develop and deploy various forms of capital as well as practices of manipulation. Although 21st-century media undoubtedly present new opportunities for attention hacking and manipulation, the masters of late 20th-century media have a lot to teach us about networked media capital. But to be clear, communicators like Limbaugh, Hannity, and O'Reilly did not really have to *hack* the media system to generate attention for their messages. While the distribution of problematic information required less enterprising techniques for the influential purveyors discussed in this chapter—they are, after all, established public figures with substantial media capital thanks to the sizable audiences their broadcast platforms afford them—they nevertheless wield various other forms of capital and exemplify many of the practices of manipulation discussed in chapter 2.

As masters of broadcast media, the right-wing pundits discussed in this chapter possess(ed) substantial capital (Bourdieu, 1993). Certainly, these pundits each held immense cultural capital—as reflected by their *institutionalized* credentials, *objectified* via the facility with which they navigated the mediatized political sphere, and *embodied* in their apparently internalized "schemes of appreciation and understanding" of the cultural landscape (Swartz, 1997, p. 76). Such embodied forms of cultural capital were often exercised through their reliance on orthodox (read: oppressive) ideologies of classism, racism, and sexism, among others. Overall, these pundits were not only smashing commercial successes who generated and benefited from extraordinary economic capital; they also built powerful reputations, or symbolic capital, as notable voices in the public sphere. Furthermore, their privileged position as mass-media gatekeepers gave them access to a great deal of social capital. These networked resources were accessible thanks to their respective channels' audiences, but also through the network of affiliated organizations—from conglomerate owners and fellow conservative political elites to corporate sponsors and advertisers on their programs—which simultaneously fueled and helped legitimate their subsequent brands and messaging.

Although it is perhaps ironic given their frequent use of antiestablishment rhetoric (Roberts, 2020), establishment institutions are often what help political media actors build social and symbolic capital in the first place. The fact that so-called mainstream media institutions such as conservative talk radio and cable news offered a platform to firebrand pundits was key to legitimating them and, consequently, their ideas. Giving them a microphone capable of reaching mass audiences also meant bestowing on them considerable media capital (Couldry, 2003). Indeed, in the late 1990s and early 2000s, radio and television news had the trust of roughly half of the American public at the time (Brenan, 2019). This media capital is built recursively by the first-order act of legitimation of being granted air and by their use of the opportunity to grow their own status among a segmented audience, which is a secondary but equally important step. When combined, these resources grant pundits the symbolic power necessary to make meaning in parts of the public sphere. Without these steps, it is unclear whether substantial portions of the public would view the mediators and messages as legitimate, especially as they stray further from media industry orthodoxy in style and substance.

Accordingly, many of the practices of manipulation outlined in chapter 2 can be found in the repertoires of the broadcast pundits being considered here. Perhaps most notable are those practices pertaining to legitimation. Legitimation is a dialectical process that involves gatekeepers, media celebrities, and the public themselves. Nevertheless, audiences' perception of mediator legitimacy is also contingent on many performative aspects, including hosts' characteristics, their selection of topics, strategic use of language and other cultural markers, and overall ideological positioning (Peck, 2019). Pundits seek to gain legitimacy not only by using pseudo-journalistic labels (i.e., Fox *News* Radio [emphasis added]) or by reaffirming the beliefs and political identities of their target audience—often through populist appeals—but also by associating themselves with in-group figures and against the "liberal media." Whether basing outlandish claims on kernels of truth, using spectacular or outrageous rhetoric, or appealing to populist or racist sensibilities, such tactics have proven essential for many prominent purveyors of problematic information on the political right. Furthermore, although most mass-media programs likely require little additional amplification beyond the tried-and-true methods of sensationalism and search engine optimization, they still benefit from utilizing practices of manipulation as they generate content. And while not necessary, establishment media outlets also utilize enterprising techniques of amplification that demonstrate how media capital is networked. This will be shown in greater detail in chapter 5.

Taken together, these tactics have enabled the broadcast media masters discussed in this chapter to generate public attention, shape issue agendas, and deploy and further amass capital of various sorts. Importantly, these pundits' propensity to draw on their diverse array of capital to enterprisingly leverage a variety of media illustrate *elementary forms* of networked media capital.[2] Additionally, by applying the practices of manipulation to mass-media broadcasts, they have not only helped cultivate a taste for problematic information among much of the public but have also inspired future generations of media manipulators. However, before we can fully grapple with how these practices play out in digital contexts, we must first consider how the structures and affordances of the hybrid media system shape contemporary media practices. This is where we turn our attention in the next chapter.

Chapter 4

What Are Platforms For? Profit, Persuasion, and (Dis)Information

On January 6, 2021, millions of Americans watched in awe as hordes of pro-Trump protestors waged an attack on the U.S. Capitol. Equipped with body armor, pepper spray, and assorted weaponry, members of the mob forced their way into Congress—roaming the halls, entering offices, and taking over the Senate chamber. Their goals were as diverse and ambiguous as they were onerous, but the overarching reason for the attack was to halt the congressional proceedings to officially certify the electoral college votes that would make Joe Biden the 46th president of the United States. Most in the mob were still hyped up from the "Stop the Steal" rally, where Donald Trump himself encouraged the crowd to march to the Capitol building and "show strength" in support of his presidency (Naylor, 2021).

Despite the rally's importance for the events of January 6, Trump's speech was hardly the most significant spark. Rather, it was his endless barrage of unsubstantiated claims that the election was being stolen—a claim he made months before any votes had been cast—that were perhaps the most consequential. While Trump certainly took advantage of his access to professional media channels, he also relied heavily on social media sites like Twitter, Facebook, and YouTube to spread his messages. Trump's most ardent followers, many of whom saw themselves as members of his digital army, relied even more heavily on digital media to access and share pro-Trump information. They also used many of those platforms to coordinate and livestream their insurrection (Heilweil & Ghaffary, 2021).

Once the rioters started waging violence against Capitol police, there were repeated calls for Trump to call off the attack. But he was uncharacteristically silent—no tweets or television appearances. It took almost two hours after the crowd breached the Capitol for Trump to post a careful message on Twitter and Facebook calling for supporters to "stay peaceful" and to "support . . . law enforcement" (Brown, n.d.). In the days that followed, Trump remained unapologetic about his efforts to incite the attack. Meanwhile, he continued to use his social media megaphones to spread baseless conspiracy theories about leftist agitators inciting violence and a stolen election.

It was perhaps this continued attempt to undermine the peaceful transfer of power as well as his celebration of violence that proved to be the last straw for social media companies. Within a few days of the attack, they finally took a stand against Trump's abuse of their platforms by suspending or banning his accounts (Fisher & Gold, 2021). Facebook and YouTube suspended Trump's account indefinitely, while Twitter described their response as a permanent ban.[1] These decisions raised the ire of his supporters and others in favor of unvarnished "free speech"—a principle that the Supreme Court has ruled does not apply to privately run spaces. However, excepting the relatively few instances where they marked his posts as "misleading" (Tyko, 2020) or "missing context" (Keegan et al., 2021), prior to January 6 social media platforms did little to stem the flow of problematic information coming from the White House.

So why did Silicon Valley fail to rein in Trump's and his supporters' manipulative use of social media? Furthermore, why are digital media so useful in efforts to spread problematic information? The answer to both questions is explained in part by social media companies' core business models, which convert user attention to advertising revenue.

Still, there's much more to the story. This chapter delves deeper into the structure of social media platforms, examining which of their affordances facilitate the spread of problematic information, and how. Building on the previous chapter's discussion of right-wing media personalities' skillful use of talk radio and cable TV, we now shift our focus from the more traditional purveyors and practices of problematic information to the platforms that provide the basis for such efforts to proliferate across the hybrid media system. Accordingly, the overarching goal of this chapter is to examine how the structures and cultures of social media platforms alter the professional media landscape, contribute to amassing networked media capital, and facilitate the spread of problematic information.

With these concerns in mind, the remainder of this chapter situates the aforementioned contests for media power in a broader political, economic, and technological context. After reviewing the political environment within which social media companies operate, the chapter delves deeper into the platforms' common business model and explores how the logic of surveillance capitalism shapes the flow of information (and power). Following a critical review of the politics of moderation leading up to Trump's involuntary departure from social media, the chapter further illustrates the growing significance of social media within the hybrid media system and considers how such developments enabled practitioners to advance new repertoires of manipulation. The chapter then offers a detailed assessment of how and why platform structures afford manipulative practices before concluding with some reflections on how these insights bear upon the remainder of the book.

Platform Logic: All Content Is Good Content (as Long as It Generates Attention)

Despite the popular assertion in conservative political circles that all social media companies are run by liberal elites (and are therefore systematically biased against them), the driving ideology of Silicon Valley is *profit*. With a fervor akin to religious fundamentalism, companies like Facebook and Twitter have long been unabashedly committed to the values of capitalism. While this assertion should come as no surprise given that most are publicly traded companies, it is a far cry from their corporate mottos to "build community and bring the world closer together" (Facebook) and to "promote healthy conversations" (Twitter). These values contrast starkly with the reality of how their platforms are used in practice, as well as how their policies are implemented.

There is perhaps no greater example of the divide between theory and practice than how the companies have handled the rise of right-wing extremism in general, and Donald Trump in particular. Following Trump's infamous May 29, 2020, post on Facebook and Twitter asserting that "when the looting starts, the shooting starts"—a thinly veiled threat to use military force to quell protests against police violence and racial injustice—Mark Zuckerberg, the CEO of Facebook's parent company, Meta, held a phone call with Trump to voice his concerns about the statement. While Twitter decided to take the rare action of hiding the post behind a warning label because it violated the company's policy against "glorifying violence," Facebook executives decided to allow Trump's statement to remain in circulation on the platform (Dwoskin et al., 2020).

This decision should not surprise those who followed the saga over content moderation and algorithmic amplification at Facebook. Indeed, at the direction of Zuckerberg and Facebook's vice president of global public policy, Joel Kaplan, a vocal Republican and former George W. Bush administration official, the company had long been working to tweak their policies in order to minimize the disproportionate effects their moderation efforts may have on conservatives (Hao, 2021; Mac & Silverman, 2021; Timberg, 2020). Some of those interventions included overriding the work of content moderators to undo penalties imposed against conservative pages for sharing misinformation, blocking company plans to minimize the visibility of "misleading political posts" on users' news feeds, limiting the scope of fact-checking measures that would notify users if they were exposed to false information, and continuing Facebook's practice of recommending political posts and pages that users did not follow (Mac & Silverman, 2021).

Such interventions, of course, do not occur in a vacuum. Rather, they are the product of a fraught political-economic climate where profit and growth are universally celebrated and policies are often applied in misguided and overly simplistic ways. Facebook executives, for example, knew that more extreme content is likely to generate more engagement, yet they allowed their algorithms to continue recommending such posts so long as they adhered to the company's rather malleable policies on acceptable content (Hao, 2021). Despite this, social media companies like Meta have performed a delicate dance of attracting public attention for steps they have taken to moderate or remove egregious violations of their policy while at the same time attempting to appear politically neutral and avoiding further public scrutiny.

As might be expected, this complex situation is in part a product of the regulatory regime that governs the U.S. digital media system (Nielsen & Ganter, 2022). Just as the repeal of the Fairness Doctrine paved the way for right-wing radicalization on talk radio and cable news (as discussed in chapter 3), the passing of the Communications Decency Act of 1996 (CDA) helped define how information would be handled online. The oft-discussed Section 230 of the CDA holds that online forums (including social media platforms) will not be held legally responsible for the vast majority of content published by third parties. Although there are limits to what forum owners are immune to—for example, they can be held liable for aiding in the distribution of extremely harmful content, such as for sex trafficking—the legislation has generally given those who administer online platforms the power to moderate their sites (or not) as they see fit. Such a regulatory approach has generally been effective in supporting innovation across the web (Nielsen & Ganter, 2022), but that innovation has come at a cost. Namely, social media platforms have been allowed to take a mostly laissez-faire approach to content moderation, focusing the bulk of their attention on developing tools to boost user engagement and advertising revenues with little concern for their latent effects. This serves as an important complement to the broader pattern of color-blindness in Silicon Valley (Daniels, 2018), which has allowed for the continued codification of racial inequality (Benjamin, 2019; Noble, 2018). As a result, companies like Facebook, Twitter, and YouTube have facilitated—and profited handily from—the proliferation of problematic information (Crain & Nadler, 2019), while at the same time further contributing to racial inequalities (Dwoskin et al. 2021; Siapera, 2022). Considering this history and their crackdown on Trump and other conservative accounts following the January 6, 2021, attack on the Capitol, the social media giants remain, as of this writing, at the center of a political controversy about a possible repeal or revision of Section 230 of the CDA.

This tension has been punctuated by recent debates in Washington, D.C., about social media companies' role in spreading disinformation and enabling the rise of political extremism. Congressional hearings are just one avenue through which social media companies have endured public criticism from a number of prominent figures on the political right, including Trump, who have criticized companies like Facebook, Twitter, and Google for being biased against conservative voices (Rosalsky, 2020; Timberg, 2020). Commonly referred to as "flak" (Herman & Chomsky, 1988/2002), this criticism is often designed to apply pressure, akin to "working the referees," with the hope of shaping future decision-making.[2] This constant barrage of flak and the threat of regulatory action further complicate the landscape the companies must navigate. In addition, the companies are working to mitigate the risk of alienating large swaths of its two most essential populations—users and advertisers—whose attention and expenditures the companies rely on for the bulk of their profits.

Although political advertisements accounted for roughly 3% of Facebook's revenue in the third quarter of 2020 (Levy et al., 2020), social media companies' advertising relationships with politicians is big business. The Trump campaign spent an estimated $44 million on Facebook advertisements during the final six months of the 2016 campaign (Clark, 2018). The strategy was so successful that Trump's 2020 campaign spent $89.1 million on Facebook ads from April 9, 2020, until the platform halted its sales of political ads a week before the November 3 election (Dumenco & Brown, 2020).[3] Those paid advertisements are not subject to the same rules as other content on the platform—a policy decision that, regardless of intention, further enabled Trump to deceive millions of Americans (Legum, 2019a).

To be clear, Facebook is hardly an outlier. While other social media platforms like Twitter and YouTube may differ—at times significantly—in their technical infrastructure, user base, and strategies for policy formation and enforcement, they also bear significant responsibility for helping to amplify problematic information. Indeed, all three share a common business model: taking advantage of unpaid labor (i.e., users uploading content at no cost to the platforms) to attract audience attention, which is then sold to advertisers for profit. This business model has a unique and evolving history, and it invariably shapes the overall strategies taken by the platform companies as well as the various communicators who use those channels.

IN THE BUSINESS OF SURVEILLANCE AND PERSUASION

Despite the very real political pressures that inevitably factor into the decisions of companies whose products constitute important parts of the networked public sphere, other forces also play an important role. The most notable and universal factor shaping corporate strategy appears to be the constant drive for (ever-increasing) profits. This is certainly the case with the development of contemporary digital media infrastructure.

All commercial media platforms are designed to attract an audience and to channel that attention toward a desired end (i.e., profit and/or persuasion). Accordingly, such platforms should be thought of, perhaps first and foremost, as *persuasion architectures*. While the term was coined in reference to websites selling commercial products (Eisenberg & Eisenberg, 2006), it has since been broadened to explain the use of information platforms to better understand, and then predict or influence, human behavior. As Tufekci (2017b) argues, social media platforms have been designed to channel users' attention toward advertising. The more time users spend on the platform, the more social media companies know about their users, and the more successful they can be at helping advertisers reach desired audiences with content customized to maximize its persuasive capacities. The burgeoning of persuasion architectures is a distinct product of mediatization and is made possible by the ongoing convergence of media forms, or hybridization.

Today's *platforms*, such as Facebook, Twitter, and Google, that serve as intermediary points between content and audience, operate according to a significantly different framework when compared to more traditional *publishers*, such as Fox News, NBC, and the *New York Times*, which are more explicitly tasked with creating and curating content for distribution to an audience (Nielsen & Ganter, 2022; Shoemaker & Vos, 2009). Whereas platforms outsource much of this work to algorithms and users, publishers remain centrally focused on gatekeeping. Accordingly, the growth of platforms along with the lack of structural awareness and visibility of the curation that occurs there has transformed the nature of gatekeeping in the 21st century (Barnard, 2018a). These same changes also make persuasion architectures that much more effective, which, as we will see, leads to some troubling implications for the dynamics of media and power.

Persuasion architectures take on a variety of forms. While most are designed to attract a broad, public audience, there are also metapersuasion architectures specifically tooled to help publishers better understand what content is most attractive to audiences, and to cater future content accordingly. Today's media companies have sophisticated methods of tracking the traffic generated by each story they publish (Christin, 2018; Petre, 2015). These analytics platforms, such as the industry-leading Chartbeat, provide a view of the kinds of issues and perspectives that resonate with audiences, which, in turn, can help media companies maximize economic and ideological returns.[4] Although such digital methods may be more valid and reliable—and provide a more holistic view—than the traditional Nielsen ratings, legacy media companies have long known, in general at least, what kinds of content will grab the attention of the audience. Digital platforms, on the other hand, have developed their own enterprising methods of tracking user behavior for the purposes of targeting and prediction, and it is this model which has reverberated across the digital media ecosystem.

Shortly after the turn of the century, Google discovered that the digital byproducts created by users' online behavior—what kinds of content they click on, what websites they purchase from, who they communicate with, their location, etc.—had a predictive power that, if used effectively, could prove highly profitable. This realization marked the beginning of a new era that Shoshanna Zuboff (2019) has termed "surveillance capitalism" (cf. Couldry & Mejias, 2019). This new economic imperative is enabled by a burgeoning technological infrastructure designed to allow consumers to make their everyday lives more efficient while simultaneously generating valuable data. This is precisely the dual function served by technologies categorized as part of the "Internet of Things" (IoT), a classification of networked technologies that include computers, mobile phones, automobiles, refrigerators, thermostats, Bluetooth speakers, and other "smart home" devices. It is estimated that there were more than 13 billion IoT devices in use globally as of 2022, and that this number will more than double by 2029 (Vailshery, 2022).

As digital technologies take center stage in everyday life, the digital traces users leave behind grow exponentially. Accordingly, companies have developed increasingly proactive strategies to generate and harvest user data. For example, one report showed Google having approximately 3 million Word documents on a single user, whereas Facebook had "roughly 400,000 Word documents" (Curran, 2018, para. 11). These data provide extraordinary and ever-increasing potential for communicators to intervene in the lives of the public with priming that increase their chances of taking one action or another.

One notable implication of this ongoing datafication of the social world is how it has encouraged advertisers to make drastic shifts in the way they reach audiences. Whereas earlier forms of communication technologies allowed advertisers to segment audiences by broad demographic types, today's digital advertising system, enabled by surveillance capitalism and artificial intelligence, allows advertisers to reach increasingly narrow slices of a given population with customized messages. By drawing on vast swaths of data to generate detailed profiles of each user, including personality types, behavioral patterns, and political leanings, advertisers are able to target users as individuals, maximizing their potential persuasive power. Such affordances, in turn, create new opportunities for the generation and application of networked media capital.

The use of personal data and predictive analytics to feed citizens' customized messages designed to prey on their emotions and ultimately persuade them to alter their behavior according to the communicator's will is not just an advancement in the techniques of propaganda and persuasion. Given the scalability of these techniques—note that Cambridge Analytica claimed to have "4,000 data points on some 230 million Americans" (Poulsen, 2018)—such developments mark a notable change in the nature of political communication (cf. Karpf, 2018). Consider, for example, the Trump 2016 election campaign strategy to demobilize likely Democratic voters in swing districts by feeding them "dark ads" that were invisible to other users (Poulsen, 2018). Such developments illustrate the potential power that can come from leveraging economic and cultural capital to propel messaging campaigns.

As a public, we lack adequate knowledge about what effects such messages have had on individual voters, let alone the overall election results. Still, combining campaigns' access to extraordinarily detailed information about individual members of the public with the powerful affordances of persuasion architectures like Facebook, Twitter, and Google, and a willingness to weaponize those tools in ways that too often lack public oversight or clear ethical grounding, creates a scenario that is ripe for media manipulation. Keeping in mind these developments as well as the shift from traditional publishers' journalistic logic to hybrid media logics driven by platforms' technological fundamentalism and commitment to surveillance capitalism (Gillespie, 2014), it is clear that the rise of the platform era marks a definitive shift in the media system and the ways power can flow from and through it. Historically, many platforms have struggled to respond with appropriate measures that help counteract undemocratic effects.

TROUBLE WITH MODERATION

Platform providers have long been grappling with the challenge of when and how to moderate the content on their sites. Starting with some of the internet's earliest public forums, moderators have struggled to set and enforce fair standards that strike an ideal balance that ensures users have the *freedom to* share as they wish while also trying to grant other users *freedom from* exposure to content that is seen as harmful. Whereas CDA Section 230 provides platforms with a supportive legal framework, decisions to moderate (or not) have often been driven by a profit-oriented desire to retain users (Gillespie, 2018; Roberts, 2019).

In the decade between social media platforms' emergence in the mid-2000s and the shifting political climate of the mid-2010s, social media companies devoted relatively few resources to content moderation. For example, while Facebook's parent company, Meta, reported spending $13 billion on "safety and security" between 2016 and 2021 (Wagner, 2021), their annual revenue increased from $27 billion to $117 billion over that time period (Statista, 2022). Given the company's increasing profitability and their failure to sufficiently address the growing problem of problematic information on their platforms, that level of expenditure appears wildly inadequate.

Then there is the question of moderation strategies. Not surprisingly, not all types of questionable content have been seen as deserving of moderation by social media companies. Copyright infringement, violence, and nudity—three types of content for which the distributor could be deemed legally and financially liable—have been treated as serious problems deserving of attention. As a result, social media companies have taken multipronged approaches, constantly updating policy, hiring and training teams of moderators, and creating artificial intelligence tools to help auto-detect content that violates their terms of service (Newton, 2019a). Many companies, such as Meta, have relied heavily on subcontractors to moderate content on their platforms, but because the subcontractors are not technically Meta employees, they have not enjoyed the same pay, benefits, and work environment as others who have worked for Meta. Structuring the labor force in this way may make legal and financial sense, but insulating moderation from other divisions of the company creates structural impediments to ethically driven decision-making. More broadly, platforms often struggle to adequately define the problem and to codify their intended response. Despite assistance from artificial intelligence as well as teams of policy and content experts, the primary challenge for corporate policymakers and moderators alike was how to clearly and consistently differentiate between ordinary public discourse and abusive, inauthentic, or otherwise harmful content (McGregor, 2020b).

Social media companies have abdicated much of the responsibility for policing such content to their users, who have been allowed to self-report or "flag" content they believed violated platform policies. Despite users performing such unpaid labor, the problematic information often persisted. For example, not only did Facebook allow many reported incidents of hate speech to remain in circulation (Tobin et al., 2017), but they also relied on policies and procedures that protected some demographic groups (i.e., White men) from hate speech, but not others (Angwin & Grassegger, 2017). Add to this a deep-seated culture of racism, xenophobia, and misogyny as well as some citizens' propensity for publicly expressing such views online, and what is left are corporate-run spaces that fail to live up to their promises to promote connection and a healthy community. Instead, too often social media platforms allow toxic discourse to spread in ways that further ostracize women and members of other marginalized groups by subjecting them to unfettered harassment and threats (Sobieraj, 2020; York, 2014; cf. Marwick, 2021).

While social media companies were focused on increasing the popularity and profitability of their platforms, cadres of nefarious actors were busy developing innovative ways to effectively spread their messages on those channels. That gap between the priorities of platform providers and the practical realities for a small but consequential proportion of their users goes a long way to explain why moderation efforts fell short (McGregor, 2020a, 2020b). For example, Facebook did not define "coordinated inauthentic behavior," its term for media manipulation, until July 2018. Twitter and YouTube were similarly slow to respond to the rise of media manipulation in the mid-2010s. When considering this alongside the platforms' affordances (discussed in greater detail below), it should come as little surprise that motivated actors have been able to hack the digital media system to spread inauthentic or otherwise manipulative messages without much resistance.

As the potential implications of media manipulation and problematic information became more apparent—most notably, in the context of the 2016 Brexit referendum and the 2016 U.S. presidential election—social media companies finally began taking more significant steps to mitigate abuse on their platforms. Twitter, Facebook, and YouTube, not to mention countless traditional and digital media companies, each played a significant role in helping cunning actors, from mom-and-pop fake news sites to political candidates and foreign adversaries, shape public perception and debate. Nevertheless, after aiding and profiting from those campaigns—both directly through the sale of advertisements, and indirectly through the increased user attention that unpaid content helped generate—social media companies began thinking more seriously about how their platforms could pose problems for the public sphere, and how to address them (Jacoby, 2018a). This led to a series of initiatives and policy changes that, although inconsistently implemented, helped the companies take more direct if measured action against what they viewed as abuses of their platforms.

After years of minimal intervention and increased use of their platforms for manipulation, Facebook, Twitter, and YouTube started to change their tone when speaking about their role in the public sphere. The shift was spurred in large part by the increased political pressure on the companies following reports that shed light on the use of social media by foreign agents—from Russian trolls looking to disrupt democratic processes across the world to Macedonian teenagers peddling fake news for digital advertising dollars. That boost in public awareness led the companies to start limiting the spread of problematic information by "down-ranking," or decreasing the visibility of posts by serial manipulators, and in some circumstances revoking account access for active members of disinformation networks (McCarthy, 2021; Talbot, 2019). Still, Facebook, Twitter, and YouTube continued to carve out exceptions for politicians, which allowed certain powerful actors to violate policies around acceptable speech that restricted other users, and only rarely posting warning labels and other vague correctives on the most egregious of violations (Rosenberg, 2019; Schleifer, 2019).[5] This approach continued until 2020, when social media companies began placing restrictions on political ads (Haggin & Glazer, 2020). Around that same time, Trump began his repeated attempts to undermine the legitimacy of the 2020 presidential election by making false claims about voter fraud on social media (Bump, 2021a).

For the most part, Facebook, Twitter, and YouTube treaded carefully with regard to Trump and largely avoided taking further action. Although they did adopt increasingly desperate measures to slow the spread of problematic information related to election integrity and the COVID-19 pandemic, research shows that by and large, their efforts fell far short of fulfilling media's democratic promise ("Facebook," 2021). Nevertheless, as discussed in the opening of this chapter, the companies were eventually driven to ban Trump from their platforms in January 2021, following his defiant statements supporting those who waged the attack on the U.S. Capitol.

Why were social media companies so slow to take action against media manipulation and other politically driven attempts to spread problematic information? There are at least three notable reasons. First, Silicon Valley companies tend to adopt a libertarian ethos (Roberts, 2019)—for example, Twitter's framing of itself as "the free speech wing of the free speech party" (Halliday, 2012)—that is often paired with a drive to "move fast and break things," as Facebook's motto initially declared. Second, the political context social media companies operate in is particularly fraught. Platforms are under constant pressure from both sides of the political spectrum to change how they play the role of gatekeeper. At the same time, the current regulatory regime governed by CDA Section 230 gives companies "the right but not the responsibility" (Gillespie, 2018, p. 31) to moderate content as they see fit. Third, and perhaps most important, the economic model driving the majority of social media companies—profitability through audience attention, advertising, and data harvesting—has led them to focus more on increasing the economic value of their products than on minimizing the social harm they could cause (Jacoby, 2018b).

Still, social media companies have assumed some sense of responsibility for what happens on their platforms. Despite significant attempts to help social media function effectively as public forums, platform-level moderation is in many ways an inherently flawed project (Sanderson et al., 2021). Those seeking to control the flow of information through social media platforms must play the role of Sisyphus, performing a nearly impossible task repeatedly with little chance of escaping the cycle. Indeed, if a platform does find success with a certain approach to moderation, manipulators with the requisite networked media capital—this includes the publishers and affiliated media professionals discussed in chapters 3 and 5—quickly adapt their tactics to avoid detection, and the cat-and-mouse game continues. Thus, it is unlikely that Silicon Valley will be able to engineer their way out of the mess they helped make of the public sphere. Even if moderation efforts succeed at drastically reducing abusive content on social media as well as the most blatant instances of misinformation, the greater challenges—political polarization and the constant spread of less cut-and-dry cases of problematic information—remain.

Polarization is in itself an extraordinary challenge for a democratic society whose abstract ideals suggest that progress should be accomplished through rational deliberation. Nevertheless, the problem of polarization is not necessarily being driven by social media but rather by larger sociopolitical trends as well as by the decades-long changes to the broader media system discussed in chapter 3 (Benkler et al., 2018; Kreiss & McGregor, 2021). Moreover, the deeper threats to democracy that social media platforms are said to contribute to—enabling the spread of problematic information and fueling polarization—are themselves deeply rooted in the companies' business models. Indeed, each of the most popular social media platforms have adopted the logic of surveillance capitalism, collecting and parsing an endless array of behavioral data in order to fuel attention-driven metrics that reward outrageous (read: shocking and emotionally engaging) content, all in the name of maximizing profitability (Zuboff, 2019).

So if inadequate moderation is not the greatest problem mediating the relationship between social media and the public sphere, then what is? The answer to this question is found in the structure of the hybrid media system and the practices it enables among users.

On the Power of Platforms: From Big Media to Big Tech

Given their location between the public and the broader world (Stoddard & Collins, 2016), media play an important role in modern societies. Whether they are used as tools of manipulation and propaganda or more straightforward mechanisms for education or persuasion, there is little doubt that media occupy a powerful position in the contemporary public sphere. Traditional conceptions of journalism have focused on the potential for media to enable honest and ethical professionals to provide members of the public with the information they need to do the work of democracy (Kovach & Rosenstiel, 2007). Nevertheless, significant portions of the journalistic field in the United States, and in many other countries, are being driven more by political and economic goals than by professional journalistic values. At best, the journalism that emerges from this context is informative (if potentially polarizing). At worst, it can undermine democratic processes.

As chapter 3 illustrates, legacy media like cable TV, talk radio, and newspapers have played and will undoubtedly continue to play a notable role in spreading manipulative political content. A 2019 survey from the Pew Research Center found that Americans get most (45%) of their political news from television and news websites/apps (25%), followed by social media (18%), radio (8%) and print sources (3%) (Mitchell et al., 2021a). Thus, despite the rise in popularity of various forms of digital media, most traditional forms of media remain essential to the political landscape. Furthermore, given their broad reach and accessibility, television and radio have also proven to be important means through which political communicators develop and deploy tactics of attention generation and persuasion (Mejias & Vokuev, 2017).

Despite the extraordinary power of traditional and broadcast media, they are increasingly integrated with newer forms of digital media (Chadwick, 2017). Furthermore, traditional publishers are growing increasingly reliant on platforms, resulting in a relationship that is tilted significantly in platforms' favor (Nielsen & Ganter, 2022). Some of platforms' growing power originates from their relatively new role as the deliverer of audience attention. For example, more than half (53%) of American adults report getting some of their news from social media (Shearer, 2021), although the majority of that news is likely to originate from establishment media outlets.[6] Beyond publishers' frequent reliance on platforms to connect them with potential audiences, platforms also have the power to shape the means and terms of communication with members of the public (i.e., by shaping affordances and behaviors). They also have the power to collect usage data and to use or share those data with other parties as they see fit (Nielsen & Ganter, 2022).

Digital media platforms provide a number of unique affordances that have proven powerful for political communicators. Perhaps most notably, social media afford users the ability to "gatecrash," or share content directly with members of the public without relying on traditional media gatekeepers (Barnard, 2018a; Bruns, 2014; cf. Nielsen & Ganter, 2022). Given the normalization of social media as a tool for citizens to build and maintain capital and to participate in the public sphere, politically motivated actors have found extraordinary opportunity online. Indeed, sharing dynamic online content (text, images, videos, links, etc.) in order to increase awareness of a message, build collective identity, and coordinate with like-minded actors has become an important part of digital activists' repertoires of contention (Etter & Albu, 2021; Liu, 2020).

What makes social media so powerful is not just how effective they are at allowing members of the public to share information with disbursed audiences but also the myriad other ways they can enable political communication efforts. For example, social media platforms allow users to identify like-minded people, to coordinate action and mobilize support among allies, and to reach new audiences through strategic sharing, algorithmic amplification, and targeted advertising (Crain & Nadler, 2019; Etter & Albu, 2021). When considered as supplementary tools for political contention, these affordances allow political actors and organizations to widen their reach and to mobilize resources in unique ways while lessening their overall reliance on traditional media to spread their messages.

As the previous chapter demonstrated, there are many ways that powerful actors can use legacy media to amass and wield capital in service of their political and economic goals. While pundits' use of traditional media often includes deceptive practices, those systems and practices are increasingly hybrid (Chadwick, 2017). Thus, social media have also proven to be essential tools to further the spread of problematic information, to strengthen political identity, and to raise doubt about the trustworthiness of political opponents (Bradshaw & Howard, 2018; Saslow, 2018). Nevertheless, many of those efforts are also bolstered greatly by the additional reach and legitimacy lent to them when amplified by traditional media (Benkler et al., 2018; Krafft & Donovan, 2020; Marwick & Lewis, 2017; Mejias & Vokuev, 2017).

The growing power of platforms has not only contributed to transformations in the political field but has also had a profound impact on publishers as well (Nielsen & Ganter, 2022). As members of networked publics have adapted to the contemporary media environment, their expectations about where, how, and how quickly information should flow inevitably evolve, leaving content providers to innovate, adapt, or fall behind in the race for attention online. Furthermore, by serving as intermediaries helping deliver audiences to professional creators' products (for a share of the profit), platforms provide creators with many of the tools necessary to reach audiences. Such circumstances not only require publishers to devote more traditional forms of capital (e.g., economic and cultural) but may also encourage them to develop and deploy more innovative forms (e.g., networked media capital) to promote their content. Given how the power and affordances of social media platforms have altered the contemporary media landscape, it is not surprising to see many, including professional creators, use clandestine or otherwise manipulative techniques to increase the visibility of their content. As we will see in chapter 5, many digital news outlets are doing just that, illustrating how the influence of publishers and platforms converge and how the normalization of such expressions of power can fundamentally alter the field for professional and amateur communicators alike. Indeed, in addition to transforming the media professions, the combined affordances of this hybrid system have also created new opportunities for less well-positioned media manipulators to spread problematic information of their own.

As detailed in the preface of this book, media manipulation tactics like bot-fueled amplification, account impersonation, and coordinated sharing have been visible in social media discourse since well before the 2016 U.S. presidential election. For example, Russia has been using media to wage disinformation campaigns in the United States and other countries since the Cold War (Ellick & Westbrook, 2018; Pomerantsev, 2019). One prominent tactic is to mobilize government-backed trolls to post seemingly organic content intended to appeal to audience emotions, encouraging engagement and amplification throughout various media channels (cf. MacKinnon, 2013). Ultimately, the objective is to generate distrust and broaden political divides (Mejias & Vokuev, 2017). A related tactic deployed by Russia's Internet Research Agency has been to utilize social media platforms' advertising tools to distribute manipulative messages catering specifically to certain types of users (Crain & Nadler, 2019).

Considering how repertoires of manipulation continue to evolve alongside political, economic, and technological shifts (Mejias & Vokuev, 2017), developments in the media system have breathed new life into information operations of both foreign and domestic origins (McGregor et al., 2021; Woolley & Howard, 2018). Still, whatever one thinks about the attempts by Russian actors to shape the U.S. political landscape, homegrown information campaigns were likely far more consequential (Benkler et al., 2018). No matter where we place our emphasis, we need a stronger understanding of the various ways social media afford manipulation, and how actors have taken advantage of such opportunities to hack the hybrid media system in pursuit of their own agendas. Accordingly, the next section examines how the structures of social media afford media manipulation and enable various kinds of media practices.

MANIPULATIVE PRACTICES AND THE MEDIA STRUCTURES THAT AFFORD THEM

All media and communication technologies have affordances that shape how they are used. Just as 20th-century media—radio, television, and print—were designed to convey audio, video, and textual information in ways that attract disparate audiences (who can then be shown advertisements), today's communication technologies blend elements from various media enabling users to create, share, and consume information in hybrid formats. Whereas a notable strength of traditional media was their ability to reach a wide and diverse array of audiences by broadcasting across vast distances, digital media make it possible to reach specific audience segments through microtargeting. They also invite participation in ways that are redefining media technologies' role in public life. Such participation ranges from sharing and commenting on a political organization's posts to grassroots campaigns organized and implemented by users. Paradoxically, social media lower the barriers to entry to the networked public sphere in ways that can strengthen democracy (Barnard, 2018a), but at the same time they make the work of propaganda and media manipulation more accessible, which ultimately undermines democratic processes.

In developing platforms designed to maximize user attention, social media companies make a variety of consequential choices—some implicit, others explicit—that shape the communicative context of their sites. Whether a company sells political advertising or does not, fact checks or does not, places clear correctives or vague warning labels on misinformation, removes or down-ranks manipulative content, recommends increasingly extreme content or does not, and so on, it is making decisions that effectively define their service and structure how users experience it. In other words, as discussed in chapter 2, each line of code and each policy decision help construct the affordances a platform makes available to users and how actors may leverage them. The amalgamation of these decisions shapes the "imagined affordances," or the perceived potential and expectations, that users ascribe to the technology (Nagy & Neff, 2015). They also provide the sociotechnical foundation for a given platform's algorithms to facilitate political organization and communication, while at the same time distorting a public's communicative process by enabling the spread of disruptive or problematic information (Etter & Albu, 2021). Such affordances not only shape users' experience on social media platforms but also help construct the strategies communications professionals deploy when creating and promoting their own content.

The notion of media channels playing host to political contests is, of course, hardly new or controversial. Despite their many flaws and varied affordances, media channels are, after all, an increasingly important part of the public sphere. In theory, these media allow communicators to engage in an equal exchange of information and ideas. Some, like public relations trailblazer Edward Bernays, have even gone as far as to argue that an ideal democracy is one where political contests are decided based on which public relations professionals can wage the most convincing campaign (Jansen, 2013). In practice, however, political battles are often staged on uneven ground, and too often media are mobilized in ways that starkly contradict ideal typical notions of rational, deliberative democracy (Gerbaudo, 2022; Habermas, 1989). Whether by misrepresenting facts, distorting context, or preying on prejudice and emotion, manipulative media creators take advantage of power imbalances in service of their own goals.

If the affordances of digital media constitute a playing field on which contests of political communication play out, then it is worth considering in greater detail the various opportunities such media provide. Certainly, not all media are created equal, and while all serve some gatekeeping functions, the rationale they apply can differ (sometimes greatly) from one outlet to another. For every outlet that takes steps to mitigate the spread of problematic information or extremist rhetoric, there are others that actively facilitate it. These media, sometimes called "alternative media" or "alt-tech" (McSwiney et al., 2021; Miller-Idriss, 2020), provide alternative opportunities for communication, often without requiring actors to adhere to norms of civil discourse. As we will see in chapter 6, such spaces provide fundamental opportunities for extremists to gather, share information, and organize for future communicative action. But regardless of their policies, all media can play a role in the spread of problematic information. On the whole, social media platforms enable or encourage political communicators' approaches to media manipulation, audience segmentation and targeted messaging, reach and amplification, as well as coordination and mobilization. Although this list is not exhaustive, it constitutes the bulk of the most consequential opportunities for political communication that social media provide political actors. The remainder of this section will address each set of affordances individually before discussing their combined implications.

Media Manipulation
As has been argued throughout this book, digital technologies are imbued with many affordances that are useful to those engaging in media manipulation. Accordingly, there is a growing body of scholarship on manipulation and its linkage to digital media. Although there are increasingly diverse definitions and approaches to such uses of media, a uniting factor is an actor's strategic approach to spreading (problematic) information via digital channels in ways that increase its visibility through covert means. While many have acknowledged the duality of motives, including profit and/or politics (Marwick & Lewis, 2017), others go further to emphasize the potential effects of media manipulation campaigns. For example, Susser and colleagues (2019) define online manipulation as "the use of information technology to covertly influence another person's decision-making, by targeting and exploiting decision-making vulnerabilities" (p. 6). Although there is undoubtedly a notable difference between documenting manipulative communication practices—those that distort reality, deceive audiences, and increase visibility in clandestine ways—and empirically demonstrating that those practices effectively change others' thoughts and actions, it is clear that acts of media manipulation, like other forms of communication, are often successful, albeit to varying degrees.

But what are the possible effects? Like the distinction between *agenda-setting*, which describes media creators' shaping of public opinion, and *agenda-building*, which is used to describe the public's ability to shape the perceptions and actions of media gatekeepers, media manipulation can itself work in multiple directions. Both functions play a notable role in the process of communication. On the one hand, there has been a concerted effort among scholars to consider how the tools of digital media allow or encourage the manipulation of public perceptions. The emphasis here is often on the first-order potential for communications technologies to shape perceptions by increasing the likelihood that members of the public engage with specific pieces of information (Golebiewski

& boyd, 2019; Tripodi, 2018). On the other hand, some scholarship has emphasized how media manipulation can occur indirectly, through other channels of communication. Thus, as Donovan and colleagues (Donovan, n.d.; Donovan & Friedberg, 2019; Nadler et al., 2018) have emphasized, online media allow motivated actors to increase the visibility of their framing of an issue within the public sphere by having their messages amplified by others.

As we have established already, social media platforms are designed to amplify (some) content, and when virality can be manufactured through concerted efforts to game algorithms and manipulate users, the consequences can disrupt democratic forms of governance (Tsfati et al., 2020). One common method involves manipulators seeking coverage from ever more influential professional media gatekeepers through a process Holiday (2013, p. 18) refers to as "trading up the chain" (cf. Marwick & Lewis, 2017). By reporting problematic information and frames, professional media enable manipulators to reach larger audiences while also lending their professional legitimacy to the cause. This process can also happen indirectly, as many users, including media professionals, often rely on social media as a source of news (Barnard, 2018a) and also as a proxy for public opinion (Lukito et al., 2020; McGregor, 2019). Consequently, if one's perception of the vox populi is skewed by intentional acts of media manipulation, or otherwise distorted due to algorithmic filtering or network homophily, then such distortions are likely to be reified through their own future actions.[7] This phenomenon is explored in greater detail in chapter 5, which examines how publishers' and media manipulators' framing of CNN correspondent Jim Acosta's unusual exchange with a White House intern as an "assault" helped generate an extraordinary amount of attention.

In the meantime, we turn our attention to other deceptive media practices and the structures that enable them. This includes considering the manipulative potential of targeted advertising. Indeed, as Zarouali and colleagues (2020) assert, "microtargeting can qualify as manipulation" (p. 3).

Audience Segmentation and Targeted Messaging
As discussed above, one of the most notable affordances of contemporary social media platforms is their ability to clearly define audiences and to reach them directly with targeted messaging. Thanks to the surveillant structure of the digital media ecosystem, the everyday behavior of users is automatically logged, and the data produced are combined with secondary data purchased or borrowed from other entities. Social media companies not only parse those data in an effort to better understand their users; they also make them available to partner organizations, as well as to customers who use the data—and the algorithmically enhanced tools that accompany them—to identify desirable audiences that can then be targeted with catered messaging. Unsurprisingly, these

tools have been used for political manipulation (Crain & Nadler, 2019; Zarouali et al., 2020).

Like many other technology-enabled practices, the growth of microtargeting techniques was driven by both supply- and demand-side pressures. On the one hand, platforms' creation of digital marketing tools was motivated by expectations of a demand on behalf of advertisers. On the other hand, targeted advertising became normalized as an everyday marketing practice thanks to the widespread availability of catered messaging features made available to advertisers by digital media companies. Despite the hype around the power of microtargeting, which has at times amounted to a moral panic, the reality is much more nuanced.

The scholarship on the efficacy of microtargeting is, like many other literatures, filled with complexity and contradiction. As Bashyakarla (2019) notes, the question "Does it work?" is far too reductive to be instructive considering the array of contextual factors that must be glossed over in order to assess the efficacy of political persuasion campaigns. Accordingly, research attempting to address the question has yielded some conflicting results. While some studies raise questions about the techniques' ability to sway political opinions, others have concluded that targeted messaging can have significant, although relatively small, effects. For example, studies have shown targeted messages to be relatively effective at increasing voter turnout among young voters (Haenschen & Jennings, 2019; cf. Kruikemeier et al., 2016). Additionally, some scholars have found that microtargeted messages can be useful in strengthening party affiliation and therefore increasing chances of retaining the allegiances of already supportive voters (Lavigne, 2021). Others have concluded that microtargeting can enhance the efficacy of other manipulative media tools such as "deepfakes"—computer-generated audio/video messages that contain words and imagery that can appear real but are not—in order to more effectively shift public opinion against a candidate. However, the effects of deepfakes were limited to a subset of the targeted population that shared multiple distinct characteristics (e.g., those who were very religious and voted for a certain political party) (Dobber et al., 2021). In the same vein, Zarouali et al. (2020) found that "psychometric profiling, or the process by which the observed or self-reported actions are used to infer your personality traits" (p. 1068), can increase the effectiveness of social media advertisements by tailoring ads to individuals based on personality characteristics. Altogether, these studies provide ample reason to be concerned about the implications of, and the lack of transparency surrounding, the use of targeted advertisements within the political field.

Beyond the debate over the effectiveness of microtargeting lies a broader recognition of the conditions that make it possible. One of the most pertinent conditions pertains to law and political culture (Bodó et al., 2017). For example, the United States is a robust landscape for microtargeting given the relative lack of consumer privacy and wide availability of user data as compared to many European countries, which often have much stricter legal limitations. Nevertheless, in some political cultures—for example, Germany—a large proportion of the public openly use social media for political debate, leaving room for those with the requisite capital to collect and parse data on their own in order to construct their own profiles of users. Those profiles could be used to send targeted messages based on network position, use of language, profile characteristics, or other common factors (Papakyriakopoulos et al., 2018). Thus, while legal frameworks undeniably shape culture and practice within a given context, they are far from deterministic.

Another set of factors that inevitably give rise to microtargeting and audience segmentation are the structural and technological affordances of a given communication platform. Whereas previous eras of analog and digital media offered advertisers with limited options the chance to reach niche audiences, contemporary social networking sites provide much more sophisticated tools (Chester & Montgomery, 2017). For example, Facebook's Audience Insights tool may enable an online magazine publishing antivaccine content to identify specific segments of the population (e.g., men in their 20s from Chico, California, who have engaged with the publisher's content) that they can then target with tailored advertisements for local events. Facebook's Lookalike Audiences tool, by contrast, allows an advertiser to expand its database of targeted users by helping to identify other users who have never interacted with its content based on shared characteristics. This may allow purveyors of problematic information to increase their reach by finding other sympathetic audiences—such as members of pro-Trump Facebook groups—to target with catered messages. Other social media platforms offer similar microtargeting tools, and when considered alongside the repertoire of other audience segmentation methods it becomes difficult to deny their potential value for publishers and political communicators.

Despite the many legitimate uses of targeted advertising for political campaigns, the practice also has numerous drawbacks. The most notable is the opaque environment in which targeted advertising takes place. Frequently referred to as "dark ads," these social media advertisements often lurk in the digital shadows where users have little knowledge about how they are being targeted or why.[8] Additionally, despite social media companies' recent efforts to increase the transparency of political advertising on their platforms, such campaigns are typically waged with minimal public scrutiny. For example, although Facebook's Ad Library does appear to list those advertisements labeled "political," the public has little knowledge about which advertisements were targeted to specific users, or why. Moreover, while creating a public database of political advertisements is a necessary and important step toward greater transparency, it is a far cry from the detailed information necessary to empower members of the press and public to offer the kind of critical oversight and investigative reporting necessary to increase public awareness and media literacy. Although Twitter has stopped selling political advertising (for now), the remaining social media companies all face similar challenges regarding a lack of transparency and a willingness to profit from deceptive political advertising. As a result, media manipulators are left with another powerful toolkit to pursue their political-economic goals.

Reach and Amplification
In contrast to the media manipulation tactics discussed above, which aim to gain and shape attention from news organizations and other media professionals, some campaigns are designed to generate seemingly organic engagement by reaching the public directly. While media professionals have traditionally served as gatekeeping intermediaries who decide which information the public has access to, the hybrid media system now enables users to communicate directly with members of the public (Barnard, 2018a). Such communicative efforts can serve numerous goals, from basic messaging and allegiance building to encouraging the viral spread of information through seemingly organic sharing campaigns (Karlova & Fisher, 2013). At the same time, campaigns' digital media usage can also have latent functions, such as to lure engagement from users in order to generate additional data that could prove useful in future targeting efforts (Chester & Montgomery, 2017).

Although digital media's public messaging affordances are now rather obvious—recall the diminishing novelty of the late 2000s refrain about all members of the networked public having their own printing press—their infrastructure has also given rise to a new array of political communication tactics. The proliferation of social networking services has enhanced communicators' ability to reach existing and potential audiences. While traditional publishers and everyday users take advantage of these affordances in characteristically mundane ways, those who are less honest have also found social media to be useful in spreading false information (Bradshaw & Howard, 2018; Nelson & Taneja, 2018). Such problematic information proliferates on social media platforms due to communicators' success in attracting audiences but also because platforms' algorithms often play a part in amplifying those messages—a function that has been shown to help fuel extremism (Berger, 2013; O'Callaghan et al., 2015; Reed et al., 2019; Waters & Postings, 2018).

Like most everything else in the social world, outcomes are a product of structure and action. When considering the spread of problematic information, that means the channels of mediation matter just as much as the communicative practices that are used to navigate them. Thus, while the repertoires of manipulation discussed in chapter 2 are notable, they cannot be divorced from the political, economic, and technological systems that gave rise to them. In the context of digital media, much attention has been (rightly) focused on algorithmic amplification due to the now all-too-common occurrence of digital platforms helping to bring fringe perspectives into the mainstream (Marwick & Lewis, 2017; Miller-Idriss, 2020; cf. Brown et al., 2022). Yet there are many other ways in which platform affordances can themselves allow or even encourage the spread of problematic information.

For example, Facebook's Groups and Stories features have proven to be particularly useful tools for those seeking to circumvent companies' limited efforts to police their platforms. Because content moderation strategies often rely on users to report harmful content, groups, which commonly cohere around shared interests—for example, Trump 2024 or Women for Trump—are often frequented by users unlikely to view problematic content as a violation, and if they do, they are also unlikely to officially report it due to the strength of in-group ties. In contrast, the short-lived nature of Facebook "stories," which expire after 24 hours, have thus far proven to be powerful vectors for the spread of problematic information. This may be due in part to technical challenges associated with the format of story posts, which commonly include images or videos along with multiple layers of superimposed text blocks, and which are frequently reshared by other users in ways that obscure the original source, such as through screen captures. Furthermore, story posts are by definition a marginal form of content—users can choose to view some, all, or none of the stories posted by accounts they follow, but historically they have not shown up on the News Feed. Thus, the ephemerality of stories creates an environment of deniability for platforms—problematic posts are gone before firestorms can mount—while at the same time discouraging action against them since the problematic content will disappear the following day.

An example of how changes in platform affordances can divert the flow of information and lead to shifts in communicative practice can be found in Facebook's revisions to their news feed ranking algorithm. In the wake of the 2016 U.S. presidential election, in which Facebook and other digital media platforms were used to spread reams of "fake news" and other problematic information, Facebook executives made the decision to prioritize "meaningful social interactions" (Hagey & Horwitz, 2021; Metz, 2021). In theory, Facebook reasoned (publicly, at least) that by increasing the reach of seemingly organic posts by average users, they could decrease the flow of problematic information and help lower the temperature of heated political exchange by encouraging greater interactions with people in users' direct friend network. In practice, the changes to the algorithm seemed to have the opposite effect. By de-prioritizing posts from influential accounts like news organizations, Facebook actually increased the influence of average users, many of whom served as vectors for the spread of problematic information to those in their network. Furthermore, the revisions to the algorithm created a reward system that incentivized divisiveness and otherwise problematic posts (Hagey & Horwitz, 2021).[9]

The existence of algorithms designed to maximize engagement on digital media platforms serves as an important backdrop against which communicative practices are iteratively developed and deployed. Many of these tactics, such as search engine optimization (SEO), A/B testing, algorithmic prediction, and bot-driven amplification, are now relatively commonplace (Diakopoulos, 2019; Woolley & Howard, 2018). Nevertheless, I would be remiss not to acknowledge the fine line that sometimes divides ordinary forms of attention-seeking from those that are dishonest and manipulative. Indeed, there are undeniable similarities between how communicators use their capital to game information systems in order to reach audiences. For example, news editors have been known to use dramatic or violent imagery and "clickbait" headlines to attract audiences, and SEO practitioners strategically use keywords to maximize their returns on users' search engine inquiries. Yet there is a distinct difference between testing multiple headlines to maximize the reach of an article and using fake accounts to artificially increase its visibility.

In the shadows of the contemporary communicative landscape, motivated political actors are constantly developing and deploying new tactics to game the system and therefore find a competitive edge. Given the growing awareness of the role confirmation bias plays in users' information-seeking practices (Tripodi, 2018), some media manipulators take advantage of gaps in online discourse, or what Golebiewski and boyd (2019) term "data voids," by seeding the communicative environment with mentions of unique phrases that help increase their visibility in search engines due to a lack of more trustworthy content. Importantly, this strategy can be effective in spreading problematic information because of how search engines are configured, which means they could also be reconfigured to limit such amplification (Golebiewski & boyd, 2019). Other amplification strategies, such as using backchannels to assist users in organizing cooperative campaigns, blur the lines between reach and amplification strategies and those that are the subject of our next section.

Coordination and Mobilization
To say digital platforms afford cooperation and political mobilization is, at this point in history, to state the obvious. Much of the hype and reductionism surrounding the so-called social media revolutions that swept across portions of the Middle East and North Africa in the early 2010s centered on the power of social networking sites to assist with activists' political action (Gladwell & Shirky, 2011). Beyond their usage of platforms like Facebook, Twitter, and YouTube to generate public attention, activists also used them to build collective identity,

organize, strategize, and mobilize resources (Castells, 2015; Tufekci, 2018). Although these and other social movement scholars have long noted the challenges posed by digital communication, there has been widespread recognition that the proliferation of social media platforms has, in a variety of ways, transformed the political field (Chadwick, 2017; Earl et al., 2013; Mattoni, 2013). This book undoubtedly speaks to numerous aspects of that ongoing transformation, but in this section we turn our attention to the ways digital communication technologies allow and encourage political actors to cooperate with and mobilize their political allies.

Social media platforms and social networking sites have proven to be especially useful tools for enabling groups of actors to collectively generate and amplify problematic information. Recognizing the relatively mundane ways media manipulators have used private and semiprivate digital spaces to strategize, research has shown how multiple actors can use social media to spread problematic information in a coordinated manner (Giglietto et al., 2020; Karlova & Fisher, 2013). In addition to the bot-driven efforts discussed previously, social media users have engaged in coordination through a variety of methods that rely on more organic participation. For example, whereas some simply share information with groups or hashtag communities along with appeals for amplification (Karlova & Fisher, 2013), others have used semiautomated tools like Thunderclap that support collaborative sharing, or what might be seen as digitally mediated mobilization (Lindner & Barnard, 2020). Similarly, White supremacist groups have been known to use digital tools such as podcasts, databases, and online forums to plan and carry out strategic amplification campaigns—a tactic they refer to as "swarmfronts"—designed to spread a specific message or ideology (Larson & McHendry, 2019).

In addition to the popular social media sites discussed throughout this chapter, there are less mainstream platforms that have proven relevant as channels for tactical coordination and political mobilization. Although the affordances of message boards like Reddit differ significantly from social media, their individual forums (or subreddits) often serve a similar function as Facebook groups, allowing communities of people with common interests to come together to share information and ideas. When the content restrictions and moderation efforts limit what users can say, they tend to seek more fertile ground. Enter alternative platforms like 4chan, Gab, Parler, Telegram, and the Trump-owned Truth Social. While these sites often lack the visibility and broad reach of mainstream platforms, their popularity among right-wing extremists makes it easier to reach and mobilize like-minded users. In other words, although alternative platforms may not afford exponential growth of social capital, they can help users and groups form fewer but stronger bonds. These spaces can also facilitate the development and conversion of other forms of capital, such as financial resources, political knowledge, or communication strategies. Indeed, as many learned in the aftermath of the January 6, 2021, attack on the U.S. Capitol, such alternative platforms have proven to be powerful sites of capital building, coordination, and mobilization for many of Trump's most vocal online supporters. Accordingly, we take a closer look at these efforts in chapter 6.

Summary

We now know unequivocally that digital media platforms are a disruptive force in the political field. As this chapter has illustrated, the political, economic, and technological structures of the contemporary hybrid media system generated new opportunities and incentive structures for those practicing political communication. The affordances of these media have, among other things, made it easier for political actors to communicate among themselves as well as with members of the public and the media. Indeed, as some tech executives have dreamed, social media have created a new "superstructure over humanity" that allows and encourages a freer flow of information than in previous epochs (Loucaides, 2022). This shift has led to a host of social changes, but it has also introduced a new set of challenges.

Recall the opening chapter's discussion of the "mediatized superstructure," a term I have used to describe the "assemblage of networked individuals, techniques, and technologies that, once populated by a critical mass, provide a relatively stable and persistent mechanism for the vetting and spreading of information" (Barnard, 2018a, p. 52). While there is plenty of evidence to suggest that many members of the networked public can and often do use media to share information, generate attention, and shape agendas in ways that adhere to widely accepted norms of democratic discourse (Barnard, 2018a; Richardson, 2020), the opposite is also true. That is, thanks to the past success of media manipulators' persuasion and capital-building efforts, other portions of the public are primed for (and capable of participating in) practices and discourses that are problematic, manipulative, or otherwise antidemocratic. This is the darker side of the mediatized superstructure spurred by the evolution of the hybrid media system, the machinations of which we will explore further in the chapters ahead.

Finally, as we pass the midpoint of this book, it seems prescient to reflect briefly on what has been accomplished thus far and what work remains ahead of us. From chapters 1 and 2 we gained an understanding of how problematic information flows in the hybrid media system, of what capital and practices political communicators employ to facilitate its spread, as well as of the potential implications for debates about media power. From chapter 3 we know that talk radio and cable TV have helped facilitate the spread of problematic information and have aided in the application (and further generation) of networked media capital. Chapter 4 has offered a critical overview of the political and economic contexts of social media, as well as how they enable media manipulation and otherwise transform the landscape of political communication. Next, we will look at multiple case studies—one in chapter 5 focusing on professional media, and another in chapter 6 highlighting volunteer activists—selected to illustrate how structure and practice combine to further the spread of problematic information, and consequently reconfigure the dynamics of media power through expressions of networked media capital.

Chapter 5

Hacking Meaning and Influence in the (Dis)Information Age

The Acosta "Assault" Case

On November 7, 2018, CNN White House correspondent Jim Acosta engaged in a tense exchange with President Donald J. Trump during a White House press conference. Hours later, Paul Joseph Watson, a contributor to Infowars—a conspiracy website popular with the alt-right—posted a video on Twitter that appeared to show Acosta striking a member of the White House staff while she attempted to take away his microphone. The video, which forensic experts have confirmed was edited, provides a misleading account of the exchange (Rothman, 2018).[1] It quickly went viral, drawing attention from publishers and publics across the political spectrum. Not surprisingly, this scandal was manufactured thanks in part to the help of many on the political right (Huppke, 2018). Just minutes after the incident, a number of influential accounts associated with QAnon, the "deep state" conspiracy community, began posting on Twitter using hashtags like #AcostaAccosts and #AccostaAssaults, among many others (Norteño, 2018).

Later that evening the White House press secretary Sarah Sanders posted a statement on Twitter announcing that the administration would be "suspending the hard [press] pass of the reporter involved until further notice" (Sink & Jacobs, 2018). Sanders's official Twitter account also shared (and later stood by) the misleading video created by Watson and the Daily Wire in an attempt to justify their decision (Rothman, 2018). Although Acosta's hard pass was later restored by order of a federal judge after his employer, CNN, filed a lawsuit against the White House, the incident provides a notable illustration of the way problematic information can flow in the hybrid media system.

The next morning, as I walked through a hallway on the sleepy university campus where I worked, already reeling from the speed at which misinformation can travel in the contemporary media ecosystem, I heard a group of maintenance staff talking about the CNN journalist's alleged "karate chop," which they had seen on Facebook. I turned to my colleagues to ask what, if anything, they had heard about the incident. It did not take us long to recognize the stark contrast in our discursive realities, and how fractured the American epistemic universe appeared to be from that vantage point. That realization led us to begin grappling with the proliferation of propaganda and the role media publishers and platforms—not to mention homophilous networks—often play in deepening the divide.

To be sure, media companies play an important part in the ongoing saga of the public sphere. But so do their audiences, who over the past decade have grown more active within, and often more disillusioned with, the journalistic and political fields. While parts of this shift may be interpreted as a strengthening of the public sphere, its appetite for outrage appears to be increasing and its relationship to truth growing more precarious. Within this context, outrage media makers and would-be propagandists have found ample opportunity to create and disseminate content to serve their own political and economic interests. Similarly, many long-standing interpretive communities appear to have grown more radical and insulated, and many new ones have formed, thanks in large part to the propaganda provided to them by platforms and overtly partisan publishers, not to mention the politicians themselves.

While there is a growing body of scholarship addressing the dissemination of contemporary propaganda (Benkler et al., 2018; Marwick & Lewis, 2017; Mihailidis & Viotty, 2017), few studies have paid close attention to the texts themselves alongside their creation, distribution, and reception by various interpretive communities (cf. Marwick, 2018). Similarly, while we have already established that both legacy and digital media play important roles in the creation and dissemination of problematic information, we still lack a detailed understanding of how they work in concert and what forms of capital are required to reach sizable audiences. Along with responding to questions raised in prior chapters, it would be helpful to know more about the (manipulative) practices employed in publishing and disseminating digital news stories about this case, and whether these practices can be traced to one's position in the political and journalistic fields.

Accordingly, through a close analysis and critical interpretation of data from the case study of Acosta's alleged "assault," this chapter examines the social, political, and technological dynamics underlying the production and dissemination of problematic information in the hybrid media system. The chapter proceeds with a brief discussion of relevant literature on meaning, interpretation, and digital distribution before addressing the research questions and methodology guiding this case study. The chapter presents findings pertaining to the production and distribution of content related to the case, paying particular attention to the ways publishers generate attention online. In doing so, the analysis considers the role capital and manipulative practices play in a story's spread, as well as what significance the publishers' political ideology may hold for the tactics deployed. The chapter concludes by considering what implications the findings hold for our understanding of media power and manipulation.

An Interpretive Approach to the Production and Reception of Spectacular News

Interpretive approaches to the study of media and meaning can be broken down into three categories: (1) production, (2) reception, and (3) media texts themselves. Despite the continued utility of this distinction, the advancement of mediatization has blurred many of the lines that separate these categories. Whereas news stories from the print and broadcast eras often mapped relatively neatly onto these categories, the social lives of contemporary media follow a nonlinear process that relies, unevenly and often unpredictably, on a variety of modes and nodes. That is, instead of a producer relying on a single channel to reach an audience, today's media often follow a cyclical trajectory that—at least for less popular stories or publishers—requires more influential actors to amplify or remix the story before it can reach a mass audience.

While many have pointed out the democratizing effects this transformation can have on the communicative process, others have raised valid concerns about the potential for such an open system to be manipulated, yielding antidemocratic ends. It is in this vein that Wardle and Derakshan (2017) developed a framework for examining contemporary "information disorder." Roughly following the production-reception-text structure of interpretive analysis outlined above, Wardle and Derakshan make the case for analyzing three interrelated "elements" of "information disorder: agent, message, and interpreter" (p. 19).

Other scholars have developed similarly innovative approaches to address the growing complexity of media and their effects in the age of mediatization. For example, Alice Marwick (2018) proposed a "sociotechnical model" of media effects, with an emphasis on the spread of disinformation, which distinguishes between actors (e.g., audiences), messages, and affordances. Following this model, Marwick utilized a mixture of qualitative methods to examine media messages as well as the contexts within which they are received and shared. Such an approach, she argues, is crucial because it allows for the consideration of coinciding forces, which all contribute to the landscape of polarization and disinformation. However, despite the many strengths of the model, its emphasis on media effects means that it does not, at least for the purposes of this chapter, pay adequate attention to the *production* of media messages. Therefore, this chapter adapts this model by broadening its consideration of "actors" to include the political and institutional factors that shape the production, distribution, and (to a lesser extent) reception of media messages.

Hacking Meaning and Visibility in a Content-Driven Digital Media Environment

The intersection of today's journalistic and political fields is a fuzzy and highly contested space. Thanks to the affordances of hybrid media, many publishers, including a slew of hyperpartisan, sensationalistic outlets, have found substantial opportunity to create and disseminate content that garners significant attention. While establishment media are still the central gatekeepers in our multimedia ecosystem, the proliferation of platforms and the computing technologies that undergird them (e.g., algorithms, application programming interfaces, bots, and data collection protocols, to name a few) is also fundamentally changing the rules about information flows, providing greater opportunities for manipulation at each stage of the interpretive process. Although the cliché "fake news" websites boosted by an army of automated bots can provide significant opportunities to game the system, the threat they pose to democracy is at times overblown (Benkler et al., 2018).

Still, the falsification of public opinion—that is, the creation of large amounts of content designed to generate (false) impressions about which views are popular, and with which types of citizens—has the potential to fundamentally alter the functioning of democratic discourse. Whether through organic campaigns run by humans to create and disseminate (mostly) original content, or artificial campaigns that produce and share large volumes of similar content driven by automated accounts, social media platforms afford users opportunities to perform, and therefore alter, public opinion. Although coordinated campaigns have a long and often legitimate political history, the use of automation, artificial intelligence, or other forms of imitation to falsify public opinion may undermine one of the key premises of the public sphere: that discourse is representative of the public (McGregor, 2019). These strategies may be said to afford the manufacturing of consent (Herman & Chomsky, 1988/2002), agenda setting by influencing what networked publics think about (Cohen, 1963), or disorientation by sowing confusion and doubt about what information is believable (Benkler et al., 2018). Accordingly, their effects, while still in need of empirical examination, are undeniable.

It is not that efforts to manipulate public opinion are a new phenomenon. Our media environment has long been filled with advertising, persuasion and public relations, pseudo-events, journalistic sensationalism, outrage politics, and the like. What is relatively new about contemporary efforts is the *process* through which actors and institutions go to manipulate public opinion. Many of today's most ambitious persuasion campaigns now involve constructing psychographic profiles of users—triangulated from numerous sources—and then taking advantage of platforms' microtargeting tools to reach particular segments of the public in opaque yet highly customizable ways (Winston, 2016). Furthermore, automated bots and sock puppets—that is, accounts made to imitate a particular identity type—play a significant role in the spread of problematic information across social media (Tucker et al., 2018). These efforts seek to imitate, manipulate, and at times manufacture entirely new interpretive communities in ways that illustrate new forms of agenda setting and agenda building. They are but a few examples of the ways that networked media capital has become key to agenda setting. But there are many more mundane and more prominent approaches that are of greater significance to the analysis advanced in this chapter.

In the hybrid media system there is a growing playbook of tactics from which political communicators can draw to spread their messages far and wide. According to the logic of the propaganda pipeline (Benkler et al., 2018), prominent publishers are often the bridge between propagandists, their fringe audiences, and the mainstream. To work, the strategy requires the complicity of other establishment media, which, wary of confirming many viewers' suspicions of "liberal bias," all too often fall into the trap of giving airtime or inches to problematic or questionable stories due to the manufactured outrage of right-leaning publishers (Yglesias, 2018). Such amplification not only helps right-wing propaganda reach mass audiences; it also helps lend legitimacy to it based on other sources' repetition of it. This is one way that media manipulation efforts fueled by "dark money" can be used to increase the visibility of extremist viewpoints (Mayer, 2017, 2021).

At the same time, many of today's publishers play an even more active role in the production and dissemination of problematic information. Whether due to the pressures of a competitive media environment, a desire to further political goals, or both, a growing number are publishing "viral journalism" that aims to maximize an article's reach (Denisova, 2022). Often driven by emotion, dramatic imagery, and surprising twists, many news sites aim to generate clicks and shares in ways that mimic "clickbait" (Denisova, 2022).[2] It is not difficult to see how today's viral strategies are similar to the "yellow journalism" produced by late 19th-century newspapers (Kaplan, 2008) and the "If it bleeds, it leads" ethos that has shaped television news in recent decades (Carter & Allan, 2000). Nevertheless, rising economic pressures have led media professionals in general, and journalists more specifically, to take a more active role in promoting their work on social media (Jukes, 2019; Tandoc & Vos, 2016). Although such strategies often conflict with traditional journalistic values (Jukes, 2019; Tandoc & Vos, 2016) and can generate tensions within the more mainstream news organizations (Denisova, 2022), American media professionals appear to be growing more accepting of journalists' marketing role (Vos et al., 2023). Such tensions are less likely to arise in smaller, digitally native outlets as well as those that routinely publish problematic information, because their position on the margins of the field typically encourages unorthodox production and promotion strategies.

Take LaCorte News as an example. In July 2017, just months after being pushed out of his position as the head of FoxNews.com, Ken LaCorte founded a news start-up, Bivona Digital Inc. (BDI). In addition to serving as the parent company of the flagship site, LaCorte News, which boasted a "free speech zone" encouraging the site's visitors to post "anything that won't get [them arrested]" (LaCorte News, n.d.), BDI also published the sites Conservative Edition News and Liberal Edition News (Perlroth, 2019). Staffed by Macedonian teenagers, many of whom cut their teeth peddling fake news in the lead-up to the November 2016 election of Trump, the websites "push[ed] inflammatory items—stories, petitions and the occasional conspiracy theory—to the American public" (Perlroth, 2019, para. 6).

LaCorte, the executive who in 2016 allegedly killed the story a Fox News reporter dug up confirming Trump's sexual relationship with the adult film star Stormy Daniels (Mayer, 2019), said the aim of his new "digital news start-up" was to "restor[e] faith in the media" (quoted in Perlroth, 2019, para. 9). Despite this ambition, his websites appeared to be more focused on stirring up partisan outrage on both the left and the right in order to drive traffic and, therefore, generate advertising revenue. Although stoking and profiting from partisan division was purportedly beyond his initial purview, LaCorte developed this approach after he learned how difficult it was to attract an audience using centrist news. When his nonpartisan Facebook pages failed to drive the volume of traffic he was hoping for, he decided to focus more attention on his other partisan "news" sites. Rather than hiring professional journalists to do original reporting, he hired a small group of teenagers with fake news experience to produce "'journalism lite'—hot takes on sensationalist stories from The Daily Caller and other right-leaning sites" (Perlroth, 2019, para. 30).

For a time, this strategy appeared to work—at least according to some metrics. Although LaCorte can lay no claim to producing substantive journalism or helping restore the public's faith in media, he was successful in increasing his company's revenue. Like countless others creating political content in today's hybrid media system, BDI relied on a complex social media strategy, including numerous clandestinely run Facebook pages, to drive traffic. While the company was initially able to keep a low profile, an exposé from the *New York Times* prompted Facebook to revoke BDI's accounts for violating its company policies (Perlroth, 2019).

As we will see, production and promotion strategies like those adopted by BDI are more common than one might think. Although the trend of amateur-generated fake news appears to have subsided (for now), there are many digital news sites producing identity-confirming partisan outrage. Furthermore, these companies often leverage substantial capital to promote their stories. This raises a variety of questions about the practices publishers employ, as well as about the political interests of those pushing problematic information.

Accordingly, this chapter analyzes the use of digital media with an emphasis on addressing questions of *who, what, how,* and *to what effect.* The sections that follow examine the flow of messages and meaning as illustrated by the online discourse pertaining to the alleged Acosta "assault" and the subsequent revocation of his hard pass. The rationale for selecting the Acosta case is twofold. First, it is a unique yet relatively mundane episode displaying many common characteristics of the way (problematic) political news is spread online. Second, the discourse represents each phase of the interpretive process and, when considered alongside the messages themselves, provides fertile ground for analysis of the flow of meaning and problematic information in the contemporary media environment. In other words, by offering a window into how a variety of relevant entities—including publishers, media professionals, and various political actors—create and disseminate content, the case and associated data reveal much about the practices and capital required to generate attention in the hybrid media system.

With these goals in mind, the research conducted for this chapter is guided by the following questions: What patterns emerged in the most influential content produced about the incident? What role did publishers, pundits, platforms, and publics play in spreading and responding to the messages? What tactics were used, and what kinds of capital did that require? What can this teach us about the workings of media power?

The Case Study

In order to address these questions, this chapter triangulates data on the Acosta case from multiple sources. Using Media Cloud, an online platform designed to help researchers "track how stories and ideas spread through media" ("About," n.d.), I collected online stories pertaining to the incident published between November 7 and December 7, 2018. Because the focus of this analysis is the spread of information in the American media ecosystem, data were sampled from Media Cloud collections for "U.S. Mainstream Media," "U.S. Top Digital Native News 2016," and "U.S. Top Online News 2017," as well as from collections of websites grouped according to their political leanings during the 2016 presidential election (left, center-left, center, center-right, and right). These collections contain a total of 1,062 online publications. From that sample, the query returned a total of 785 stories published by 225 sources.[3]

The data were analyzed using a variety of quantitative and qualitative measures. First, I used the metrics generated by Media Cloud to familiarize myself with and observe patterns in the data. After examining the types of stories published by various outlets and how much attention they received (i.e., number of Facebook shares, and links from other stories in the corpus), I collected the Alexa website rankings for the most influential publishers from each of the five partisan categories. I used Tableau to uncover additional patterns and to generate visualizations based on cross-comparisons of various measures.

I drew a subsample of the top three stories from the five most influential publishers within each of the following categories: (1) left-leaning sites, (2) right-leaning sites, and (3) sites in or near the center (this includes those coded as center-left, center, and center-right).[4] This amounted to a subsample of 44 stories. Analyzing media artifacts from opposing sides of the political spectrum makes it possible to test the claim that right-leaning political communicators have been more successful in boosting visibility relative to their position in the field due to enterprising deployment of networked media capital. In addition to drawing comparisons by political leaning and publisher, the analysis also involved a close examination of particular themes and frames emerging from individual stories. Accordingly, the analysis drew upon the tools of digital ethnographic content analysis, examining both the form and the content of mediated communication pertaining to the event (Barnard, 2018a). Beyond examining the structure of media platforms as well as the flow of information through them, the research entailed a close reading of texts from news and political sites. The content analysis focused largely on the "*frames* (what is being discussed, and how), *themes* (patterns in the text), and *discourse* (fields of meaning, relevance, and audience)" (Barnard, 2018a, p. 198; also see Altheide & Schneider, 2012). Finally, the analysis incorporates supplementary data from CrowdTangle, which aggregates user-engagement metrics from Facebook, Instagram, Twitter, and Reddit, to trace the spread of influential stories on social media.

Overall, the research conducted for this chapter yielded numerous insights pertaining to the production, distribution, and reception of varying types of information in the contemporary digital ecosystem. The main findings are summarized below.

PRODUCTION, RECEPTION, AND (RE)DISTRIBUTION

As expected, the majority of stories in the data set were published within the first few days of Acosta's exchange with Trump. Although coverage declined steadily thereafter, there was a slight resurgence of media attention following major developments in the story—namely, CNN's legal filing, Fox News' surprise statement of support for CNN, and the court ruling ordering the administration to reinstate Acosta's press pass (see Figure 5.1).

Although many stories inevitably received a boost from publishers' multimedia promotion efforts as well as links from other articles, the primary measure of attention for this analysis is the number of Facebook shares a story received. The combined sample of 785 stories received a collective 8,754,742 shares on Facebook. But the reach of the stories was not distributed equally. The two most shared stories came from legacy publications with mass audiences: CNN and Fox News, respectively. A majority of the top 20 most shared stories were from similarly mainstream outlets (*Washington Post*, ABC News, NBC News, CNBC, BBC, and *New York Times*), though a few were published by sites outside the mainstream, including The Daily Wire and Axios.

Even though the most trafficked websites typically received the most attention on Facebook, there were times when relatively marginal sites were able to generate a disproportionate amount, or to "punch above their weight," considering their place in the information ecosystem. Of the 72 sites with 2,000 or more average shares per story, many low-traffic sites were able to reach mass audiences—tens of thousands of shares per story—on Facebook.[5] These sites included the conservative LifeZette and liberal Shareblue, among many others. As will be discussed in greater detail below, this finding suggests that there was something remarkable in these stories that attracted extraordinary attention (i.e.,

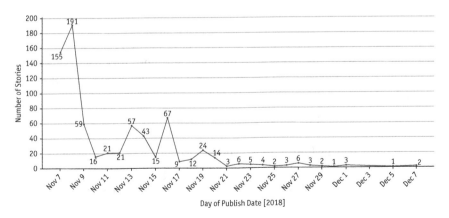

Figure 5.1 Number of stories per day.

spectacle), but also that the sites had dedicated user communities on Facebook (i.e., social capital), that publishers paid to promote them (i.e., economic capital), and/or that there were entities deploying media-hacking strategies to artificially amplify them (i.e., networked media capital).

Political leaning proved to be another revealing indicator of attention. Collectively, sites on the right produced 300 stories on the Acosta incident (0.6 stories per publisher), followed by left sites with 141 stories (0.8 per publisher), center-left sites with 81 (0.65 per publisher), center sites with 56 (0.6 per publisher), and center-right sites with 33 (0.3 per publisher) (see Figure 5.2). While articles from the center-left received the greatest number of shares (3,687,908, or 42.1%) that group also had the largest share of influential websites—five of the top 10, and 7 of the top 20—according to Alexa.com.[6] Stories from the right (2,834,123, or 32.4%) and left (1,301,396, or 14.9%) received the next greatest proportion of shares, while those in the center (870,326 or 9.9%) and center-right (60,989 or 0.7%) received the fewest (see Figure 5.2).

Stories from the center-left were most likely to be shared on Facebook (an average of 45,530 per story), followed by stories from the center (15,542 per story), right (9,447 per story), left (9,230 per story), and center-right (1,848 per story). Nevertheless, given the extraordinary proportion of stories included in this metric—300 out of a total 611 classified stories were from publishers on the right—as well as the number of fringe publications punching above their weight, it would be a mistake to gloss over the attention-getting power of the top-performing right-wing outlets. Indeed, while center-left sites had the top 4 (and 6 of the top 30) average shares per story, right sites had 3 of the top 10 (and 14 of the top 30) (see Figure 5.3).[7] The Daily Wire's position as the most-shared right-leaning site is particularly noteworthy, since it is suggestive not only of its popularity with online audiences and of its success at creating outrageous, identity-confirming content, but also of a strategic campaign to promote their stories.

Of course, the attention these stories receive is dependent on many factors. This includes the popularity (i.e., social capital) and perceived legitimacy (i.e., symbolic capital) of the messenger, the framing of the story itself, as well as the promotional strategies used by the publisher and by members of the networked public (i.e., economic capital and networked media capital). Having addressed the role popularity plays, we now turn our attention to the remaining factors.

According to data from CrowdTangle, Facebook and, to a lesser extent, Twitter and Reddit played a key role in distributing information to networked publics. By focusing on the most influential publishers from each political grouping, it is clear that although trajectories often varied by story and publisher, there were some common trends in the way information flowed through the network.

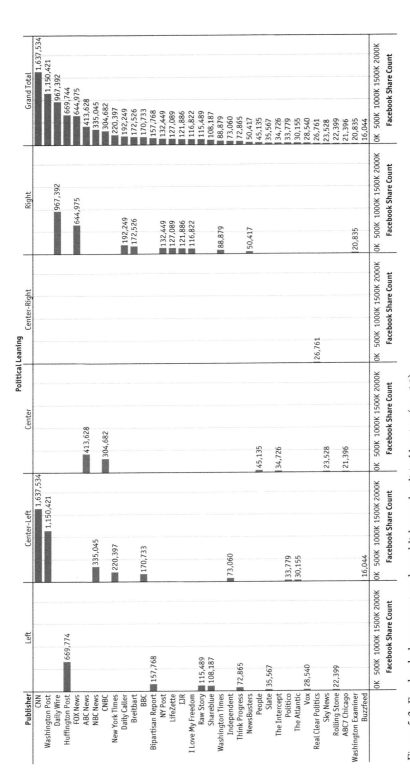

Figure 5.2 Facebook shares per story by publisher and political leaning (top 35).

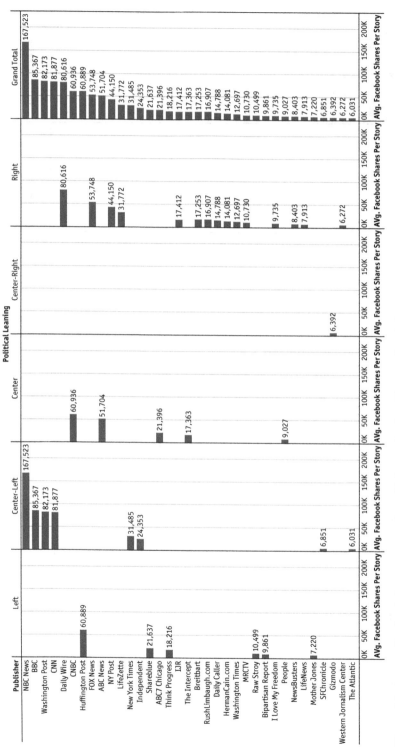

Figure 5.3 Average Facebook shares per story by publisher and political leaning (top 35).

Publishers and publics on the right employed a variety of novel methods to get their messages out. The most established outlets appeared to rely primarily on relatively orthodox publicity practices, which is not surprising given that their substantial economic, social, and symbolic capital make enterprising promotional efforts largely unnecessary. For example, while the bulk of attention to Fox News articles was driven by the organization's social media accounts—its main Facebook and Twitter accounts, as well as those affiliated with various programs—members of its audience also played an integral role in amplifying its stories. The Daily Caller used a similar strategy to distribute its content, relying on numerous posts from their main Facebook and Twitter accounts, as well as many of their smaller, affiliate accounts which helped with cross-promotion. They also benefited from shares by other influential conservatives as well as a variety of politically focused Facebook pages and users. This trend of leveraging social and symbolic capital was common among other publishers within and beyond partisan groupings.

Stories from the Daily Wire followed a different distribution path, relying primarily on its charismatic leader, Ben Shapiro, who at the time had over 5 million Facebook followers, to generate the bulk of their attention.[8] A strategy Shapiro deployed consistently was to share the same article several times over the course of a few days. This helped reach different audiences by maximizing returns from the Facebook algorithm. Notably, Daily Wire used undisclosed paid partnerships—for example, with the Facebook page "US Chronicle"—to promote its content. Daily Wire also benefited from amplification by conservative political action committees (PACs) like Future In America (see Figure 5.4). Like many other publishers, the remainder of attention to Daily Wire stories on Facebook was generated by posts from influential public figures, politically focused Facebook pages, and ordinary social media users, especially on Facebook and Twitter. These promotional efforts not only signal the presence of substantial economic (i.e., paid partnerships), social (i.e., Shapiro's and the PAC's large social media following), and symbolic (i.e., reputation) capital but also indicate considerable networked capital, as illustrated by their clandestine partnerships and gaming of the Facebook algorithms (Legum, 2019b).

Stories from other influential publishers on the right followed somewhat different paths. Whereas the *New York Post* received more traffic from Facebook and Twitter influencers than their own Facebook pages, Breitbart relied on a large cohort of political social media pages—including some associated with the QAnon conspiracy group—alongside Twitter influencers and Reddit pages. This pattern of distribution is illustrative of the power of social capital, and of the sensationalism, populism, and xenophobia reflected in many of the stories, which clearly resonated with right-wing audiences. Additionally, Breitbart's boost from fringe conspiracy groups is indicative of the enterprising amplification strategies

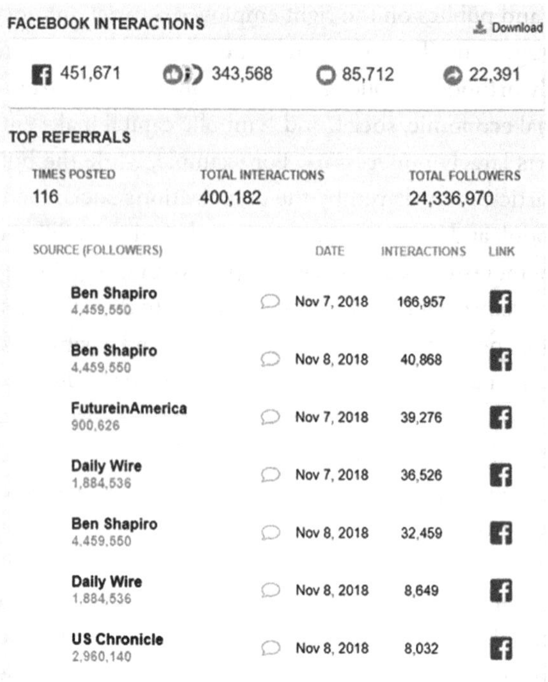

FACEBOOK INTERACTIONS				Download
451,671	343,568	85,712	22,391	

TOP REFERRALS

TIMES POSTED	TOTAL INTERACTIONS	TOTAL FOLLOWERS
116	400,182	24,336,970

SOURCE (FOLLOWERS)	DATE	INTERACTIONS	LINK
Ben Shapiro 4,459,550	Nov 7, 2018	166,957	f
Ben Shapiro 4,459,550	Nov 8, 2018	40,868	f
FutureinAmerica 900,626	Nov 7, 2018	39,276	f
Daily Wire 1,884,536	Nov 7, 2018	36,526	f
Ben Shapiro 4,459,550	Nov 8, 2018	32,459	f
Daily Wire 1,884,536	Nov 8, 2018	8,649	f
US Chronicle 2,960,140	Nov 8, 2018	8,032	f

Figure 5.4 Screenshot of CrowdTangle data showing flow of web traffic to Daily Wire article.

employed by far-right networked publics, which will be examined further in chapter 6.

On the left, top publishers generated attention through means that were largely mundane but occasionally distinctive. Like many on the right, the bulk of traffic to Raw Story was driven by its main Facebook account. Raw Story also relied on numerous posts from its Twitter account, from influential social media users, and from political Facebook pages along with ordinary users. Bipartisan Report relied on a number of highly influential Facebook pages in addition to its main social media accounts. Most of Shareblue's traffic was driven by their repeated social media posts—an average of seven per story— over the course of multiple days. While the bulk of ThinkProgress's attention on social media came from its own accounts, it also relied on influential social media users as well as Reddit's "politics" discussion board. As expected, each of the stories analyzed also relied on amplification from other political social media pages and users.[9] Overall, these trajectories are largely reflective of the publishers' social and symbolic capital, though Shareblue's approach to viral sharing is also indicative of networked media capital (i.e., how to maximize algorithmic amplification).

Stories from the center also followed noteworthy paths to their audiences on social media. The most influential publisher considered for this chapter, CNN, received the bulk of its traffic from multiple posts on Facebook and Twitter, as well as from numerous affiliate accounts. They also received added attention from influential accounts, including politicians and left-leaning political organizations, as well as from Reddit. By contrast to its distribution of news stories, an opinion piece from CNN was not shared at all by their social media accounts, and instead was distributed primarily through Reddit as well as by various political groups from across the political spectrum, including those affiliated with QAnon.

Other publishers near the center also had their content shared by a wide array of social media accounts with varying political affiliations. For example, the *Washington Post*, which relied primarily on its own social media accounts, employees' personal Twitter accounts, and foreign media personalities to generate attention, also had stories shared by pages and users from the right and left. While some ABC news stories also received similar treatment, the bulk of their attention came from their numerous Facebook and Twitter posts—both from their primary and affiliate accounts as well as from the personal Twitter accounts of reporters at their local affiliate stations. This illustrates, once again, that influential publishers rely primarily on their substantial social and symbolic capital to generate attention online.

Interestingly, there were notable differences in the way two outlets from the same conglomerate generated attention. While both NBC and CNBC drew in readers from across the political spectrum, NBC's traffic was mostly driven by constant promotion on Facebook and Twitter. Indeed, 16 of the top 17 sources of social media engagement on its most shared story came from Facebook and Twitter posts by its primary account (NBC News), as well as by affiliate accounts, including MSNBC and those dedicated to its nightly news program. By contrast, when CNBC stories drew large audiences (i.e., tens or hundreds of thousands of shares on Facebook), it was not due to their own promotion efforts on social media. Rather, the primary driver of attention to their stories came from Reddit, as well as from pundits and political pages on the right and left. This points to a notable, albeit predictable pattern: stories from publishers near the center were more likely to be shared by a more diverse group compared with stories from publishers on the left or right.

Content
The content analyzed for this chapter followed discernable patterns according to partisan grouping. While stories from the top-performing sites on both the right (Fox News) and left (HuffPost) were framed in ways that generally conformed to the journalistic norm of objectivity, other publishers in both groups

stretched the convention in unique ways. On the right, some sites appeared to strike a tone of straight reporting in some stories, while also emphasizing aspects that would appease their target audience and ignoring those likely to challenge them. For example, both the *New York Post* and the Daily Caller published influential stories that ignored the controversy over the press secretary's sharing of an edited video. Breitbart's mixing of wire content from the Associated Press with their own interpretation, subtle mentioning of minority media organizations supporting Acosta, and heavy use of quotes from Trump and Sanders (62% of the article) fulfilled a similar function. When compared with their quoting of Acosta, whose words made up a mere 9% of the story, it is clear how the Breitbart story prioritized Trump's perspective over others'. Relatedly, the fetishizing of Trump's conflict with the press was a common theme in many of the stories from publishers on the right. This theme often appeared alongside the liberal media frame, which purportedly functioned to simultaneously smear those in the media establishment while also aiming to boost the credibility of right-wing media.

Some of the most extreme, advocative stories on the right would perhaps best be described as "outrage porn." The Daily Wire, which received the most shares for any site on the right, appears to have mastered this style. Their initial story on the topic—the third most-shared in the sample—was a mixture of inflammatory statements (e.g., calling Acosta "obnoxious" and accusing him of "lying"), propaganda from the press secretary, and sensational critiques cribbed from tweets by right-wing pundits. Other stories from the Daily Wire, while less influential, were similar in style and substance. Taken together, these examples illustrate many of the practices of manipulation discussed in chapter 2, including how content creators' use of sensational framing, kernels of truth, appeal to emotion, association, and dissociation can help them generate attention, therefore converting social and networked media capital into revenue. They also illustrate the identity-confirming function of many right-wing media outlets in the United States (Benkler et al., 2018), as well as the delicate line some publishers walk to produce agreeable content for their audience while attempting to maintain their credibility.

Whereas stories from publishers on both sides of the political spectrum were similar in their (often heavy) reliance on tweets from public officials, they sometimes differed significantly by which sources they quoted—government officials, reporters, or partisan pundits—and to what ends. That is, publishers on both the left and the right selected tweets that helped frame the story according to their narrative, as well as to lend legitimacy to it. HuffPost took an even broader tack, focusing their second most influential story on the fact that, as the headline read, "People on Twitter Call for Sarah Huckabee Sanders to Resign for Jim Acosta Video."

In addition to issue selection, many stories on the left appeared to target their intended audiences by emphasizing other related areas of concern (e.g., Trump's treatment of minority reporters during the same press conference), as well as through the use of carefully crafted language that walks a line between accuracy and sensationalism. For example, Bipartisan Report described the incident as Acosta "refus[ing] to back down against the president's lies," while HuffPost emphasized that the video "appears to be doctored." Although the majority of articles on the right skirted the questionable origins of the viral video, those on the left and in the center often made it a central focus of their reporting. Similarly, some publishers on the left, including Raw Story and ThinkProgress, framed stories around the ongoing conflict between Trump and the press, often emphasizing the "lies" from the president and his spokespeople. These examples leveraged sensationalism, kernels of truth, identity confirmation, association, and dissociation to appeal to the target audience, though the stories and the strategies employed in distributing them were far less deceptive than many found on the right.

Not surprisingly, stories from publishers near the center struck a more objective tone and often followed the "he said, she said" frame (Rosen, 2009). However, many stories also included gentle correctives—likely a measured response to the Trump administration's history of dishonesty and combativeness toward the press. Another notable trend was how long and detailed stories from the center tended to be, often providing substantial background on the timely controversy surrounding Acosta as well as the heightened tensions between CNN and Trump. This not only suggests investment of reportorial resources but also reinforces the perception of liberal and moderate audiences as being more trusting of fact-based reporting (Mitchell et al., 2014), which may help explain the popularity of these stories.

Implications and Conclusions

The analysis of information flows following the Acosta incident yielded multiple findings pertaining to the production, distribution, and reception of news and political communication. First, news about the Acosta incident flowed in a relatively predictable manner, and the bulk of coverage largely conformed to the styles audiences have come to expect in a polarized political climate. Whereas news outlets on the left and near the center were both critical of the Trump administration, with some striking a more adversarial tone than others, the bulk of coverage from the right was much more supportive, and at times overtly propagandistic. It is tempting to interpret this finding as being indicative of conflicting values: on the one hand, a press courageous enough to persist in fulfilling its

Fourth Estate functions, to fight for truth, and to stick up for those, like Acosta, who are caught in the crossfire; on the other hand, one willing to abandon its professional responsibility in pursuit of their own interests. There may indeed be some truth to such a narrative, but there is certainly more to the story.

A more fruitful and empirically demonstrable explanation comes from a more nuanced consideration of the interests of these publishers. Some are undoubtedly driven by political ideology. This tends to be especially true of digital news sites, which often produced the most sensational coverage. Nevertheless, political and economic interests are deeply intertwined, and profit orientation is perhaps the greatest common denominator among the publishers included in this study. Just as there is big business in the horse race frame and other forms of sensationalism (Searles & Banda, 2019), there is plenty of profit to be made by feeding division through so-called partisan journalism. In doing so, publishers from all sides may be helping define and defend political lines and facilitating the spread of problematic information, while simultaneously serving economic ends.

One common response media outlets offer to such criticism is that they are just *giving the public what they want*. Increasingly, it seems many want what Benkler et al. (2018) refer to as "identity-confirming" news, which is defined by a characteristic lack of information or perspective that challenges a group's preferred narrative. Certainly, of those stories analyzed for this chapter, many of the most shared from sites on the left served this key function. Nevertheless, as indicated by this and other research (Benkler et al., 2018; Hiaeshutter-Rice & Weeks, 2021), propaganda or otherwise problematic information was found to be much more prominent, and to have a much greater reach, on the right than elsewhere on the political spectrum.

The pressures on publishers are undoubtedly more than political. Media outlets have long had incentives to use spectacle, sensationalism, propaganda, and other forms of deception, whether egregious or mundane, to generate audience attention (Kaplan, 2002, 2008). But in response to increased competition, shrinking profit margins, and a need to do more with less (Littau, 2019), many publishers may feel torn between their ideals and extinction. Thus, in a time of political polarization and market segmentation, when clickbait and other forms of problematic information can generate substantial traffic (and therefore advertising revenue), the strategy may also be driven by economic demands.

These pressures clearly manifest in the methods publishers employ to attract attention. Indeed, the trend of news professionals using frequent and at times emotionally charged social media posts to promote content is supported by prior research (Tandoc & Vos, 2016). But, as the findings of this analysis indicate, in the era of the participatory web, content is distributed not only by creators but also by members of the public who share content across a variety of channels. This work, which Axel Bruns (2014) has termed "gatewatching," entails the "sharing and commenting on existing news stories" (Barnard, 2018a, p. 86). Given the increasingly active role played by "the people formerly known as the audience" (Rosen, 2006), it is clear that members of the public also bear responsibility for what flows through our news feeds. Indeed, the effects of public participation can be seen in the results of this analysis, which found that a committed base of social media users played a significant part in the amplification of information—a phenomenon I will examine further in chapter 6.

This analysis did not directly measure the relationship between accuracy and the size of the audience. Nevertheless, it was clear that while more widely trusted sources tended to be shared most, there were a number of cases—mostly on the right—where false or misleading accounts reached mass audiences thanks in part to network effects. This conclusion is bolstered by other studies that have found false information spreads faster than the truth in online social networks (Vosoughi et al., 2018) and that right-leaning audiences are more susceptible to problematic information (Garrett & Bond, 2021).

Still, publishers are more than complicit in the amplification process. Like the omnipresent "share" button, the ideology of (maximum) attention is embedded in the logic of hybrid media. Not only do publishers produce mass amounts of content in hopes that some go viral; they also invest financial resources (i.e., economic capital) to promote their content across the web, and they track the effects with detailed web analytics (i.e., cultural capital), the results of which are used to guide future content and promotion decisions (Petre, 2015; cf. Christin, 2018). While such methods of attention hacking may be mundane today, their ubiquity illustrates the powerful role that various forms of capital play in the contemporary media system.

To be sure, media companies have long been in the business of luring and selling attention. The skills of "attention merchants" are rooted in their knowledge of their audiences (i.e., habits and preferences) and technologies (i.e., logics and affordances of their media), as well as their capacity to produce attractive content (Wu, 2017). This knowledge, and the facility with which actors employ it, is the basis of networked media capital. Manifestations of this capital are visible in many of the enterprising production and distribution practices discussed throughout this analysis.

In the hybrid media system, attention hacking takes many forms. Although influential entities rely on their field position to lure consumers, the amount of competition has also driven even the most established publishers to adopt novel approaches to increase the chances their targets see and take the bait. Whether to improve or maintain their position, this was precisely the strategy employed by many established outlets under consideration for this chapter, including CNN, Fox News, and Daily Caller. A related and often complementary strategy entailed harnessing the collective power of their social networks (i.e., social capital) to generate attention. For publishers on the left and the right, this often involved sensationalism and partisan outrage. In addition to mobilizing shares from their core networks, including celebrity employees and influential affiliate accounts, as illustrated by ABC, the *Washington Post*, and others, publishers also relied on the reach of their audiences to help distribute their products. This frequently included transpartisan and nongovernment organizations in addition to celebrities, influential political pages, and members of the public—a trend that simultaneously helped amplify and legitimate the information being shared. Such uses of social and symbolic capital were common across many of the stories analyzed for this chapter.

Beyond those media-hacking strategies discussed above, the data examined in this chapter also illustrate several practices of manipulation introduced in chapter 2. Some, like fabrication, reliance on kernels of truth, appeals to emotion, association, and dissociation, were directly observable in the content analyzed for this case study. Others, such as cooperation, viral campaigns, and bootstrapping, were shown through the consideration of CrowdTangle data, which helped reveal how the stories were amplified through social media. Practices like paid promotion and SEO were less discernable in the data collected, although they undeniably played a part in many of the stories included in the sample.

These media-hacking tactics, like the attention they help generate, are not reserved for those in positions of power. While some publishers may occasionally punch above their weight, whether thanks to their own promotion efforts or a boost from networked publics, their viral successes are mostly attributable to the facility with which they use the tools of the hybrid media system to enterprisingly create and disseminate information—a capacity I have referred to as *networked media capital*. Certainly, knowing which issues or frames will generate the most attention is a marker of networked media capital, as is knowing how to balance timing and repetition of posts to maximize visibility without sacrificing perceptions of credibility or authenticity among their target audience.

Perhaps the most deliberate display of such capital came from Daily Wire, which, in addition to using all the above methods, also relied on PACs with shared political goals as well as popular Facebook pages that were paid to cross-promote their content.[10] Daily Wire's deceptive use of separate Facebook pages to increase the visibility of their content is not only the most extreme deployment of networked media capital identified in this chapter. It also appears to be a brazen violation of Facebook's rules relating to "coordinated inauthentic behavior" (Legum, 2019b, para. 21). Nevertheless, the primary source of Daily Wire's influence was its charismatic leader, Ben Shapiro, who frequently parlayed his influence on social media to attract the attention his outlet desires. As this example illustrates, possessors of networked media capital rely on their field position, dispositions, and other forms of capital to attract attention online. In doing so, they can realize such capital's fundamental power: its potential to be further generated and converted from one form to another (Bourdieu, 1986). This conversion process operates in multiple directions but is perhaps most apparent in an actor's ability to leverage social and networked media capital to generate economic capital.

Despite the limitations of this analysis, much can be learned from it. First, although it did not include detailed data on the actions and motivations of publishers and audiences, the analysis offers a clear view of where information pertaining to this incident flowed, and how. Second, the case selection and data collection methods inevitably painted an incomplete picture. For example, the few Fox News stories analyzed for this chapter looked more like objective news than the right-wing propaganda the network is known for. Thus, we should keep in mind the larger patterns that may be obscured by this one, relatively narrow analysis. As Marwick (2018) argues, "Many of the narratives and talking points that appear frequently in problematic information work seamlessly with the metanarratives and themes pioneered and honed by Fox" (p. 495). Similarly, the emphasis on the role of well-known publishers and prominent social media sites, as well as the reliance on available data, may have concealed other important factors in the dissemination of problematic information. For instance, while stories from extremist sites like the Nazi-affiliated Daily Stormer do not appear to have been shared on Facebook, the content moderation and public backlash such users have come to expect on social media have led them to adopt other channels for discussion and distribution of their materials. In light of that shift, and of the substantial role members of the networked public play in generating and amplifying problematic information, we now turn our attention to a critical analysis of a politically homogeneous web forum where manipulative practices and networked media capital are on full display.

Chapter 6

We Are Trump's Digital Army!

Capital and Practices of Manipulation on The_Donald

> We have an army of digital soldiers.
> —Lt. Gen. Michal Flynn (Young America's Foundation, *2016*)

In the lead-up to the 2016 U.S. presidential election, many avid supporters of Donald Trump began flocking to the social news aggregation site Reddit, specifically its message board "r/The_Donald." By the summer of 2020, when Team Trump was in the midst of its campaign for reelection, the forum had reached 790,000 subscribers (Timberg & Dwoskin, 2020).

The_Donald (TD) was a relatively homogeneous space where fellow Trump supporters could share information and memes, hone talking points—which often reeked of racism, sexism, ableism, and xenophobia—and plan next steps in the ongoing information war. Indeed, in an era defined by Republican voters' extraordinary and disproportionate distrust in legacy news media ("American Views," 2020), TD enabled the networked public that formed there to construct an "epistemic bubble" (Nguyen, 2018). Enforced by downvotes and moderation efforts, users effectively insulated themselves from more mainstream forms of news and political discourse. This, in turn, enabled users of TD to build and maintain a collective identity, defined by its opposition to other social groups like Muslims and the political left (Gaudette et al., 2021), while at the same time amassing capital as digital activists in preparation for battle as part of Trump's volunteer digital army.

Despite the constant barrage of challenges posed by Trump's unorthodox and scandal-ridden presidency, the political momentum driven by incumbency and right-wing populism appeared to be in their favor. But in 2019, Reddit began taking action against TD for repeated violations of its policies on hate speech and inciting violence, and by June 29, 2020, the platform issued a permanent ban on the forum (Harwell & Timberg, 2019; Isaac, 2020; Peck, 2020). Anticipating this move, avid users had already begun migrating to a platform of their own. Ironically named TheDonald.win, devotees developed their own online community where there was less scrutiny and lower expectations for moderation than what they experienced on Reddit.

By January 21, 2021, in the aftermath of the January 6 attack on the Capitol, TD users were again making contingency plans given the increase in public scrutiny of far-right activists' use of digital media. While users discussed backup plans, developers installed a redirect (Thedonaldbackup.com) that would usher visitors to the new site if the existing version was taken offline. A few weeks later, amid strife between the site owner and its developers and moderators, the site reemerged once more as Patriots.win (author's digital archive). Despite the new address, the forum was nearly identical, and although some were concerned that users may fail to migrate to the new site, those that did quickly resumed their practice of sharing and discussing bits of (mis)information. Of course, users were also quick to resume their practice of swapping political memes, which they deemed essential to group morale, as well as sharing strategies and mobilizing action in support of their overarching cause: spreading their preferred forms of problematic information across the networked public sphere. Although their reach was somewhat limited after losing the consistent boost from Reddit's algorithms, which showed popular threads from TD on the Reddit homepage (Peck, 2020), the split freed the forum from other constraints while also seeming to provide extra motivation for devotees to amplify their content using other platforms.

This chapter provides a detailed assessment of political actors' use of digital media as a tool to develop and deploy networked media capital as well as practices of manipulation. Although it centers discourse from alternative platforms like TD, the chapter also remains attuned to the ways ideas and practices from alternative media spill into the mainstream. This dual focus is appropriate due to the multitudinous ways members of the networked public utilize digital media. On the one hand, mainstream platforms like Facebook, YouTube, Instagram, TikTok, Reddit, and Twitter are obvious sites of interest, not only because of their unique affordances but also because of their popularity and broad public reach. On the other hand, following mainstream social media companies' crackdown on nefarious uses of their platforms, extremists have increasingly migrated to alternative platforms like Parler, Gab, Telegram, 4chan, and other community-run discussion boards (Holt, 2022). These online spaces are also of interest because of the relatively unmitigated flow of extremist discourse that occurs there, due in part to their disproportionate concentrations of fanatical users as well as a relative lack of interest in content moderation. Thus, whereas mainstream platforms present obviously relevant opportunities for political actors to spread their message and recruit supporters to join their cause, alternative platforms often function as "set spaces" (Reid & Valasik, 2020) where extremists can convene to, among other things, build collective identity, strategize, and mobilize. As such, these spaces are increasingly central to right-wing political actors' media power.

Relatedly, it is important to understand the significance of alternative and popular media in this research, and in the media and political fields more broadly. Studying problematic information exchanges on mainstream channels allows us to more closely examine the *products* of media manipulation campaigns, while alternative platforms offer a window into the *processes* that shape what is shared, and how. This chapter places a special emphasis on metadiscourse (Barnard, 2016, 2018a;Carlson, 2016; Liu, 2020) because of the uniquely revealing light it can shine on networked publics' communicative practices, how they obtain, share, and wield capital, and the value systems that shape their actions. However, before we examine data from the case study, it is necessary to provide an overview of what is known about digital activism in general, and right-wing forms of media manipulation in particular. Accordingly, the chapter begins with a brief discussion of common patterns within networked activism. After contextualizing TD and its supporters within the broader array of right-wing organizing—from the Tea Party to QAnon—I (re)introduce some of the most notable media-related practices for the current context. I consider the chapter's driving questions and offer an overview of the methodological approach taken to address them. The focus then shifts to the findings from two years of research on TD. Here, the chapter examines the significance of the forum's format, assesses the discursive boundaries constructed by the community of users, presents the most common themes and practices found in prominent threads, and analyzes the processes of capital-building and exchange. The chapter concludes by discussing TD's role in the agenda-setting efforts of the right-wing media ecosystem and by considering the most noteworthy practical and theoretical implications that emerge from this analysis.

Media-Related Practices of Networked Activism

Media have long played an essential role in the public sphere. As discussed in previous chapters, media provide important opportunities for political actors to manage impressions, shape agendas, and recruit and mobilize supporters. And in the contemporary political climate, the importance of digital media appears to be growing. Driven by the ongoing mediatization of everyday life (Couldry & Hepp, 2017), which has itself been spurred by an era of physical distancing required by the COVID-19 pandemic, political discourse is increasingly taking place in digital space. Furthermore, social media platforms enable political actors to develop and deploy new strategies. By combining their own capital and habitus (Bourdieu, 1990, 1993) with the technological affordances at their disposal, networked activists form repertoires of contention (Liu, 2020), which they selectively enact based on the political opportunities presented to them.

The scholarship on networked activism and political communication is wide-ranging and transdisciplinary. What is most relevant for the purposes of this chapter are those studies that contribute to our understanding of how political actors' communicative practices are developed and deployed in digital media. One important study by Jun Liu (2020), for example, demonstrates the essential role that various forms of communication play in social movement organizing in China. Liu examines how the combination of face-to-face communication, mass media, and networked/mobile communication allow social movement actors to identify political opportunities and mobilize, frame, and build collective identity. Most notably, Liu finds that information and communication technologies in general, and *mobile* forms of communication in particular, play an essential role in networked movements' repertoires of contention. While activist practices vary across movements, cultures, and political contexts, there is a broad agreement among many scholars that media's relation to practice can shed important light on dynamics of political action and, therefore, processes of social change more broadly (Mattoni, 2020).

Political actors' media-related practices serve a variety of important functions. Although the long-standing need to gain and shape attention from news media (Gitlin, 1980) remains relevant, members of today's networked public increasingly utilize digital media for public outreach. Whether through their use of mainstream (Barnard, 2018a) or alternative (Lievrouw, 2011) platforms, digital media have been shown to enable communication within and beyond activist networks (Castells, 2015; Earl & Kimport, 2011; Richardson, 2020; Tufekci, 2017a). While the hybrid media landscape and the organizational structures they afford certainly create challenges for social movement organizing (Tufekci, 2017a), there is little question that activists' repertoires evolve alongside the technologies at their disposal (Earl & Kimport, 2011; Liu, 2020). Thus, although the proliferation of tactics and technologies has led many to celebrate their potential for ushering in revolutionary, progressive change,[1] it would be a mistake to overlook other countervailing forces.

One such force has been found in conservatives' use of digital media. Indeed, while the disproportionate attention paid to progressive social movements has led many to conclude that those groups hold the advantage in digital media, a closer look at right-wing movements' media practices paints a different picture. In her study of how actors and grassroots organizations participated in local and state-based politics, Jen Schradie (2019) found that conservatives have a number of advantages, especially when it comes to digital media. In short, Schradie found that whereas progressive activist groups often failed to engage in effective digital political communication, "conservative hierarchical groups had the infrastructure and political motivation to use the internet" (p. 147). Furthermore, while the media-related practices varied significantly within and across platforms, organizations, and ideologies, Schradie discovered that those on the right often "normalized social media into their organizing practices because of their ideas around the internet as an evangelizing tool for the Truth" (p. 173). By using digital tools like email, blogs, Facebook, and Twitter, activists on the right were able to share information—much of which was often misleading or questionable—to a supportive audience in ways that both circumvented and exploited establishment media. Although the political context and technologies have inevitably evolved in the years since Schradie's research was conducted, we will soon discover that many of the tactics championed by the Tea Party, Patriot, and (doomsday) Prepper movements popular in the early 2010s remain common today.

As the Tea Party movement waned, right-wing activists began coalescing around other compatible causes. Enabled in part by innovations in the hybrid media system and driven by rapidly shifting political opportunities, many media-savvy conservatives began forming a new, loose coalition of compatriots that is now commonly referred to as the "alt-right." As Reid and Valasik (2020) describe it, "the alt-right is a confederated movement composed of a variety of factions that are generally against feminism, globalism, immigration, multiculturalism, establishment politics, and political correctness, but are supportive of President Trump" (p. 7). While the media-related practices of the Tea Party and the alt-right differ somewhat—the former focusing on Facebook and blogs as spaces to build collective identity and mobilize support, not to mention their rudimentary attempts to manipulate online ratings (Hiar, 2010), and the latter trolling political opponents and seeking to convert or confuse persuadables with memes and disinformation—there is much that they share in common. Indeed, as Rohlinger and Bunnage (2017) find, Tea Party organizing contributed to the political success of Trump and, by extension, the alt-right.

There are notable remnants of Tea Party politics in contemporary right-wing discourse, such as advocating for small government and deregulation and furthering the ideology of White supremacism. Nevertheless, the distinctive approach to political communication that members of the online right have developed in recent years has brought new practices into the repertoire. For example, digital media provide opportunities for activists to develop and enact methods for radicalization, recruitment, intimidation of opponents, and manipulation of online discourse (Kohler & Ebner, 2019), as well as deliberation and collective identity formation (Gaudette et al., 2021; Juarez Miro & Toff, 2022).

In other words, in addition to amplifying extremist content, digital platforms like those discussed throughout this book "help those on the far right communicate with one another, broadening networks; building resources that support activism, violence, and movement growth; and bridging online connections with off-line engagement and networks" (Miller-Idriss, 2020, p. 145). Furthermore, the use of digital media by members of the alt-right not only helps generate support for their primary causes but can also advance other, more extreme agendas. As Davey and Ebner (2017) put it, "[A]lt-light activists, free speech warriors, Southern rights advocates and libertarians play an instrumental role in mainstreaming white supremacist and even neo-Nazi thought. They are at the heart of the cross-pollination that allows for the normalization of fringe ideologies" (p. 18). Accordingly, the advancement of information and communication technologies in general, and social media platforms in particular, helps networked social movements generate capital, strengthen their communicative practices—in terms of improving public outreach as well as in-group ties (Castelli Gattinara & Bouron, 2020)—and shift the political landscape by helping normalize fringe ideologies (Daniels, 2018).

Another notable development in American right-wing politics is the growing significance of extremists. In addition to the White nationalist and antiglobalist groups that helped organized the January 6, 2021, attack on the U.S. Capitol, another staunchly pro-Trump group has emerged under the label "QAnon." Following their anonymous, self-anointed leader, who goes by "Q," adherents of this "big tent conspiracy movement" (Conner & MacMurray, 2021, p. 7) gather in various online forums, including those hosted on 4chan, 8kun, Reddit, and. win. QAnon followers use the forums to identify the cryptic trails of information (referred to by supporters as "crumbs") and to work together to interpret the info drops, to follow related leads, and even to coordinate sharing their conspiracist ideas in other forums. Operating (and openly identifying) as "digital soldiers" (Conner & MacMurray, 2021), many of the most ardent followers of Q work together to develop and carry out communication strategies intended to increase their visibility and grow their supporter base. Much like TD, QAnon forums often focus on fostering a participatory culture and developing capital among participants. This capital is later put to use through mobilization efforts calling on group members to help spread supporting content using a variety of platforms and practices.[2]

AGENDA-SETTING TACTICS POPULAR AMONG THE (ALT-)RIGHT

As has been discussed in previous chapters, many of the most passionate participants in contemporary (digital) politics draw from a broad repertoire.

Depending on the combined implications of technological affordances, political opportunity, and available capital, networked activists seeking to gain discursive advantage through deceptive means can utilize digital media to develop and deploy various practices of manipulation. Such manipulative uses of media to spread problematic information—from memes and trolling to coordinated sharing and disinformation—have become especially popular with alt-right activists. In this section, we review some of these practices and consider how the structure of the hybrid media system affords media influence by less powerful political actors.

At an elemental level, effective (political) communication campaigns hinge on their ability to frame issues and to disseminate those frames in ways that shape the agendas of others: "Agenda-setting is the power of the media to tell the public what to think about, and framing is their ability to tell us how to think about it" (Lindner & Barnard, 2020, p. 152). This understanding of communication as a matter of agenda-setting and framing has long been widely applied in studies of media and politics (Entman, 1993; McCombs & Shaw, 1972; Terkildsen & Schnell, 1997). While scholarship on agenda-setting has largely focused on the ability of legacy media to shape the public's awareness and prioritization of issues, the growing prominence of social media has led to other avenues where agenda-setting can occur. For example, studies have demonstrated how effective social media sites like Twitter can be for shaping legacy media coverage (Conway et al., 2015; cf. Barnard, 2018a). Still, such intermedia agenda-setting works in multiple directions, suggesting that newspapers, for example, also exercise power over politicians' (and certainly the broader public's) communications (Conway-Silva et al., 2018). These examples make it clear that the communicative practices useful in helping shape public consciousness can work in multiple ways, by speaking directly to members of the public (i.e., gatecrashing) or indirectly by obtaining amplifying coverage from others in the hybrid media system. Yet despite the potential value in distinguishing between direct and indirect forms of communication, and even in comparing *who* is responsible for helping set or accomplish particular framing and agenda-setting goals, the hybrid media system affords multidirectional communication and influence.

One prominent example of political actors' use of networked media capital to shape agendas can be found in the communications of Trump. In addition to my own prior research demonstrating how Trump's use of media like Twitter helped shape the agendas of professional reporters (Barnard, 2018a), more recent work has illustrated how Trump's use of media to raise doubt about the 2020 election helped generate similar coverage among prominent right-wing media like Fox News (Bump, 2021a). The synergy among right-wing media is so strong that some have labeled it a "right-wing media ecosystem" (Tripodi & Ma, 2022), and even a "propaganda feedback loop" (Benkler et al., 2018). In such an environment, influence flows in multiple directions. For example, in their analysis of 15 months of legislative communication from the Trump administration's official newsletter, *1600 Daily*, Francesca Tripodi and Yuanye Ma (2022) found that the administration relied heavily on right-wing media coverage to help frame the issues they chose to highlight in their email messages: "By encouraging their readers to 'do their own research' but providing the hyperlinks directly, the White House emails reveal an intricate structure whereby conservative news producers work in tandem with elected officials, bouncing signals throughout their information networks" (p. 12). Although those with less capital lack the agenda-setting power of the presidency, they often deploy comparable methods in hopes of reaching similar ends (Rønlev & Bengtsson, 2022).

Another revealing instance of media manipulation by members of the alt-right can be found in the infamous #GamerGate saga. Beginning in late 2014, a group of digital activists began a deceptive media campaign that aimed to clap back against feminist messaging about inequalities in the gaming industry. In response to the positive attention feminist actors were receiving, antifeminist gamers began creating and amplifying counternarratives on sites like Twitter, YouTube, and Reddit, frequently including the #GamerGate hashtag. By taking advantage of biases within news industry—for example, fairness and "he said, she said" framing (Rosen, 2009)—they were able to get their message before a public audience. As Blodgett (2020) found:

> News stories put the movement's name front and center and drove home the main points that the gamergaters were trying to argue, that there was corruption in games journalism resulting from the relationships between reporters and video game developers, and that this was just a heated online discussion. (p. 191)

The relative success of the #GamerGate movement was not accidental; it was a strategic campaign of media manipulation coordinated in various online set spaces. The campaign not only harassed feminist detractors but also relied on carefully crafted rhetoric, spectacle, and disinformation to attract media attention. Although the tides eventually turned after journalists grew wise to their manipulative tactics, #GamerGate activists began waging other attacks (Blodgett, 2020). One of the most consequential was "Operation Disrespectful Nod" (Dewey, 2014). Coordinated on anonymous online forums, this campaign encouraged supporters to wage email and social media messaging campaigns chastising reporters and outlets that were critical of #GamerGate, with a goal of doling out punishment (e.g., encouraging sanctions from employers and advertisers) while applying public pressure to yield more flattering coverage.

The #GamerGate campaign marked an important inflection point in the history of right-wing media manipulation efforts. The case was a testing ground that provided proof of concept for future alt-right messaging campaigns, which may explain why many of the tactics mirror those discussed on TD. Furthermore, #GamerGate also illustrates the *negative* power that can be wielded by those in possession of networked media capital. Not only did the campaign succeed at further eroding journalistic autonomy as well as a portion of the public's trust in media. It also contributed to the reduction of some media outlets' advertising revenue and disrupted other capital-generating opportunities within the media professions (Blodgett, 2020; Dewey, 2014). Such efforts to boost manipulators' influence while eroding the power of democratic actors and institutions offer a revealing window into the role media play in contests for power, especially by those operating on the margins of the political field.

To be clear, the tactics discussed in this section are just a few of the most common media-related strategies used by alt-right actors to shape public awareness. But as we will see, there are many other useful methods being developed and deployed in digital spaces. From memes and trolling, hash-targeting and coordination, to sensationalism and identity confirmation, many of the practices of manipulation discussed in chapter 2 and elsewhere in the book are on full display in the data analyzed from TD. But before examining these discursive practices in greater detail, it is first necessary to provide an overview of the analytical approach that guides this analysis.

Studying Practices of Manipulation via Alternative Media

Thus far, this book has examined expressions of media power and practice in multiple settings and from a variety of angles. While our attention has focused primarily on popular platforms and relatively high-profile political actors, there is also much to gain from looking at how practices of manipulation manifest in alternative set spaces like TD, and the role that exchanges of capital play in the process. Accordingly, the remainder of this chapter is focused on addressing the following questions: What themes and practices of manipulation are most prominent on The_Donald? How are these practices developed, discussed, and deployed? What can this tell us about the workings of networked media capital, and about the power of digital media more broadly? To address these questions, the analyses presented in this chapter critically examine digital discourse to gain a greater understanding of how networked actors use media to amass and deploy capital as part of their communicative practice.

Like the previous chapter, the analysis presented here employs digital ethnographic content analysis (DECA) (Altheide & Schneider, 2012; Barnard 2018a) in order to expose the ways political actors organize and mobilize in digitally mediated space. Specifically, the analysis focuses on how online forum users develop, debate, and deploy media-related practices, and what role those practices play in shaping the broader political culture in which they exist. In addition to gleaning insights from sustained participant-observation in online forums (described below), the content analysis portion of the research examined the technological structure and affordances (or *format*) of TD, as well as the most salient "*themes* (patterns in the text), and *discourse* (fields of meaning, relevance, and audience)" found there (Barnard, 2018a, p. 198; see also Altheide & Schneider, 2012). In light of the research questions, the analysis focused on those aspects of the forum that pertain to practices of manipulation and expressions of media capital.

While this methodological approach shares much in common with chapter 5, one aspect that makes this analysis distinct is its focus on metadiscourse. In the context of this chapter, *metadiscourse* is politically focused discourse about the production and dissemination of political information, which manifests as a reflection of capital and (political) practice. Previous studies have already established the value of examining metadiscourse in order to reveal the composition of actors and practices in the journalistic and political fields (Barnard, 2018a; Carlson, 2016). For example, my previous research on journalists' use of social media (Barnard, 2016, 2018a) showed how posts discussing strategy and values can shed light on normalized sets of practices among particular social groups. What is unique about the research presented here, however, is the express focus on strategizing and mobilizing discourses that clearly aim to increase the viability and popularity of manipulative media practices. As such, this metadiscourse helps reveal not only manipulative practices themselves and the capital and habitus that enable them but also the meaning actors attach to them.

Given the emphasis on metadiscourse as a representation of manipulative media practices, the analysis presented here focuses on an online forum popular with web-savvy Trump supporters. As I have alluded to in previous sections, alternative platforms frequently serve as important spaces of deliberation for fringe political groups (Castelli Gattinara & Bouron, 2020; Hawkins & Saleem, 2021; Juarez Miro & Toff, 2022). This description is particularly applicable to TD, which has been shown to play a fundamental role in facilitating group identify formation as well as in helping proliferate hateful discourse (Gaudette et al., 2021). Indeed, although it may be possible to gain relevant insights about the creation or distribution of manipulative media by focusing on other spaces— for example, private Facebook groups or Discord channels—TD offers a unique opportunity to examine the practices contributing to the production and dissemination of problematic information. Furthermore, given the forum's longstanding role in increasing the power of Trump's brigade of online support (Peck, 2020), it provides an important window into the flow and functioning of capital.

The research process included regular observations of TheDonald.win between August 1, 2020 (in the lead-up to the 2020 U.S. presidential election), and January 22, 2021 (when the site shut down). I resumed observations when the site reemerged as Patriots.win and continued sporadically until August 2022 (following the conclusion of primary elections featuring many Trump-backed candidates).[3] Drawn from within this time period, the data included in the analysis presented here are based on a purposive sampling of highly upvoted posts with salience to media-hacking practices, capital, and political metadiscourse—in other words, those discussion threads listed on the front page of the site and that pertain to the research questions.

Structures and Practices of Manipulation on The_Donald

The remainder of this chapter offers a detailed examination of TD and the various ways users leveraged its affordances to facilitate the spreading of problematic information and the amassing of networked media capital. Thus, the following sections address various aspects of the communicative structure and practices present on TD, organized according to the specific components of DECA. Taken together, they provide a broad overview of the culture of TD as well as of the practices and capital driving Trump's digital army. As a result, we glean a variety of insights about the workings of contemporary media power.

FORMAT: COMMUNICATIVE FORMS AND AFFORDANCES

As with all manner of communication, media formats play an important role in structuring the meanings and interactions they facilitate (McLuhan, 1964). TD is no exception. Despite the aforementioned turmoil surrounding TD's home on the web, the structure of the forum has remained largely consistent. Indeed, while not necessarily original, the versions of the site launched on the user-developed dot-win site largely mimic those of the forum's original host, Reddit, which is ranked as the 20th most popular website in the world, and by far the most popular discussion forum ("Most Visited Websites," 2022).

Much like Reddit, the dot-win platform that now hosts TD serves as a primarily text-based forum for users to share and discuss various topics. Discussions are organized by topics in user-generated threads, which themselves play host to comments—presumably related to the thread's stated topic. In addition to titles, the links to each thread are accompanied by other information, such as the number of comments and upvotes it has received, the name of the original poster, information about the source of the original information being shared (a news website, a social media site, etc.), and any HTML encoded images or "flairs" that the poster selected to accompany the thread (see Figure 6.1). In addition to written text, posts are often accompanied by other embedded content such as static images (typically memes), GIFs, videos, and weblinks. Within a given thread, users will also find an array of nested comments, each operating as a unique conversation.

Threads and posts are given priority on the site (e.g., if they are shown on the front page, and in what order) based on recent activity, the number of upvotes and downvotes they receive from users, as well as the number of points (what Reddit refers to as "karma") the original poster has accumulated on the site. In addition to the community- and algorithmically driven prioritization of content, moderators are responsible for deciding which threads (typically between three and five) are "stickied," or anchored at the top of the page. On top of privileging recency, this structure also tends to reward identity-reinforcing content while disincentivizing whatever challenges the community's existing beliefs and values. In other words, users of TD leverage the site's affordances in order to continually co-construct an epistemic bubble in which shared ideology is reinforced and unorthodox ideas are marginalized. Moderators reinforce this effect by deleting posts or banning users that violate forum rules—of which support for Trump is most important.

DISCOURSE: MEANING AND AUDIENCE

Given the anonymous structure of online forums like TD, we lack a clear understanding of exactly *who* frequents and contributes to the forum. Nevertheless, the relative homogeneity of TD, as well as the practices it prohibits, provides a clear indication of the values that define the space. This homogeneity is codified in the forum rules as well as in its "welcome" message: "Welcome to the forum of choice for President Donald J. Trump! Be advised this forum is for serious supporters of President Trump. We have discussions, memes, AMAs [Ask Me Anything], and more. We are not politically correct" (author's digital archive). When the forum was relaunched as Patriots.win, the list of rules accompanying this welcome message had been updated (see Figure 6.2). Although most rules were the same or slightly revised, there were a few significant changes. Most notably, a new rule labeled "High Energy" instructed visitors, "No forum sliding, consensus cracking, topic dilution, etc." This rule included a link to additional

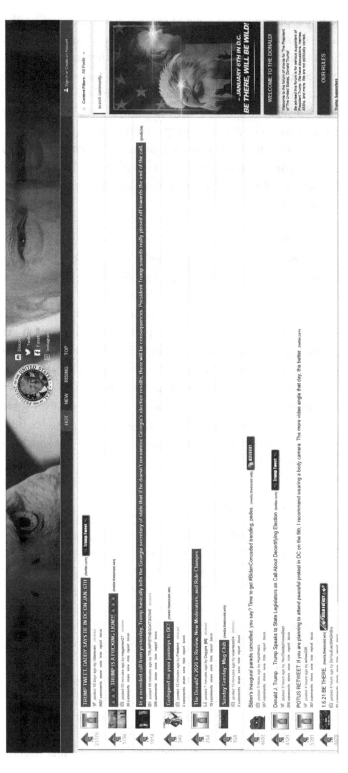

Figure 6.1 Screenshot of TheDonald.win homepage on January 3, 2021.

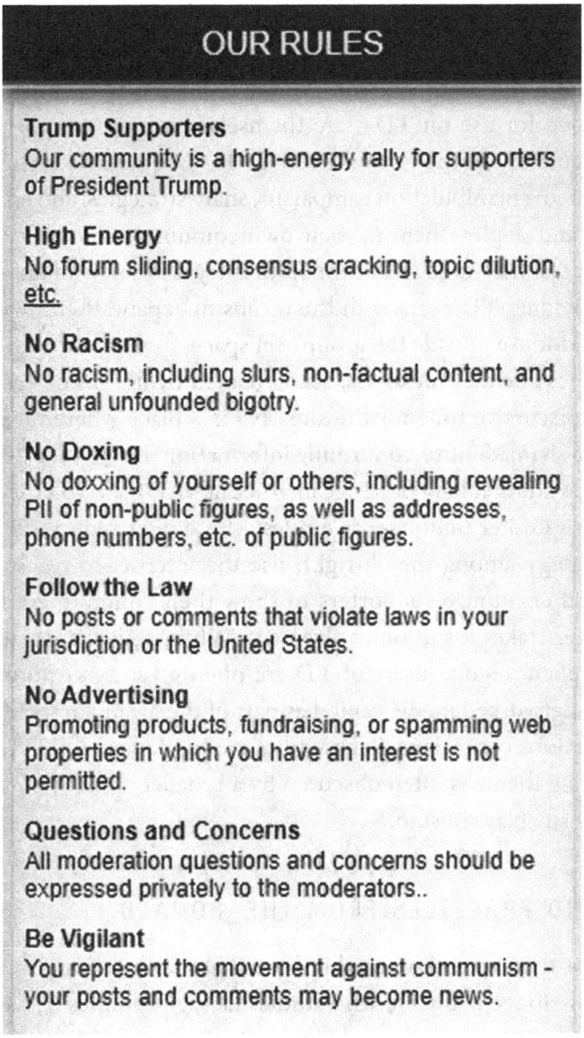

> **OUR RULES**
>
> **Trump Supporters**
> Our community is a high-energy rally for supporters of President Trump.
>
> **High Energy**
> No forum sliding, consensus cracking, topic dilution, etc.
>
> **No Racism**
> No racism, including slurs, non-factual content, and general unfounded bigotry.
>
> **No Doxing**
> No doxxing of yourself or others, including revealing PII of non-public figures, as well as addresses, phone numbers, etc. of public figures.
>
> **Follow the Law**
> No posts or comments that violate laws in your jurisdiction or the United States.
>
> **No Advertising**
> Promoting products, fundraising, or spamming web properties in which you have an interest is not permitted.
>
> **Questions and Concerns**
> All moderation questions and concerns should be expressed privately to the moderators..
>
> **Be Vigilant**
> You represent the movement against communism - your posts and comments may become news.

Figure 6.2 Screenshot of Patriots.win rules on January 30, 2021.

information about these and many other (presumably banned) disinformation tactics ("The Gentleperson's Guide," n.d.).[4]

Beyond providing a brief definition of media manipulation techniques like forum sliding, consensus cracking, and topic dilution, the site linked to by TD moderators also provided detailed instructions and examples—enough information for users to learn and adopt the strategies. Presumably, this information serves multiple functions. On the one hand, it provides users with relevant descriptions of tactics that may allow them to spot when their own communication channels are being manipulated. It may also have a deterrent effect. That is, by signaling that moderators of TD possess the networked media capital necessary to spot these techniques, would-be manipulators may be discouraged from using them in this particular space. On the other hand, many of the practices outlined in "The Gentleperson's Guide to Forum Spies" (n.d.)—practices that are banned for use on TD—are themselves subject to substantial (often positive) discussion on the forum. Users of TD frequently use the site to plan and discuss media manipulation campaigns, share strategies, and encourage others to adapt and deploy them in their own communications. Thus, linking to "The Gentleperson's Guide to Forum Spies" may also serve an important latent function, providing TD users with the means to expand their own networked media capital for use outside the group's set space.

Overall, these banner messages, accompanied by images of Trump himself, help set the discursive tone for the site: TD is a place where members of the alt-right go to share identity-confirming information. But in June 2022, the site's creators added another banner image instructing visitors to volunteer as an election judge or in other public service roles. This advice reflects an increasingly common strategy among the alt-right: use the internet to reach like-minded audiences and encourage supporters to show their commitment to the cause through higher-stakes forms of involvement. While such calls to action are not always so explicit, regular users of TD are often given opportunities to build and leverage networked media capital as part of the group's ongoing (dis)information operations campaigns. Such efforts are fundamental to TD, even if the capital-building theme is often obscured by a broader array of topics and functions that the site plays host to.

THEMES AND PRACTICES FROM THE_DONALD

Much of what this research unearths about TD may be shocking, but perhaps not surprising. Indeed, anyone who studies far-right politics or has spent time in obscure web forums could easily guess the kinds of content that dominate TD. The forum is essentially a prolonged, asynchronous rally for Trump, most threads and posts calling attention to the issues deemed important by his most vocal supporters.

Although the research conducted for this chapter did not seek to confirm (or dispel) stereotypes commonly associated with pro-Trump political actors, this analysis uncovered a number of predictable patterns. For example, one clear theme from TD is the nearly ubiquitous presence of *conspiracy theories*, ranging from specific claims about the 2020 election being stolen or the September 11, 2001, terrorist attacks on the World Trade Center being an inside job, to QAnon-adjacent conspiracy theories about Pizzagate, Jeffrey Epstein, and the so-called deep state. Similarly, many posts also seemed focused on *sowing doubt*, whether about the integrity of the elections, establishment institutions, or American democracy more broadly. Therefore, users of TD not only relied on the forum to share information about Trump and their support of him, but also to *discuss other hot-button political issues*.

Given the ongoing culture war, where members of the political right and left compete to shape public agendas and mobilize voters by generating outrage over cultural issues of interest to their base, there was no shortage of threads that fit this description. One common theme that ran across these discussions was that of *bigotry and hatred*. Whether targeted at specific political opponents or at broader societal trends, TD frequently served as a vehicle for racism, misogyny, homophobia, transphobia, xenophobia, and anti-Semitism. Although this bigotry was typically aimed at women and minorities, contributors to the forum typically spoke in similar ways about anyone who was not an avowed Trump supporter, but especially those on the political left. This finding resonates closely with earlier research on TD, which illustrated how consistent themes of othering helped Trump supporters build and maintain collective identity (Gaudette et al., 2021).

Hypermasculinity was another prominent theme running throughout much of the content on TD. In addition to a recurring tendency to degrade and objectify women, especially if they are left-leaning, there was also a tendency to use emasculating rhetoric when discussing progressive men. Unsurprisingly, other, related themes frequently accompanied such rabid displays of (hyper)masculinity— particularly the *celebration of violence*. In addition to the general love for guns displayed through the popularity and prominence of weekly "Sunday Gunday" threads, where users bragged about the size of their arsenals and their Trump-loving militias, these threads were also used to coordinate action and identify potential targets. For example, just days before the insurrection on January 6, 2021, one of the top "stickied" threads carrying a "Sunday Gunday" heading was used to discuss Washington, D.C., gun laws and to share strategies for making illegal (more lethal) modifications to weapons and sneaking weapons into or near the U.S. Capitol. Of course, such violent fantasies sometimes included naming would-be victims, which ranged from left-leaning citizens to top-ranking Democrats, and even Vice President Mike Pence.[5]

It would be a mistake to assume that discourse on TD is defined by widespread agreement. There are, in fact, a number of debates and disagreements that play out on the forum every day. Nevertheless, one primary function of the forum—in addition to helping organize and facilitate the spread of pro-Trump propaganda, discussed in greater detail below—is to boost morale among Trump's volunteer digital army. Through moderation, algorithmic amplification, and user-driven actions, those who visit TD are presented with a cacophony of comments affirming their pro-Trump identity and encouraging them to keep up the fight in the ongoing "meme war" (author's digital archive). In line with prior research on the power of *identity confirmation* in the right-wing media ecosystem (Benkler et al., 2018; Tripodi, 2018), TD provides a haven where the core beliefs of even the most extremist users are rarely questioned.

Instead, users rely on the homogeneity of the TD to collectively *criticize political opponents*. In an environment that requires and rewards a pro-Trump stance, one way users show their allegiance is by maligning those they disagree with. (Recall the bigotry, hatred, and hypermasculinity.) At times, the attacks seemed personal, such as when users and moderators derided Reddit after being quarantined and removed from the site. More often, users of TD engaged in collective pile-ons where they reveled in skewering their opponents. Some of the most frequent targets of this criticism were, predictably, Democratic politicians, legacy media outlets, and social media companies, and anyone who supported these was typically fair game. While their criticisms were often profane and lacked a factual basis, this did not stop users from taking the opportunity to act out what appeared to be one of their true callings: using the digital tools at their disposal to "own the libs."

One of the most prominent themes found on TD is *information sharing*. While one would expect information sharing to be a significant practice in online forums, it is hard to overstate how central this function is to the site. Information can come in many forms, of course. Although many prominent threads begin with an identity-affirming meme, others include links to outside sources, such as news articles, videos, and social media posts. As indicated elsewhere in this chapter, the forum also helps users circulate unconfirmed rumors and conspiracy theories, as well as legally questionable information. In addition to the countless posts promising proof that the election was stolen or offering advice to those considering using violence to stop Biden from taking office, others used the forum to share voter information. For example, in a November 20, 2020, post, a user shared a link to a database of all Wisconsin voters, which they claimed to have purchased themselves for $25,000, along with instructions for how to save and share the data with others. This is one illustration of how information sharing also functions as a form of group education.

Building on the information-sharing theme, users of TD also engaged in occasional discussions about the community itself, or what I refer to as *metadiscourse*. Given what we know about the occurrence of metadiscourse in other digitally mediated communities (Barnard, 2018a; cf. Carlson, 2016), it is hardly surprising that users at times reflect on the forum and its norms. These metadiscursive reflections often occurred sporadically, although there were numerous threads explicitly devoted to such discussions. Some posts, like those that offered a history of TD, shared statistics about site usage, or reflected broadly on moderation issues, were noteworthy opportunities to build a sense of shared ownership and commitment through transparent communication.

Others reflected on technological affordances or specific moderation issues, which often emerged in direct response to challenges faced by the group. For example, a number of metadiscursive posts appeared after the forum changed hosts (from Reddit to TheDonald.win, and eventually to Patriots.win). In the days and weeks surrounding these transitions, users were more likely to discuss opportunities or challenges facing the group, to criticize perceived opponents of the forum (Reddit, moderators, etc.), and to facilitate planning in the event of future site disruptions (outlining site protocols, sharing links to mirror sites, etc.). Yet, in characteristic fashion, these discussions often devolved into a blend of cheerleading, critical reflection, and conspiracy theorizing, as evidenced by posts suggesting TD was banned from Reddit because of its success or raising concerns about the new forum being surveilled or controlled by outsiders seeking to undermine the group's efforts.

Of all the functions TD serves, *capital-building* may be the most significant. While posts explicitly emphasizing capital-building make up a relatively small proportion of comments on the forum, and the aforementioned themes occur more frequently, TD still plays a fundamental role in facilitating the spread of problematic information within and beyond the forum. It does so by helping its members generate capital, and also by encouraging them to put that capital to use in support of the cause. When threads do aim to share information or facilitate a dialogue about how users can better leverage digital tools, discussions of these topics are frequently derailed or diluted by numerous replies that are of little value or relevance to the topic as initially framed. Ironically, these disruptive conversations often occur in a troll-like manner that imitates many of the forum manipulation tactics, like "topic dilution" and "anger trolling," that are listed as violating community standards.[6] As a relatively mundane but representative example, consider an April 14, 2021, thread about how users can elect to enable "beta features" on the Win platform.[7] Presumably, visitors to the thread were able to obtain most of the relevant information from the initial post. However, this quickly became a self-fulfilling prophecy, because the vast majority of the 220 replies on the thread were nonsubstantive comments focused on reinforcing group identity, insulting the out-group, and even floating conspiracy theories about what may happen to users who enable the beta features. The relative lack of technological literacy on display in this and many other forum conversations points to an important truth about TD users, and the alt-right more generally. That is, although a notable portion of individuals' communicative actions do display substantial networked media capital, many others lack the requisite capital to wage sophisticated attacks from the front lines of the information war. Furthermore, while some who lack such capital express a willingness to obtain it, others are more likely to play the role of supporter or observer. This gap in actors' capital reinforces the importance of capital-building efforts among their ranks. Given the extent of capital-building efforts on TD and their centrality to the research questions driving this analysis, the following section examines this theme in greater detail.

Divisions of Labor and Conversions of Capital according to a User-Generated Typology

One of the primary functions of a social network is the way it affords the leveraging and exchange of capital, and TD is no different. Beyond addressing the aforementioned themes, discussions on the forum frequently centered on building group members' capacities for influence in the hybrid media system. The multipronged approach that sorts, trains, and deploys troops based on individuals' skill sets is clearly on display by the most dedicated users of the forum. Indeed, one digital flyer that circulated on TD, 8kun, and other QAnon-affiliated sites, offers a breakdown of the group's tactical approach (see Figure 6.3). Using the acronym STFU (short for "shut the fuck up," an apparent nod to their goal of drowning out or silencing legacy news and other media content they deem undesirable), the flyer breaks down the group's approach to information warfare into four distinct roles. Due to its cogent summary of the way media-related practices and exchanges of capital are made manifest in Trump's digital army, this section will closely examine the digital flyer while also considering related exchanges discovered through the research process.

To start, it is helpful to consider the hierarchical division of labor outlined in the flyer. As relatively low-skilled supporters, "Scouts" search the web for content that may be helpful to the group's cause, whether by boosting morale or skewering opponents, which they then post to social media and web forums to notify others. Those playing the role of "Tactical Assault" are "troll master[s]" and "highly skilled social media warrior[s]" that use their networked media capital to create and share content on social media to reach targeted audiences and avoid having their accounts suppressed by platforms' moderation efforts. Once the content is initially shared on social media, those working the "Flanks" help amplify their messages and suppress opponents'. This work can range from liking and sharing content on social media as the user deems appropriate, to more coordinated action like boosting viral campaigns through social media, polls, and online petitions, with an ultimate goal of increasing visibility and even creating an impression among the public that such views are normal or even popular. Thus, the more supporting content that can be created and shared online (assuming it is not tagged for removal by moderators), the greater chance the digital army has of normalizing their ideology. Finally, those serving in "Unit Operations" help plan and orchestrate future communicative actions. Using their substantial capital, they create and curate content; develop strategies for dissemination (including creating or identifying hashtags); coordinate action

Figure 6.3 Digital flyer circulated on TheDonald, 8kun, and other QAnon-affiliated sites.

among Scouts, Tactical Assault, and Flanks to maximize visibility; gather information and assess the effectiveness of the group's information operations; as well as recruit and train reinforcements.

As an artifact of TD's view of networked capital and its division of labor, the digital flyer depicted in Figure 6.3 is a helpful illustration of the approach to information warfare taken by this so-called digital army, and from it we can glean many things. First, given the common use of media-related practices, language, iconography, usernames, and even cross-posting information from one forum to another, there is a clear, synergistic relationship between TD and many QAnon-affiliated sites. Indeed, throughout the digital ethnographic portion of this research I witnessed countless instances of links between TD and other

QAnon-related forums—a finding that resonates with prior research (Zeeuw et al., 2020). While examining the structured relations among far-right activists is beyond the scope of this study, it is clear that contributors to TD, QAnon forums, and other alt-right groups share common goals. More important for the purposes of this analysis, they also share common communicative practices.

Second, the flyer shows the clear presence of military tactics within pro-Trump political groups. There is a visible presence of military members within alt-right groups, most prominently Lt. Gen. Michael Flynn, whose ties to QAnon are so strong that he even trademarked the phrase "digital soldiers," which is now common parlance within the conspiracy theory community (Rondeaux, 2021). There are also numerous elements of military psychological operations (PsyOps) tactics discernable on the digital flyer and in related forum posts. For example, discussions on TD frequently use language or refer to online materials that indicate military training. Such participation by members of the military (current or former) is common among other alt-right and right-wing extremist organizations (Reid & Valasik, 2020).

Third, the flyer's purported emphasis on activists "providing plain facts and straight truth reporting" in an attempt to counter popular narratives mirrors a strategy outlined elsewhere on TD (author's digital archive). For example, in an August 2020 thread from TheDonald.win asking if users were "doing their part," many emphasized the importance of remaining respectful and to the point and relying on widely trusted sources when engaging in political debates on social media. As one user put it:

> [E]veryone needs to realize that every thread on Facebook or comment section in youtube or instagram ect. its not just about the person you are replying to, there is ALWAYS an audience of however many people just reading and not replying. THIS is who its really for.
>
> Just be polite, to the point, and dont get taken off course. If they see one person calmly saying "No that isnt true, heres proof that x happened" and the other person is having a shit fit saying "SHUT THE FUCK UP YOU [insert political insult] THATS JUST PROPAGANDA!" They will by default believe the calm one and think the other person is just some unhinged loon. (Author's digital archive)

This strategy of seeking to win over hearts and minds through rational discourse was on display in many posts to the forum. Of course, some others advocated for different approaches to information warfare. For example, in an October 2020 post to TheDonald.win about the "art of the troll" in which the creater dubbed themselves "resident Shitpostmaster General of .win," there appeared to be widespread agreement about the value of trolling (author's digital archive). Rather than approaching exchanges from a place of intellectual honesty, where activists raise and address various points using evidence and reasoning, users suggested that it was better to engage dishonestly. That way, they may confuse, distract, and perhaps even demoralize their political opponents. Such approaches resonate closely with other practices common on the forum, such as the production and dissemination of edgy memes, which are more grounded in internet culture than in traditional tactics of political communication. Additionally, the contradictory nature of such practices provides an opportunity to acknowledge another important reality about TD and other alt-right groups: they often lack a cohesive, organized structure that makes the most of the group's collective capital. As is typical of many contemporary movements, especially those operating primarily in a digital environment, they tend to be loosely stuctured or leaderless and are fueled by laypersons who act in relatively autonomous ways (Gerbaudo, 2017; Tufekci, 2017a).

Fourth, the QAnon-connected digital flyer circulated on TD and other alt-right sites (Figure 6.3) offers advice both similar to and different from other such training and recruitment material. Consider a page from the Trump campaign's Army for Trump website shared numerous times on TD (see Figures 6.4 and 6.5). The page featured step-by-step instructions (with accompanying videos) of how to stay updated on Trump-approved talking points, and how to disseminate them on various social media sites. While some of the trainings offer relatively basic information (e.g., how to create a Facebook account), others help users adopt more sophisticated tactics that require greater knowledge of the various technologies involved, and in doing so they also help users generate networked media capital. A video about Instagram instructs users to deploy workarounds or hacks in order to share the campaign's content.[8] Another encourages users to include a variety of preapproved pro-Trump hashtags when posting on social media. Although this advice differs significantly from the more extreme practices of manipulation outlined in Figure 6.3, users of TD celebrated the resource for its "production quality" as well as for its ability to provide accessible instructions for activists to join the digital fight using similar tactics (author's digital archive).

Fifth, and perhaps most important for the purposes of this analysis, Figure 6.3 offers a useful illustration of many of the most common tactics discussed on TD, as well as of the various forms of capital and dispositions required to put them into practice. The digital flyer serves as a clear example of what is perhaps the most noteworthy aspect of the *capital-building* theme. That is, by engaging in knowledge-sharing practices on sites like TD, users with more capital are able to help those with less develop their capacities for influence in the networked media system.

Figure 6.4 Screenshot of "Become a Digital Activist," from ArmyforTrump.com.

Before proceeding with our analysis of the capital-building theme, it is important to examine the limitations and strengths of Figure 6.3 and to clarify the purpose of referring to it throughout this section. There are several noteworthy limitations to consider. For starters, the stated roles—Scouts, Tactical Assault, Flanks, and Unit Operations—appear to be mostly informal categories. Based on the data analyzed for this study, it seems unlikely that more than a small minority of TD users would self-identify with a particular role outlined in the STFU framework. As is typical for networked activists, many are more likely to work with relative autonomy, and even to blend practices from various roles according to their own capital and dispositions. Instead of a fully operational training manual developed by a highly organized communications team, it is a typology created by a small group of devoted digital activists and organizers to develop an ordered description of an otherwise hybrid set of practices with an ultimate goal of shaping the actions and perceptions of others. Indeed, there is good reason to view the flyer itself as an article of propaganda and disinformation. Nevertheless, the STFU framework serves as a useful typological device to

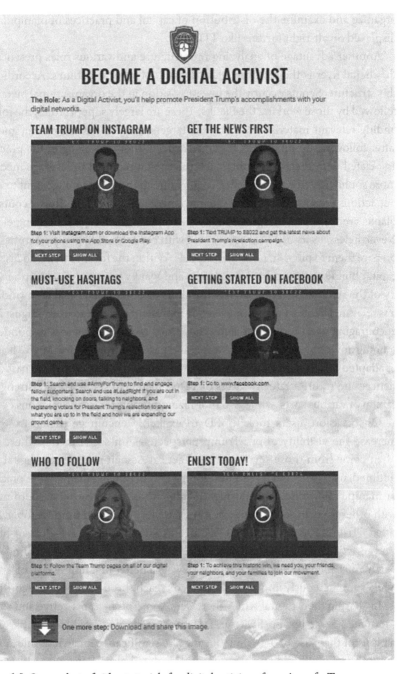

Figure 6.5 Screenshot of video tutorials for digital activism, from ArmyforTrump.com.

organize and examine the distribution of capital and practices of manipulation displayed on alt-right forums like TD.

Another advantage of analyzing the structure and various roles presented in the digital flyer is the relatively clear division of labor it outlines. According to this structure, Scouts occupy the lowest position in the organizational hierarchy, followed by those working the Flanks. These are largely support roles, the former finding relevant material and potential targets in the information war, and the latter following up on attacks for added effect. Those engaging in the practices associated with these roles often lack the capital required to leverage media in more sophisticated ways and often require direction and encouragement to carry out actions seen as beneficial to the movement and its leaders. Thus, Scouts and Flanks are frequently the intended audience for others' capital-building efforts. Nevertheless, users of TD are presented with capital-building opportunities that prepare them to pitch in, no matter the role. Within the forum threads focused on capital-building, comments from Scouts and Flanks frequently make up a majority of the replies, asking follow-up questions or otherwise engaging in (more or less relevant) banter. For example, in one representative thread from August 2020 encouraging users to join the fight, numerous rank-and-file users responded to training advice by swapping war stories and passing on strategies they've learned or adapted during their time in the digital trenches. By discussing those past experiences and future strategies, users of TD were able to showcase and strengthen capital of various sorts, while also mobilizing support for future missions.

On occasion, users took to TD to explicitly encourage digital troops to increase the visibility of pro-Trump perspectives on social media. These calls often come from those serving in the Tactical Assault role. As the digital flyer outlined, users are tasked with developing and deploying many of the practices of manipulation discussed throughout this book, and also with coordinating with other users to solicit support. For example, in a thread from October 2020 titled "Trump's new viral video. We need reinforcements guys, lots of liberal trolls. LETS GO!" users were instructed to like and comment on a Trump campaign YouTube video in order to give viewers a better first impression of Trump while simultaneously improving the video's reach through YouTube algorithms.

In sharing their capital with other users, some of the most active and skilled social media warriors on TD (e.g., Tactical Assault) also provided notable explanations of their use of digital media and the significance it carries. Thus, examining the capital-building theme in greater detail also allows us a closer look at some of their most salient practices. Many practices discussed in previous chapters, such as those intending to maximize amplification, were also visible in TD discussions analyzed for this research. While I discovered few instances of users talking openly about leveraging the technical affordances of digital media to boost visibility (e.g., using automated bots, paid promotion, or search engine optimization), there were numerous discussions of other tactics that could reasonably help achieve similar results. Most commonly, users of TD were presented with suggestions about how to select appropriate topics and creatively frame attacks to appeal to specific audiences, as well as about how to appeal to emotions and to associate with members of the in-group while dissociating from those less desirable.

Most capital-building efforts aimed to increase the volume and creativity of pro-Trump content, and then to foster its spread through relatively low-tech efforts at (coordinated) amplification. For example, in a series of related threads, users were encouraged to share and comment on positive content and were also offered advice about other creative ways to reach desired audiences. Many of the suggested strategies were rather mundane, such as finding appropriate images, videos, or links to accompany text, posting at peak times, simultaneously directing comments to individuals and the broader public (e.g., by using ".@" at the start of a Twitter reply), and customizing aspect ratios to optimize the impact of images on various platforms. Users were often encouraged to come up with pithy hashtags in the hopes they resonate with audiences and, ideally, grow into mimetic trends themselves. As a more extraordinary example, numerous threads offered advice about how to effectively carry out "hash-targeting," where users identify popular, more or less relevant hashtags, and then spam them with pro-Trump content in order to reach different audiences. Such tactics varied in sophistication. Some suggested identifying swing states and then posting comments on local news outlets' social media accounts, with the goal of reaching passersby. Others encouraged users to take advantage of bot-detection software to identify hashtags (an apparent proxy for recognizing prominent but already boosted topics) for use in their posts. However different or deceptive, each of these entail sophisticated practices of manipulation that require substantial networked media capital.

While some of these strategies focused expressly on increasing the visibility of desired content, many could also be used to dilute conversations or suppress perspectives deemed counterproductive to their cause. Like other acts of propaganda and disinformation, which aim to advance a certain narrative or to muddy the waters enough to raise doubt and disrupt rational deliberation, hash-targeting can be used to "flood the zone with shit" (Lewis, 2018). In some threads, users of TD were instructed to do just that, while others encouraged disrupting or diverting undesirable discussions using slightly different tactics. Sometimes, as discussed above, they were taught to troll users, often through the use of anonymous or misleading online identities—much like the sock puppets discussed in the book's preface. Alternatively, visitors to another thread were instructed to report supposedly inauthentic accounts advancing agendas they disagree with, thereby (hopefully) decreasing the visibility of opposing perspectives.

On numerous occasions, experienced media manipulators offered advice about how to circumvent social media platforms' moderation infrastructure. For example, when a widely disputed *New York Post* article sought to tie President Biden to an international conspiracy benefiting his son, and was being removed from most major social media platforms due to concerns it contained illegally hacked materials, users were taught enterprising techniques to push the problematic narrative—in part by overwhelming the moderation systems platforms had in place. After learning that attempts to share standard links to the article were ineffective, organizers shared more novel techniques, such as creating duplicate versions hosted on other websites, and sharing uniquely edited screenshots of the story (adding a filter or pixel, recropping the image, changing the file type, etc.) from numerous accounts, therefore hoping to slip past the sites' automated moderation tools. This approach to circumventing censors is similar to the methods used by the digitally savvy far-right activists who helped spread the video of a 2019 mass shooting targeting Muslim mosques in Christchurch, New Zealand (Klonick, 2019). Altogether, these discussions illustrate the variety of manipulative media practices deployed by users of TD, as well as the persistence of the capital-building theme among those seeking to fuel the information war.

The capital-building theme also emerged in even more explicit forms from users clearly seeking to train and mobilize new members of Trump's volunteer digital army. Indeed, one of the most visible positions displayed on TD has to be the organizers themselves, or Unit Operations. By definition, many of the most useful capital-building efforts come from those who have the requisite capital to share with others. This, of course, begins with those actors who, as the flyer states, "make training bulletins, spreadsheets and graphics," such as the STFU flyer itself. A majority of these training threads appeared in the months before the 2020 election. For example, in a series of "meme classes" hosted on TD and cross-posted to other platforms, more experienced users shared step-by-step guides to help those with less capital learn how to create and share pro-Trump memes. Beyond teaching volunteers how to find the necessary software, the trainings also offered technical instructions for formatting memes and advice about how to identify relevant topics and images, and detailed suggestions for how to craft the most compelling messages (read: humorous and potentially persuasive to a broad audience). Rather than simply provide a series of one-way instructions, the organizers encouraged active-learning strategies such as holding interactive conversations with users and offering detailed feedback on the technical makeup and cultural connotations of memes. In addition to discussing ways to increase humor or specificity and clarify meaning, users received guidance on how and where to share their finished products. While the series of "meme classes" were perhaps the most formal and explicit places where capital-building work occurred, countless other threads helped accomplish the goal in less explicit ways.

The digital flyer depicted in Figure 6.3 also emphasizes the importance of building, maintaining, and converting *social capital*. In addition to helping boost the networked media capital of digital army volunteers (discussed in greater detail in the following section), many training threads like the "meme classes" serve another function: recruiting and mobilizing supporters to take additional actions on behalf of the movement. While the processes of capital generation and mobilization are not mutually exclusive nor temporally ordered, once users have developed sufficient networked media capital, the next step is to encourage them to put their skills into (communicative) practice—a process they hope not only shapes political agendas of those who engage with their content but also inspires future recruits to join the fight. Thus, although the process operates recursively, with capital-building efforts supporting recruitment and mobilization, and vice versa, the group's lofty goals come with a clear, ever-present need to recruit and rally the troops.

By helping to foster and strengthen social ties and to convert potential support into political action, those contributing to recruitment, coordination, and mobilization efforts are playing an important role in helping users of TD build social capital. Many mobilization efforts focused mostly on straightforward instructions, like "spreading #stopthesteal information to . . . friends and family" or posting a link and instructing supporters to "make sure to like and comment" on it (author's digital archive). Other mobilizing posts combined instructions with requests for information or volunteers, such as when a thread asked supporters to commit themselves to further in-person (violent) action ahead of the January 6 attack on the Capitol. Still others sought to mobilize support while at the same time bridging gaps to build social capital across network boundaries. This occurred most clearly in cases where users from TD were directed to other far-right forums (or vice versa).

As with all forms of social action, effective participation in the political field requires more than just social capital. In order to wield influence, one must possess and convert other forms of capital as well, including *economic capital*. Political actors have long relied on economic capital to generate other forms of power, as illustrated by the enterprising (if troubling) use of "dark money" to advance political agendas (Mayer, 2017, 2021). There are smaller-scale equivalents of anonymous injections of money to finance group initiatives, such as a user's purchase of voter data (discussed earlier in the chapter), which they made available to all site visitors. This process of capital conversion is also clearly illustrated by the way TD is funded: through the financial support of users. Political organizations frequently use digital media to help them generate economic capital (e.g., donations) (Auter & Fine, 2018), and by doing so they demonstrate the potential economic value of social capital. However, online forums, even popular ones with a relatively organized leadership team, are often run quite differently (and more cost-effectively) than formal political campaigns.

Despite the parallel investments in capital-building made by the Trump campaign, as evidenced by the Army for Trump website discussed above (see Figures 6.4 and 6.5), TD has remained relatively independent. Although TD has a murky history of support from wealthy benefactors, including a former tech executive (Collins, 2016), the forum is apparently run by an ad-hoc collective of Trump supporters who have declined previous funding offers and have no direct ties to the Trump campaign (Bossetta, n.d.). Considering this, we would not expect users to focus as much on raising money as we would professional political operatives. Indeed, there was little discussion of money on TD. Barring occasional admissions that the forum was financed by site moderators, very few posts called on users to help fund political efforts, and when they did, such calls often took a backseat to the site's primary mission. For example, while one contributor encouraged users to consider donating to the Trump campaign as well as to other like-minded candidates, these requests were pitched as an alternative for those who lacked the time, skills, or disposition to help spread their content across the networked public sphere.

While economic capital is helpful in building and sustaining effective messaging campaigns (Mayer, 2021; Schill & Hendricks, 2016), in the era of digital activism, money (or lack thereof) is far from a deterministic factor. What is often more important is an individual's or group's ability to reach large audiences through social capital, to command their attention and respect through symbolic capital, and to leverage the political, cultural, and technological tools at their disposal through expressions of *cultural capital* (Barnard, 2018a; Nissenbaum & Shifman, 2017). To understand how this applies to the case study at hand, it is helpful to more closely examine the distribution of capital among members of the digital army based on their designated roles.

As illustrated in Figure 6.6, each role in the digital army can be said to require its own unique combination of social and cultural capital. Recall that while Scouts represent those relatively less-skilled users performing background research and Flanks represent those who follow up on (dis)information campaigns to help amplify them, those working in Tactical Assult play the primary role of creating and initially disseminting content, while Unit Operations are largely responsible for planning, training, and mobilizing support. Furthermore, if social capital manifests in the size and power of one's social networks and cultural capital in one's knowledge of political and technical systems, then there is a clear hierarchy in terms of capital distrubition across ranks of the digital army.[9]

Given the relative lack of social ties and technical or political knowledge required to find information online, it generally requires the least capital to

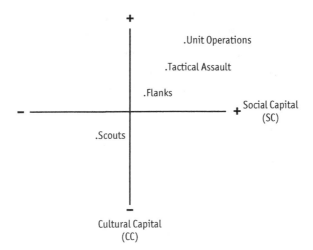

Figure 6.6 Distribution of capital in digital army roles.

carry out the work of Scouts. Those working the Flanks clearly require greater knowledge and social reach in order to effectively amplify messages supporting the movement, but such generalizations become more complicated at the upper levels of the capital distribution matrix. For example, it would appear that social and cultural capital are greatest among those working in Unit Operations because they must possess substantial technocultural knowledge and maintain strong social bonds with fellow activists in order to effectively plan and organize digital campaigns. Nevertheless, it is clear that those working as Tactical Assault need considerable cultural capital in order to plan and execute information campaigns. Furthermore, Tactical Assualt accounts also require greater social capital in the broader (digital) public sphere given that, by definition, their accounts should have substantial followings and, therefore, a greater ability to reach larger (outside) audiences.

Of course, it is important to acknowledge that representations like the one in Figure 6.6 oversimplify what is otherwise a complex interaction of numerous factors. First, the roles outlined in the STFU framework do not fit neatly within a distinct typology but are better understood as a hybrid amalgamation of skills and practices. Second, a closer examination of Figure 6.6 illustrates why attempts to explain digitally mediated practice using Bourdieu's (1990, 1993) classic typology of capital fall short. Indeed, the skills required to create and carry out practices of manipulation cannot be fully explained by actors' possession of traditional forms of cultural and social capital. Finally, while Couldry's notions of "media capital" (2014b) and "media meta-capital" (2012) bring us closer to understanding how media-related skills allow actors to wield power across various fields, they do not adequately explain the hybridized set of skills and practices required of actors to effectively wield power across the contemporary media landscape. Rather, such power is better attributed to the unique combination of knowledge and skills spanning hybridized fields like media, culture, technology, communication platforms, journalism, and politics, which I describe throughout this book as *networked media capital*. Indeed, when actors combine and leverage multiple forms of capital to navigate the hybrid media system in enterprising ways, they are drawing on networked media capital.

Regardless of which form of capital is being deployed or converted, each plays an elemental role in shaping social action. Given the group's goals to elevate pro-Trump perspectives throughout the public sphere, such a wide distribution of capital illustrates both the need and the capacity for capital-building, especially on forums like TD. The chapter's final section grapples with the significance of these findings for broader dynamics of media power.

Shaping Media Practice and Attention on The_Donald and Beyond

Media are viewed as powerful largely because of their ability to shape what people know, or at least what they think they know, about the social world. This is precisely the kind of power that Herman and Chomsky (1988/2002) were concerned about when they wrote *Manufacturing Consent*. But gone are the days when the information landscape was dominated by a relatively small number of corporate publishers who could ensure—inadvertently or intentionally—that elites maintained power over such an extraordinary institution. As this analysis has shown, the deepening of mediatization and hybridization have opened the gates to the political and journalistic fields, and to many others (cf. Barnard, 2018a). With fewer barriers to entry, less well-positioned actors have demonstrated an ability to wield influence that their counterparts—let alone Herman and Chomsky—could hardly have imagined just a few decades ago.

On top of the shifts in media structures, affordances, and relations of power, there are questions about how to adequately capture flows of power in the hybrid media system (Chadwick, 2017). Although some studies have sought to measure the influence of less well-positioned actors (Barnard, 2018a; Meraz, 2009), hybridization has made the agenda-setting process more complex. Given the at times powerful role that intermediaries play, it can be difficult to attribute influence to individual actors or entities. This is especially true in cases like this one, where many are working in a range of (un)official capacities and more or less in concert to accomplish similar goals. Because the campaigns organized on TD during the period under study were largely user-driven efforts to anonymously share persuasive posts and provocative memes and to undermine the opposition's influence—actions that are themselves hard to glean direct effects from—and because Trump, his campaign, and the entire right-wing media ecosystem are pushing similar narratives, it is necessary to consider the combined effects of these efforts.

Like many populist politicians, Trump's rhetorical strategy has long sought to mobilize members of the public to campaign on his behalf. Consider the (now defunct) Army for Trump website depicted in Figures 6.4 and 6.5, which sought to train and mobilize supporters to increase the visibility of pro-Trump content. Also recall the White House social media summit discussed in chapter 1, which aimed, among other things, to provide a boost of capital and encouragement to media-savvy supporters and political influencers. Then there is Trump himself, who not only used the bully pulpit of the presidency to campaign but who also leveraged his extraordinary networked media capital to direct media attention (Tripodi & Ma, 2022). Perhaps most infamous, Trump's use of Twitter expertly leveraged spectacle to his advantage (Barnard, 2018a). Although much of Trump's social media content was original, he also frequently amplified posts from fringe accounts, including those associated with QAnon, Proud Boys, and other extremist groups (Gregorian et al., 2022). Lest we forget, alongside these efforts exists an entire right-wing media ecosystem committed to pushing identity-confirming (read: pro-Trump) content to an audience of (mostly) loyal partisans (Benkler et al., 2018; Tripodi & Ma, 2022). Each of these instances not only increases the visibility of campaign-supported talking points within the hybrid media system but also provides a model for practices that less well positioned actors can adopt or adapt to fit their own communicative endeavors. In other words, capital-building and mobilization were latent functions of many communicative acts. It is on top of this cacophony of influential voices (and many more) that TD users join in the fight for media attention.

Some of the most visible evidence of the group's agenda-setting power beyond the TD forum comes from the media coverage of the site and their related work. Like Trump himself and the #GamerGate supporters discussed earlier in the chapter, the battle for attention did not favor TD in the end. That is, while they succeed in attracting extraordinary attention, the bulk of the media coverage they received was critical of their methods and messages. According to MediaCloud, there were 348 digital news articles mentioning "TheDonald" published between October 1, 2020, and January 31, 2021. Over 90% of those stories were published in the wake of the January 6 insurrection, and many attributed the size of the Stop the Steal rally and subsequent attack on the Capitol to the media prowess displayed on TD and related platforms (author's digital archive). This did not amount to the outcome activists desired, as many users were vocal about their frustration with the coverage and with their inability to ensure Trump was reelected. Nevertheless, it does raise an age-old question about media: Is all press good press?

While I can offer no definitive answer to that question, the analysis conducted for this chapter does reveal much about the repertoires of communication and practices of manipulation that have grown popular among the (alt-)right. In addition to the clear taste for propaganda illustrated by the sheer volume of false or misleading information that circulates on TD with little resistance, many users of the forum also display a strong affinity for trolling, media manipulation, and other disinformation-like communication strategies. When considered alongside the typology of manipulative practices discussed in chapters 2 and 4, the communicative strategies displayed on TD run the gamut. Indeed, as mentioned above, discussions on TD demonstrated how users drew upon many practices of manipulation, including impersonation, trolling, sensationalism, viral campaigns, coordination, hash-targeting, and, of course, memes.[10]

Users of TD are clearly not representative of the average American's political views, or perhaps even the average member of the Republican Party. But it is fair to say that discussions on the forum both reflect and reinforce the communicative norms of the alt-right. Given the ongoing mediatization of the political and journalistic fields in general (Barnard, 2018a), as well as the extraordinary role that digital communication plays in political campaigns, whether professional or volunteer driven (Karpf, 2016; Kreiss et al., 2018), it is clear that the taken-for-granted norms or "doxa" (Bourdieu, 1990, 1993), continue to shift. Although we will grapple with the implications of these findings to a much greater extent in the book's final chapter, recent scholarship supports the conclusion that the "Overton window" appears to be shifting toward greater acceptance of portions of the far-right agenda (Bouko et al., 2021; Conway, 2020) as well as of the propagandistic forms of communication discussed throughout this book. Such discursive shifts within the public sphere are a clear result of the manipulative media strategies discussed and deployed on TD. Having addressed the potential agenda-setting influence of TD, the remainder of this section will consider what implications these findings have for our understanding of capital and other related dynamics of media power.

The analysis of data from TD highlighted many noteworthy themes and involved discussions or illustrations of numerous practices of manipulation examined in previous chapters. Prominent themes included sharing conspiracy theories, sowing doubt about democratic institutions, discussing hot-button political issues, amplifying bigotry and hatred, celebrating violence and hypermasculinity, criticizing political opponents, and confirming right-wing political identities. Through participation on the site, users gather and share relevant information and engage in metadiscursive exchanges where they reflect on the culture and technologies that define the community. They also discuss, develop, and enact practices of manipulation designed to further their cause.

When considering the broader implications of this work, it is important to keep in mind that TD is just one of many digital "set spaces" (Reid & Valasik, 2020) popular with the alt-right. Indeed, in addition to Patriots.win, many devotees to the cause continue to use online forums like Reddit, Discord, and 8kun, as well as Facebook Groups, group messaging apps, microblogging platforms, and similar technologies to develop shared understandings and coordinate actions. Given how widely these sites' affordances and audiences can vary, it is also necessary to recognize the hybridity of political communication practices, which frequently blur the lines between internal and external forms of communication (Castelli Gattinara & Bouron, 2020).[11] Like many of those who stormed the Capitol on January 6, 2021, members of Trump's digital army are devoted to relaying messages in support of their chosen leader. On TD and beyond, supporters play the role of "surrogate message carriers" (Jamieson, 1996) and "citizen marketers" (Penney, 2017), continuously remixing and reiterating claims in ways that broaden their reach and strengthen their influence in the public sphere. By observing these communications within the confines of a set space, we gain insight not only into the norms and practices prominent among the alt-right but also into their broader implications for the "elements of practice" (i.e., capital, habitus, doxa) that undergird their work in the field (Barnard, 2018a).

The transformations in norms and practices are directly reflected in the dispositions or habitus (Bourdieu, 1990, 1993) displayed by contributors to TD. As I have argued previously, due to the deepening of mediatization in everyday life, participants in the digital public sphere are developing a "networked habitus" marked by a "growing acceptance of digital, interactive values and practices" (Barnard, 2018a, p. 74; see also Barnard, 2016). Other studies have further established the hybrid dispositions of journalists (Chen, 2022; Russell, 2016) as well as those participating in networked social movements (Liu, 2020; Reid & Valasik, 2020; Schradie, 2019; Treré, 2015). Certainly the bulk of digital interactions examined as part of this research can be seen as further indication of activists' disposition toward planning and carrying out political action using digital communication technologies. It is through these displays of habitus that we also find indications of capital being put into practice. Indeed, within and beyond discussions of capital-building, there were repeated indications that many users were enacting "hacktivist sensibilities" (Russell, 2016) in their practice.

As established in chapter 3, prominent right-wing media outlets and their most successful pundits have spent decades amassing capital and honing their craft. The success of these actors is reflected not just in the size of their audiences and earnings but also in the extraordinary extent to which their fans have developed a taste for consuming, sharing, and even creating problematic information to further the cause. These influential media makers work in concert with media-savvy politicians, TD thought leaders, and other members of the right-wing media ecosystem to facilitate supporters' capital development. That is, beyond the inspiration rank-and-file activists inevitably draw from professional media personalities, many undeniably advance their own capacities by observing other political actors' practices, especially those developed and deployed by Trump himself. Trump and his official campaign have leveraged their own capital to help supporters develop theirs—whether by following the instructions laid out on the Army for Trump website (see Figures 6.4 and 6.5) or by heeding his calls for media-related activism promoted at the social media summit and elsewhere—all in service of Trump's broader political-economic goals. Indeed, although some members join forums like TD already possessing the capital required to enact practices of manipulation, many others need support and encouragement. The identity formation, skill-building, and mobilization work carried out on sites like TD appear to play an outsized role in helping the group amass capital and to translate their vision for media manipulation campaigns into practice. By training the next generation of digital soldiers, the most skilled and dedicated contributors to TD, alongside the like-minded pundits and politicians flush with networked media capital, provided additional means and motivation for future trolls and media manipulators. Such exchanges are to be expected given that a fundamental characteristic of capital is that actors can convert one kind of power to another (Bourdieu, 1986).

Overall, this chapter has provided a detailed examination of the format and discourse of The_Donald as well as the forum's most salient themes. Through this analysis, we have developed a clear sense of what norms and practices are most prominent among its users, and what role the forum plays in building and exchanging capital. By focusing on alternative platforms like TD, the analysis inevitably failed to capture whatever other values and practices were being championed by political communications professionals and campaign officials, as well as those displayed by activists in other channels. Nevertheless, the abundance of metadiscourse available on TD made it an ideal research site, given how frequently users engaged in and reflected on practices of manipulation. Furthermore, the supplementary data and literature incorporated in this chapter, which include secondary data from official political campaigns, demonstrate both a clear overlap with the approach taken by volunteer members of Trump's digital army as well as an obvious pattern of putting the approach into practice on popular media channels. Thanks to this analysis as well as the broader bodies of literature on political communication and media manipulation, it is now abundantly clear that the right-wing mediatized superstructure—from politicians and pundits down to average members of the networked public—appears to be just as "stable and persistent [a] mechanism for... vetting and spreading ... information" as I previously theorized it being on the political left (Barnard, 2018a, p. 52). The catch is that, at least for those represented on forums like TD, the goal is often to do so in ways that manipulate information, the media, and the public more broadly. Considering the pattern established throughout this and prior chapters, the book concludes with some broader reflections on what we now know about how actors hack hybrid media, and what implications that holds for the future of media, power, and public life.

Chapter 7

Trouble with Power, Practice, and Information in the Hybrid Media System

Social theorists have long grappled with questions about the complex relationships that exist between thought and action, between representation and materiality, and between knowledge and power. In much of this theorizing, there is a tendency to place significant emphasis on the role played by media—whether through language, communication, or other sociotechnical processes. Perhaps this is because, as Stoddard and Collins (2016) put it, media occupy a unique and deeply important social position "between us and the world" (p. 67). In other words, people rely on media to *mediate* their relationship with the people and events that have been deemed to carry personal or societal relevance. Of course, as one would expect in a hybrid media context, many also rely on media's productive affordances, helping actors create and disseminate messages to audiences of interest. While these messages rarely have the direct, "hypodermic" effects that propagandists likely aspire to, media undeniably have the power to shape publics' perceptions. This capacity to shape what we (think we) know, how we communicate, and with whom, means that media play a central role in many aspects of power relations.

In a time marked by historic levels of media usage and political polarization, there is little doubt that the dynamics of media power continue to fluctuate. While many early assessments of the relationship between digital media and civic engagement were overly optimistic (Shirky, 2009), more recent events have made it clear that this relationship is at best tenuous. For every example of digital media serving as a boon to democracy, there seems to be a counterexample where similar tools are used to further erode the health of our public sphere. This book has not sought to weigh the evidence for or against these contradictory claims; others have done that more effectively, and in a much timelier manner.

Rather, it has focused on providing a critical assessment of how the structures and cultures of the hybrid media system allow and encourage those with the requisite capital to enact manipulative, antidemocratic practices, which in turn threaten our ability to effectively understand and distribute information.

Ever since 2009, when I began researching my first book about the role social media played in contestations of power at the intersection of the political and journalistic fields, I have struggled to reckon with the contradictory power of information and communication technologies (ICTs). In line with Couldry and Curran's (2003) metaphorical view of media as a processing plant, I believe media serve simultaneously as a channel through which more traditional (read: political and economic) power flows as well as a novel means of generating power in its own right. Although we know such power is often shaped by ambient *structures* and expressed through media-related *practices*, there is still much to be discovered about this relationship. Through my previous work, I showed how the boundaries separating the journalistic and political fields were blurring, and how practices were growing increasingly hybrid thanks to incursions from networked publics (Barnard, 2016, 2018a, 2018b). Certainly there were signs that increased participation in the public sphere could lead to greater accountability for our institutions and their leaders, and to a healthier society overall.

But by the mid-2010s, the tides were clearly beginning to turn. It quickly became apparent that the structures and cultures of communication which make up the hybrid media system would generate fundamental challenges for the public sphere. While a sizable portion of the American public remained engaged in good-faith political discourse, sharing and discussing information according to the ideals of deliberative democracy, the system enabled and even encouraged users to develop new practices that would threaten democratic ideals. Following the relative success of the decades-long strategy to undermine public trust in establishment media (Hemmer, 2016; Lane, 2020) and to instead cultivate a widespread taste for (right-wing) propaganda (discussed in chapter 3), much of the networked public were forming practices and communities that leveraged the affordances of social media to further amplify such information. Rather than "we media" (Gillmor, 2006) helping citizen journalists hold the powerful accountable, networked publics' use of digital media was now also helping circumvent traditional gatekeeping structures and undermining public accountability measures. As it turned out, journalistic doxa as well as the libertarian ethos that drove the ICT sector left the systems—and the broader public sphere—vulnerable to manipulation.

The overarching argument advanced throughout this book is that the structures and practices of the hybrid media system have given rise to a new form of networked media capital, which is being deployed to facilitate the spread of problematic information, thus transforming the relations of (media) power. As the structure and culture of social media platforms evolve, so too do the affordances available to users. As a result, tools that were once seen as bastions of democratic communication grew increasingly weaponized and today serve as key battlegrounds for (dis)information and democracy. Whether publics take advantage of opportunities for targeted messaging, coordinated sharing, or algorithmic amplification afforded by popular social media platforms or use more homogeneous digital "set spaces" (Reid & Valasik, 2020) to train and mobilize digital soldiers, ICTs have proven extraordinarily consequential for the functioning (or dysfunction) of the contemporary public sphere.

Despite the increased emphasis being placed on media literacy—or perhaps, as some have argued, in part because of it (Banaji et al., 2019; boyd, 2018)—we have witnessed a proliferation of practices and producers that undermine traditional processes of democratic communication, therefore upending the structures through which knowledge and power are produced. Although gatekeeping structures undoubtedly play an important role in maintaining the playing field on which political contests are waged, much of the analysis presented here has focused primarily on the actions of the players themselves. By homing in on political actors' media-related practices while remaining attuned to their place at the intersection of the political, journalistic, technological, economic, and cultural fields, we are able to render visible many of the meso-level factors shaping (and being shaped by) relations of power.

One concern that has served as a driving force throughout this book has been the need to develop a greater understanding of the dynamics of media power. On this journey, affordance theory has proven to be a useful tool given the recursive relationship that often exists between structures and practices. More important, the book has leaned heavily on prior theorizing about media practice, because it is there that we can see the machinations and manifestations of power. In what follows, I review and reflect on some of the most notable implications emerging from this analysis.

Power

There is little doubt that the hybrid media system, with its myriad affordances, has contributed significantly to the proliferation of problematic information, and to the accordant practices that generate and facilitate its spread. Chapter 3 explored the various ways that broadcast media enabled firebrand pundits to draw on their substantial media capital to reach mass audiences. Through their work, legacy media pundits like Bill O'Reilly, Rush Limbaugh, Sean Hannity, and, most recently, Tucker Carlson leveraged the affordances of broadcast and digital media to generate, amplify, and legitimate countless problematic narratives while at the same time further building (and drawing on) their own capital. By providing a steady flow of outrageous, hyperpartisan, and often deceptive content, these pundits helped their sizable audiences cultivate a distinct taste for problematic, identity-confirming information. The broadcast media allowed for audio, video, and textual content to be shared with audiences in engaging ways, and later to be repackaged in a variety of formats for distribution across the web. The approach taken on these programs not only further eroded the boundaries between news and opinion (or journalism and politics) and of the public's trust in institutions, but also helped inspire future generations of media manipulators like those discussed in chapters 5 and 6.

Although financial incentives are certainly an important driver behind much of what publishers do, they are also an essential factor shaping practices on digital media platforms. Chapter 4 offered a critical assessment of how the structures and practices of manipulation have shifted as our media system grew increasingly hybrid. In addition to the at times perverse incentives surrounding "surveillance capitalism" (Zuboff, 2019) or "data colonialism" (Couldry & Mejias, 2019), the analysis considered how platforms' affordances allowed and even encouraged the spread of problematic information. By enabling dishonest actors to circumvent traditional gatekeepers in order to serve their own economic or political agendas (or both), social media platforms further normalized a kind of political culture defined (at least in part) by manipulation. This is less a matter of technological affordances requiring such an outcome and more a mix of sheer complexity and willful blindness from Silicon Valley. Nevertheless, political actors seized the opportunity to develop and deploy sophisticated practices of manipulation to pursue their desired ends.

While power is often expressed through practice (as outlined in the following section), its essence and manifestation in mediated forms is often visible in structural arrangements. One such expression (and bestowment) of media power is to be seen in the *affordances* of ICTs (Davis, 2020). As this book has made clear, the capacities that are coded into technical systems contribute to patterns of behavior, thereby making some courses of action more or less likely. For example, the onset of hybrid, participatory media encouraged users to share information in a variety of modes and formats, including sharing across platforms and audiences. The structure of many social media platforms also allowed users to work collaboratively to create and moderate content, while algorithmically driven ranking systems encouraged motivated users to hack (read: manipulate) the system to maximize their reach. This concern about the ways sociotechnical structures and affordances function as expressions and reifications of power has given rise to a growing body of scholarship intended to call attention to—and disrupt—such unequal systems of power (Benjamin, 2019; Couldry & Mejias, 2019; Noble, 2018; O'Neil, 2017; Zuboff, 2019).

Just as sociotechnical systems can be calibrated to reinforce dominant ideology, they can also be used to challenge them. In fact, such effects are not mutually exclusive. Consider the case of Twitter. On the one hand, Twitter has long served as a noteworthy tool in activists' efforts to contest the power of established individuals and institutions and to otherwise advance unorthodox views (Barnard, 2018a; Tufekci, 2017a). The same could be said for many other platforms and practices discussed in this book—even those that espouse manipulative methods. On the other hand, Twitter, like other social media companies, has also been lambasted by many on the political right for censoring or "shadow banning" (officially known as "down-ranking") certain kinds of online discourse that are deemed harmful or inappropriate.[1] Yet motivated actors continued to leverage these tools in their fight to shape public consciousness. The point is: the affordances put in place enable and at times impede networked publics to engage in individual and collective forms of (anti)democratic communication. Altering these affordances would have their own implications with different distributions of power.

I have argued previously that networked publics' use of ICTs can be considered a *mediatized superstructure*, or "an assemblage of networked individuals, techniques, and technologies that, once populated by a critical mass, provide a relatively stable and persistent mechanism for the vetting and spreading of information" (Barnard, 2018a, p. 52). Whether by deploying gatecrashing practices that circumvent traditional media gatekeepers and communicate directly with other members of the public, or by working collaboratively in other ways to share information deemed trustworthy and relevant, activists from across the political spectrum continue to leverage the affordances of digital media to direct public attention toward issues and frames that serve their interests. Yet in an information environment marked by remarkably low trust in establishment media (Gallup & Knight, 2020), manipulators have seized the opportunity by establishing themselves as a trustworthy alternative.

Following the lead of propagandists whose views have been legitimated by professional "news" organizations or other authorities trusted by members of their respective in-group, countless amateur manipulators have joined the fight for public attention. Of course, the *effects* of media differ widely and depend notably on the dispositions of individual citizens. Broadly speaking, studies have shown how exposure to certain messages can shape issue agendas and reinforce existing beliefs (Bolin & Hamilton, 2018). Although such effects can occur more or less directly, studies have shown that the effects of publicly generated problematic information (i.e., not published by professional media outlets) are experienced in interactions with larger partisan media sources (Guo &

Vargo, 2020; Vargo et al., 2018). This suggests that problematic information is more likely to be effective when it reinforces existing beliefs. In addition to the individual-level effects that exposure to problematic information can have on members of the public, there are broader consequences stemming from the rise of media manipulation. For example, members of the public have developed a heightened sense of what information is trustworthy in a so-called post-truth environment, leading many to be broadly skeptical of all information, especially that which is not shared by an already trusted source (Gottfried, 2021; Gottfried & Liedke, 2021; Hameleers, 2022; Luo et al., 2022; McIntyre, 2018; Van Duyn & Collier, 2019; Warner & Neville-Shepard, 2014).

In an environment rife with problematic information and distrust, it makes sense that media professionals themselves would be affected. Beyond the obvious implications that coordinated inauthentic behavior has for the governance of online platforms, the practice and profession of journalism is also being reshaped. As has been discussed previously, media manipulation efforts have proven successful in shaping what news organizations cover, and how (Ehrett et al., 2021). Furthermore, as the cat-and-mouse game of manipulation unfolds, journalistic norms are also (constantly) shifting, and media professionals are (in need of) recalibrating their own practices to limit their susceptibility to manipulation (Carlson, 2018; Donovan & boyd, 2021; Michailidou & Trenz, 2021). Nevertheless, the broader partisan media environment, and the incentives for manipulative media campaigns, remain intact. Given the privileged position of media in social and political life, this has extraordinary implications for the functioning of democracy and society.

Overall, the efforts by political and journalistic interlopers to build legitimacy in the political and journalistic fields should certainly be seen as expressions of power in their own right. Yet, given the nature of media power, where abilities to shape information flows also afford actors power over other aspects of social life, the structures and practices of the hybrid media system provide a means to amass and express power in new ways. Whether we view such shifts as traceable to the structures, cultures, or practices is largely a matter of emphasis, because they are all interrelated. As the next section will show, much can be learned when we consider how power is reflected in media-related practice, and vice versa.

Practice

As discussed throughout this book, the affordances of the hybrid media system have created novel opportunities for politically driven actors to develop and deploy new practices of manipulation and to amass and express new forms of capital. We have long known that media play an important part in political practice, and scholars from a variety of fields have contributed key insights to our understanding of how political communication manifests, and to what effects (Chadwick, 2017; Penney, 2017; Schroeder, 2018; Weeks et al., 2017). In recent years, scholars working at the intersection of sociology, communication, political science, journalism, and media studies have generated additional knowledge about the tools and techniques political actors deploy in digital media environments (Gil de Zúñiga et al., 2020; Liu, 2020; Mattoni & Treré, 2014; Woolley & Howard, 2018). Building on this work, this book has sought to take account of various manipulative media practices and to situate them within the broader "repertoires of communication" (Mattoni, 2013). Given the need to bring examinations of propaganda and deception into closer conversation with media practice, I developed the concept of "repertoires of manipulation" to account for the variety of manipulative practices that political actors had at their disposal in an era of mediatization where (problematic) information is abundant. Although these repertoires are ever-evolving, we see them being deployed throughout the examples discussed in this book—and, of course, in a great many more instances not (yet) discussed.

These repertoires are made up of individual *practices of manipulation*, which signify the deceptive actions that political actors and organizations may take in their pursuit of power. Chapter 2 spelled out many of the ways that various practices can assist in the generation, amplification, and legitimation of problematic information. Chapter 4 further considered how the affordances of social media platforms enable and encourage political actors to engage in the following practices: media manipulation, audience segmentation and targeted messaging, reach and amplification, and coordination and mobilization. Through two unique case studies, chapters 5 and 6 provided empirical opportunities to consider how many of these practices are brought to life. In chapter 5, we saw how relatively unknown members of the public, popular pundits, and digital media start-ups deploy similar tactics to distort narratives and drive attention. Chapter 6 further illustrated many of these practices (and more), while also showcasing how Trump's so-called digital army of propagandists discuss and deploy deceptive communication strategies.

Whereas chapter 2 introduced many of the core theoretical concerns driving this book and foreshadowed many that would emerge out of it, chapters 5 and 6 offered opportunities to see them in context. Through these case studies, we also see how the elements of media power manifest in practice. Building on my own prior theorizing (Barnard, 2016, 2018a, 2018b), as well as that of many other scholars, I explored what the development, discussion, and deployment of practices of manipulation can teach us about the dynamics of media power. Furthermore, drawing on the "elements of practice" framework encapsulating much of Pierre Bourdieu's theorizing, we can consider how individual practices are made possible by various forms of power or *capital*, are indicative of distinct dispositions or *habitus*, and are reflective of various taken-for-granted norms or *doxa* (Barnard, 2016, 2018a; Bourdieu, 1990, 1993).

The norms underlying contemporary political communication are in some ways drastically different than they were just a few decades ago. The same could be said of the everyday practices and the dispositions of those actors who deploy them. The proliferation of problematic information is both a cause and a consequence of these shifts. As this book has shown, actors with the requisite skills and motivation are leveraging the affordances of hybrid media to advance their own agendas. To be sure, the means political actors use to pursue agenda-setting goals have always been shaped by the tools available to them. Nevertheless, the practices of manipulation on display in the previous chapters provide a clear demonstration of how normalized they have become across significant portions of the American public sphere (and beyond).

The rise of manipulative practices constitutes not only a shift in taken-for-granted norms among members of the networked public (think: greater distrust in journalism and continued propagation of problematic information), but also a shift in the norms shaping how media structures are governed. As chapters 3 and 4 illustrate, the past few decades have brought about drastic changes to the standards driving gatekeeping decisions by platforms and publishers alike. In response to the shifting norms of political communication, participants in the mediated public sphere continually develop and adapt a "networked habitus" (Barnard, 2016, 2018a), wherein they are predisposed to interpret and respond to communicative practices in ways that are deeply informed by the evolving structures and cultures of contemporary media. In other words, shifts in media, technology, and politics shape the actions, attitudes, and experiences of individuals in the public sphere.

There are clear illustrations of this process throughout this book. For example, chapter 6 offers a detailed look at information consumption and production practices on display in a prominent far-right discussion forum. Of course, these developments are the product of many years of inter- and intrafield relations. Certainly that includes the economic and technological forces that make up and shape the hybrid media system and the structures and practices that emerge therein. Furthermore, the actions and dispositions on display in the media manipulation tactics described throughout the book are a (more or less direct) response to the forces shaping the journalistic and political fields. That is, the long-standing attempt by right-wing ideologues to decrease trust in journalism was a political strategy developed to make up for their disadvantageous treatment by much of the journalistic field. As former Breitbart editor and Trump White House official Steve Bannon put it, "The real opposition is the media. And the way to deal with them is to flood the zone with shit" (quoted in Lewis, 2018).

Other illustrations of how actors' networked habitus is mutually shaped by the structures and practices emergent in their respective field contexts can be seen in chapters 5 and 6. Many of the viral campaigns discussed in chapter 5 were successful in part thanks to consumers being digitally disposed toward amplifying problematic information. Similarly, the hybrid production and consumption (or "prosumption") practices that make up The_Donald are the result of its users' digitally oriented dispositions. In both cases, it is fair to say that such politically and technologically savvy capacities are the cultivated effect of years of (informal) preparation. In addition to learning tactics from others on The_Donald, many users borrow communicative strategies from the legacy media pundits discussed in chapter 3, adapting them to the current political climate as well as the hybrid media system. Indeed, many of the contemporary attitudes about establishment media's supposed untrustworthiness and liberal bias can be credited to the relative success of conservatives' decades-long campaign to undermine public trust in media (Hemmer, 2016; Lane, 2020). Other practices and dispositions are the result of additional forces shaping action within and across fields, such as the pressure that profit orientation puts on media production, or the ways new social media features create unique affordances that allow or encourage practices like viral sharing or clandestine, coordinated action.

When grappling with the relevance that practices hold for the norms and dispositions of actors in a particular field, it is also important to consider the broader context. While this study might be said to be sampling on the dependent variable by focusing primarily on digital manifestations of political practice, the findings reached here are in line with political communication practices more broadly. Indeed, as discussed in previous chapters, the myriad affordances of ICTs have led a variety of political actors—from ad-hoc activists to professional campaign managers—to adopt increasingly novel digital media strategies. Thanks in part to a rapidly expanding industry of experts and technologies, campaigns throughout the United States and across the globe are taking up the tools of digital media for a variety of communicative ends (Chester & Montgomery, 2017; Schradie, 2019). Given the facility with which people use the techniques and technologies of the digital public sphere, it is clear that prior findings about the rise of networked habitus (Barnard, 2018a) extend well into the fields of journalism, politics, and beyond. Overall, the normalization of hybrid dispositions operates in a recursive, mutually shaping fashion where actors' production of problematic information leads to public engagement, inspiring future iterations of information to be produced and consumed, ad infinitum.

In a changing environment where norms and practices evolve along with political and technological shifts, one might expect to find accordant shifts in power relations. Although this book has examined such relations and manifestations of power at various levels, the form most visible at the level of practice is capital. If *capital* represents actors' individual and collective capacities to put power into practice, then media are undoubtedly central to the way many express and generate such capital. Consider, for example, the organized sets of actors and practices used to shape the discourse around CNN White House correspondent Jim Acosta's press conference debacle, discussed in chapter 5. In this case, many content creators relied on their mastery of American political discourse (i.e., cultural capital) as well as their prestigious reputations as noteworthy pundits and publishers (i.e., symbolic capital) to (attempt to) shape public awareness and set the agenda. Additionally, many used paid promotion (i.e., economic capital) to increase the visibility of their content, while also benefiting from significant engagement and amplification from portions of their follower base (i.e., social capital).

While each of these forms of capital played a central role in the relative success of these information campaigns, chapter 5 also demonstrated how Bourdieu's (1986, 1990, 1993) classic typology of capital falls short of fully accounting for the success of some campaigns—in particular those who garnered extraordinary attention relative to their position in the political and journalistic fields. That is, in addition to the combined deployment of traditional forms of capital, the actors examined in chapters 5 and 6 exchanged and enacted capital in ways that allowed them to collaboratively create and amplify information using manipulative media practices. It is the combined influence of such an industrious, media-savvy approach that indicates the presence of networked media capital.

More broadly, in each of the cases discussed throughout this book, we have seen how political communication campaigns have been waged to gain traction in the networked public sphere. These analyses address the gap left by prior theorizing about propaganda (Herman & Chomsky, 1988/2002; Jowett & O'Donnell, 2014) and agenda-building (Conway-Silva et al., 2018; Parmelee, 2014), which do not account for the enterprising ways less well-resourced actors combine and convert capital in order to wield influence through media (cf. Barnard, 2018a). Furthermore, the focus on how affordances are leveraged within the hybrid media system has illustrated the ways techniques and technologies shape media-related practices as well as the broader power relations that follow.

It may be tempting to rely on prior theorizing to make sense of contemporary media practices. Yet the ongoing transformation of the hybrid media system requires new analytical tools. Consider how recent developments have altered the way media-related capital and media capital operate (Couldry, 2014b). In an era of "deep mediatization" (Couldry & Hepp, 2017), some actors may develop media capital that allows them to exercise power over other forms. Yet, as this analysis has shown, such influence is often meted out not directly but through enterprising efforts to hack the media system by creatively navigating the changing, interdependent logics of media as they flow through and across fields. At the same time that practical manifestations of media power are increasingly contingent on their ties to networked communication, they can enhance more traditional capacities. For example, the deepening of mediatization and the expansion of hybridization makes Couldry's (2014b) conception of generalized media capital more powerful, even if there is a need to further consider how such capital is *networked* across an array of actors, fields, and media logics.

Although we may be approaching a time when generalized media capital allows actors to wield power across all social fields (Barnard, 2018a), the analysis presented in this book demonstrates how it is the unique combination of networked practices, the relatively sophisticated knowledge of hybrid media systems, and the enterprising ways that actors leverage these affordances in practice—often collaboratively—that allow them to effectively wage media manipulation campaigns. Additionally, by taking advantage of portions of the publics' proclivity toward identity-confirming problematic information, networked actors are able to generate (original) manipulative media and contribute to the further amassing of individual and collective forms of networked media capital. This points to one common characteristic linking the myriad media manipulators discussed throughout this book. Whereas chapter 3's more traditional pundits drew on the classical forms of capital to shape public discourse, it was their enterprising combinations of techniques and technologies—in addition to their position and status in the political and journalistic fields—that granted them influence in the public sphere. In contrast, chapters 5 and 6 demonstrated how the participatory campaigns advancing problematic narratives about Acosta and Trump benefited somewhat from legacy media amplification, but also employed a variety of unorthodox, enterprising practices that allowed them to manipulate the hybrid media system for their benefit. The unique power of these manipulative practices points to the need for new conceptual tools, such as those presented in this book. In the sections ahead, we continue tracing this line of argumentation while broadening our scope to consider the implications of these conclusions within and beyond the American political and journalistic fields.

MEDIA CAPITAL BEYOND THE POLITICAL FIELD

Not far from the politically charged online spaces where actors craft and carry out their campaigns sits another kind of media manipulator, one focused more on selling widgets than winning political contests. Although the goals may differ, the practices are often eerily similar. For example, consider Ryan Holiday, a self-professed media manipulator whose somewhat unorthodox marketing strategies have helped many, from aspiring media professionals to major corporations, gain attention through the use of enterprising yet highly deceptive tactics. While Holiday's approach to media manipulation entailed many of the practices discussed throughout this book, his overarching method is best understood as "trading up the chain" (Holiday, 2013, p. 18; see also Marwick & Lewis, 2017). Through countless examples, Holiday demonstrates how actors can generate significant media attention with a little planning and a lot of deception. Much like the "pseudo-events" (Boorstin, 1962/2012) discussed in chapter 1, media manipulators frequently start by manufacturing controversy, which they then share with select micro-influencers (e.g., bloggers). With the seeds planted, the ground is ready for fertilization. Using fake or anonymous identities, manipulators can then circulate outrageous comments to help generate additional spectacle, which can then be used as justification to larger media outlets that theirs is a newsworthy story that needs to be covered. With a little luck (and a lot of manipulation), this formula may allow them to reach large portions of their targeted audience without having to purchase a single advertisement or make any official public relations pitches.

Such media manipulation campaigns undoubtedly require substantial networked media capital. In addition to having strong technical knowledge, Holiday also displays intricate knowledge of the media industry. This includes having a keen awareness of the recursive relationship publishers often maintain with one another as well as the incentives driving practice in the field (i.e., profit and status). Effectively trading up the chain also requires extensive knowledge of digital publishing platforms (in Holiday's case, blogs), of the infrastructure that drives influence across them (i.e., search engines and aggregation sites), as well as of the cultural toolkits at play. Perhaps most important, success also requires an ability to combine these capacities and opportunities in enterprising ways to create and shape media and, in consequence, public perception.

Given how hungry creators are for content that will drive page views, it is relatively easy for manipulators to exploit this vulnerability. Of course, practices inevitably evolve as the context changes, and given the ongoing proliferation of social media, media manipulators are now likely to start with social media "influencers" rather than "bloggers." Although digital marketers like Holiday operate in a different context than those politically driven actors who have been the focus of this book, there is little doubt that their successful forays in media manipulation entail developing and deploying similar practices. Whether it is guerrilla marketers like Holiday feeding "scoops" to bloggers in hopes they will get the attention of larger publishers or alt-right provocateurs like Mike Cernovich creating sensational hashtags in hopes they will spark a viral trend, the methods are largely the same (Holiday, 2016).

Consequently, the actors who put them into practice must also adopt a similarly manipulative habitus and draw on similar kinds of capital. By acknowledging this, we are also forced to reckon with the implications such shifts in practice have for the taken-for-granted norms—or, as Bourdieu would describe them, *doxa*—of a given field. Holiday's (2013) reflections on the matter offer a useful illustration:

> I'm not so foolish as to expect bloggers to know what they are talking about. I no longer expect to be informed—not when manipulation is so easy for bloggers and marketers to profit from. I can't shake the constant suspicion that others are baiting, tricking, or cheating me, just as I did to them. It's hard to browse the Internet when you are haunted by the words of A. J. Daulerio, the editor of the popular sports blog *Deadspin*: "It's all professional wrestling." (pp. 6–7)[2]

Perhaps this deeply cynical description, like Holiday's other creations, is a gross exaggeration. Or perhaps his cynicism is warranted, and the erosive potential of contemporary media power is helping usher in a post-truth world where reliable knowledge is increasingly fleeting (McIntyre, 2018). More likely, both extremes are illustrative, and the future—of society, of our public sphere, and of democratic governance more broadly—hangs in the balance. If this description is more or less accurate, then we are sitting on the precipice of a future where our institutions have been (further) hollowed out in favor of private interests; where the public lacks the will or ability to recognize and reject deceit; where life-and-death decisions are made not on the basis of shared ethics, reasoned evidence, and collective deliberation, but on dubious terms manufactured by a relatively small, shadowy class of manipulators with the power to "grind out the reality of [their] choice" (Goffman, 1974, p. 5).

At this point in history, the tactics Holiday describes are not new or novel. Rather, they are increasingly normalized in the professional spaces of marketing, advertising, PR, and of course media and politics. Thus, while this book focuses largely on the implications of media manipulation for politics and journalism, there is good reason to consider the broader implications that are likely to emerge as these practices creep across social fields. As such, we now grapple once more with the issue of problematic information and the consequences its proliferation spells for the public sphere.

Problematic Information

This book has offered a critical examination of the structures and practices that facilitate the production and amplification of various forms of problematic information. In democratically oriented societies like the United States, with broad conceptions of free speech, one can and should expect there to be countless instances when false or misleading information spreads through some portion of the information ecosystem. After all, former president Trump is said to have made over 30,000 false or misleading claims during his four years in office (Kessler et al., 2021), and this is to say nothing of his or his supporters' tendency to amplify such claims without adhering to broader standards of democratic communication (Jensen, 2013). When viewed as a matter of individual agency, this may be seen as little more than a necessary, if unfortunate, trade-off of life in a free (speech) society. Nevertheless, the proliferation of problematic information spells potential difficulties for the future of democratic communication and governance.

To be sure, many legacy media have been shown to have propagandistic elements and systemic shortcomings that have contributed to the public's skepticism of professional journalism (Barnard, 2021; Herman & Chomsky, 1988/2002; Jensen, 2015). But the rise of manipulation and propaganda in recent years demonstrates how the problem has metastasized as media grow more hybrid. Increasing levels of problematic information may be a somewhat inevitable consequence of social media platforms' gatecrashing affordances and the further hybridization of the media system (Barnard, 2018a). Thanks in large part to the rise of ICTs, social media platforms, and user-generated content, the "people formerly known as the audience" (Rosen, 2006) have substantial power to shape the flow of information, but they do so from different positions and with different practices than media professionals. This is to be expected. Nevertheless, as scholars and critics of the contemporary hybrid media environment, we should be cognizant of the myriad ways that divergent and unorthodox forms of communication can have far-reaching implications.

Some of the most obvious and potentially troubling consequences are visible when we look beyond the level of practice. From a macro-level perspective, the proliferation of problematic information (and responses to it) interact in a dialectical fashion. As Figure 7.1 illustrates, the *dialectics of (dis)information* is a relational process wherein addressing the rise of problematic information by increasing the availability of trustworthy information does not necessarily inoculate audiences from manipulation but instead can serve to reinforce the view that the information environment is one defined by "post-truth" (McIntyre, 2018). Indeed, given the seeming inevitability that interest groups will challenge the facticity of a particular claim, as well as the commonality of "deep disagreements" (Kappel, 2018) where parties are divided not just by ontology (what is known) but by epistemology (how something can be known), the issue of (dis)trust in institutions is central to this conflict. Although there is a long history of conflict and persuasion at the border between the political and journalistic fields (Kaplan, 2002), the mediatization of public life coupled with the growth of manipulative communication practices has further contributed to a crisis of

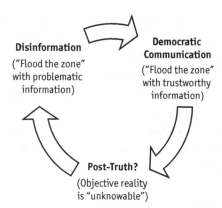

Figure 7.1 The dialectics of (dis)information.

distrust wherein democratic forms of communication are rendered ineffective for a sizable portion of the public, whose political beliefs are shaped more by allegiance than by facticity.

Consider, for example, the distrusting relationship much of the public has with the journalistic field. According to a June 2022 Gallup poll, Americans' trust in news institutions hit a record low, with only 16% expressing confidence in newspaper and 11% in television news (Brenan, 2022). Alternatively, a study by the Reuters Institute and the University of Oxford found that Americans' trust in the news overall was substantially higher, at 44% (Newman et al., 2021). While this raises obvious questions about *actual* trust levels, it is noteworthy that Gallup and Oxford found that Americans' trust in news ranked last among 46 countries surveyed (Newman et al., 2021). One trend that holds across many countries is the "trust gap," whereby many members of the public appear to be more skeptical of news found on social media than they are of news overall (Newman et al., 2021).

Given many citizens' distrust of institutions, whether journalism organizations or platforms, we might expect to see relatively higher levels of trust in people and organizations more closely connected to individuals' daily lives. For example, people tend to place greater trust in news when they are more actively engaged in seeking out the information, even through social media platforms (Newman et al., 2022). Similarly, Americans' trust in local television news was comparatively high, 44%, although Democrats remain much more trusting than Republicans (Fiorini, 2022). The latter finding suggests that Americans' trust in local television news makes it a potentially lucrative site for media manipulation campaigns (Nyhan, 2019). Americans' general distrust of news institutions illustrates how insulated many citizens are from receiving the factual information necessary to make informed decisions, whether about the media, politics, public health, or a host of other social issues. For example, Fox News, the most-watched American news channel (Katz, 2022) and Republicans' most-trusted source for news (Gramlich, 2020), has mastered the art of feeding its viewers identity-confirming information while frequently isolating them from that which may challenge their worldview, however factual or misleading (Benkler et al., 2018; Bump, 2021b).

Clearly, the symptoms of the post-truth mindset, where propaganda and "alternative facts" trump factual information and deliberative discourse, are not experienced equally from all positions of the political spectrum. As Rhodes (2022) demonstrates, although Democratic- and Republican-leaning citizens are both susceptible to trusting fake news that confirms previously held beliefs, exposure to contradictory (factual) information often leads Democrats to trust factually accurate information, whereas Republicans are much more likely to trust in identity-affirming accounts even when they are false. Thus, while many in the "reality-based community" (Danner, 2009, p. 555) are likely to place their trust in factual accounts of the world, Americans on the political right—the sector of the public that has been most strongly affected by the decades-long campaign to sow distrust in news institutions—are disproportionately more likely to display a taste for problematic information even when presented with more truthful options.

The problem of (dis)trust in media undoubtedly spans beyond the thorny issue of fake news. Nevertheless, the exposure to fake news provides a useful illustration of how problematic information (and attempted correctives) are disproportionately partisan in effect. Indeed, considering the fact that the vast majority of fake news—like many other expressions of problematic information discussed in this book—tends to convey politically conservative ideals, attempts to counter problematic information by increasing exposure to trustworthy information are likely to prove inadequate (Rhodes, 2022). For this reason, the recursive relationship depicted in Figure 7.1 is likely to continue as long as problematic information remains a salient part of our public sphere. This is especially applicable to those on the political right.

Some of the most cited strategies for countering such manipulative communication include "flooding the zone" with trustworthy information and attempting to build up public resistance to information-manipulation campaigns before they occur. Despite the plethora of competing pressures, such as the political and economic incentives driving cable television and social media discussed in chapters 3 and 4, gatekeepers have long been responsible for ensuring that the information they publish is trustworthy. Yet, in response to the growth of manipulation campaigns, we have seen a variety of countermeasures emerge, ranging from stricter content moderation policies and revised journalistic standards to information intended to highlight and amplify democratic forms of communication. The latter strategy, known as "pre-bunking," attempts to "preemptively build resilience against anticipated exposure to misinformation" (Roozenbeek et al., 2022, p. 1). Pre-bunking follows the logic of inoculation theory, which purports that people can build up resistance to manipulation through exposure to small, carefully measured information treatments. Pre-bunking campaigns use a variety of methods—from short video advertisements to online games—to raise public awareness about common practices of manipulation, therefore increasing the subjects' media literacy.

Certainly, media literacy plays a central role in enabling and facilitating political participation and is therefore an essential component to every democratic society. How can we expect the public to decipher truthful from untrustworthy accounts if they are not literate in the myriad ways that information is created and disseminated across the contemporary hybrid media system? Nevertheless, if increased literacy has also enabled some actors to design and carry out more sophisticated media manipulation campaigns (Banaji et al., 2019; boyd, 2018), then it is not a viable, universal solution to the problem of problematic information. Furthermore, inoculation theory does not address the fact that many knowingly prioritize political identity over facticity, choosing to believe what they want as long as it suits their (perceived) interests (Tandoc, 2019). In the final section, I discuss some potential structural and cultural efforts that could help counteract the effects of problematic information and reflect on what the future of (anti)democratic communication may look like as the dialectical process of (dis)information continues.

The Future of Media Power (and What Might Be Done about It)

This book has offered numerous lessons about the ongoing changes taking place at the intersection of the political, journalistic, and technological fields. It has also made the case for a critical, nuanced assessment of political communication practices and power structures in a hybrid media context. Given the recent moral panics over fake news and foreign interference in American politics, we have been distracted from the more mundane ways that (often domestic) actors use the tools of everyday communication to direct public attention. Hence, as I hope this book makes clear, more attention needs to be paid to the ways that media manipulation works as well as how it functions as an arbiter of social, political, and cultural power. In what follows, I offer some closing reflections on what the book has (and has not) accomplished, as well as on the challenges that lie ahead and how we might go about addressing them.

Despite the growing body of scholarship and public inquiry regarding the relationship between (dis)information and democracy, there is still much to learn about these interrelated phenomena. Not only are these relationships generally opaque and ever evolving, but the way they manifest in practice often varies significantly across contexts. Such an acknowledgment calls attention to an obvious limitation of this book. That is, the story of the United States is in many ways exceptional. For one, America's journalistic and political cultures and institutions at times differ greatly from otherwise similar nations. Furthermore, the fact that many social media platforms with a global reach are also based in the United States means that companies tend to place greater emphasis on monitoring national political discourse and less emphasis on what takes place abroad. Accordingly, although many of the findings and assertions discussed throughout this book—namely, the ways that media power and capital manifest in practice—likely apply far beyond the United States and other Western democratic nations, others have limited applicability outside the American context. Indeed, recent research has shown how the structures and practices underlying the production, dissemination, and potential disruption of problematic information contain many similarities as well as distinct differences across the world (Bakir et al., 2019; Chernobrov & Briant, 2022; Woolley & Howard, 2018).

It is important to recognize another notable limitation of this book—namely, that it is focused largely on the manipulative media practices enacted by Americans *on the political right*. While some critics might suggest that such a focus indicates a troubling blind spot in scholarly analyses of disinformation studies, the disparity in attention paid to left-wing media manipulation has less to do with a sampling bias than it does with disproportional representation (cf. Mayer, 2017). Indeed, the clear lack of collectively organized efforts from the political left to manipulate the hybrid media system in order to more persuasively represent their cause is a primary reason why this book does not examine progressive media manipulation campaigns (cf. Freelon et al., 2020). Thus, the decision to focus on problematic information practices from the right was made in part to avoid perpetuating a false equivalency about the left's and right's use of media for manipulation. This is not to say that progressive political actors have not deployed similar tactics in their fight for power; there are isolated examples where liberal political actors used similar practices and capital to spread disinformation (Shane & Blinder, 2019). Although there is reason to question the validity of claims regarding widespread disinformation campaigns from actors on the left, we would nevertheless benefit from a greater examination of what those campaigns entail as well as how, and how frequently, they are waged (Freelon et al., 2020).

Having discussed the tactical and organizational advantage many right-leaning movements have (Schradie, 2019), as well as the "hack gap" meant to highlight the disproportionate number of "organized, systematic propaganda broadcasters" found on the American political right (Yglesias, 2018), there is good reason to focus our attention in that direction. Furthermore, this disparity may be exacerbated by the visibility with which right-leaning political actors engage in and discuss their practices of manipulation, as evidenced by the prominence of metadiscourse discussed in chapter 6. A related consequence of the significant emphasis being placed on manipulation (from this work and others) is that readers may leave with an impression that information campaigns are universally effective in shaping public consciousness. There are plenty of reasons to believe that media messages matter. Nevertheless, the fact that users exercise agency at various points in the communicative process and that media have frequently been shown to be more effective at reinforcing rather than changing existing beliefs means that the *effects* of media are hardly deterministic or homogeneous (Shehata & Strömbäck, 2013; Weeks et al., 2017).

Thanks to the flurry of recent scholarship, we have a strong and ever-growing body of knowledge about our rapidly changing hybrid media system. But there is still *so much* to learn about our media structures and practices, as well as how their interactions shape the flow and functions of information—especially since these dynamics are constantly evolving. Although I have offered a rather detailed assessment of problematic information *practices* and the *platforms* that play host to them, they will undoubtedly change between the time of this writing and the time this book reaches you. The same can be said for the *policies* that govern networked communication, the field *positions* and *professions* that are represented in (dis)information campaigns, and the *political opportunities* that actors respond to as they vie for influence in the contested public sphere. While the consequences of these exchanges will be endlessly complex, altogether they amount to the manifestations of media power discussed throughout this book.

Each of the six *p*'s listed above (practices, platforms, policies, positions, professions, and political opportunities) represents an array of challenges that will linger for years to come. Certainly, communicative *practices* will evolve as mediatization deepens, and it would be a mistake to speculate too wildly about the frontiers that lie ahead. Nevertheless, I am confident that artificial intelligence (AI) will have a greater role to play in the generation of problematic information (think: deep fakes, automated bots, and propaganda campaigns where content creation, dissemination, and search engine optimization strategies are driven by AI), as well as in the detection of it. Obviously, the *platforms* that play host to these information exchanges will also change—in form as well as in function. Whereas Meta (Facebook, Instagram, WhatsApp) and Google (YouTube) appear to be taking more active (albeit unique) approaches to content moderation, there are signals that X (formerly Twitter) is heading in a different direction under Elon Musk's ownership. Newer platforms like TikTok provide yet another illustration of how the sites for political manipulation may shift along with culture and collective behavior. There are also larger forces at play, as platforms form or empower "content cartels" to make moderation decisions in ways that span networks (Douek, 2020).

Policies are another deeply important factor that will drive the changes in platforms. As U.S. lawmakers continue to fight over which legal frameworks should be used to govern digitally mediated communication—should we overturn, reinforce, or just revamp the infamous Section 230 of the Communications Decency Act?—the results will bear heavily upon the platforms and their users. There are also related questions about the influence other legislation will have, and in what direction it will flow. On the one hand, the European Union's Global Data Protection Regulation (GDPR) privacy protections, which tighten restrictions on companies' use of personal data, have changed the way business is done in the EU. Although there was once hope that the GDPR restrictions would trickle out to reform companies' handling of American users' data, that has not (yet) happened. On the other hand, shifts in U.S. law promise to upend the status quo around content moderation. For example, Texas lawmakers have passed House Bill 20, which, if upheld, will drastically alter the legal frameworks that inform content moderation decisions in that state, limiting companies' ability to restrict abuses of their platforms (H.B. 20, 2021). Such policy changes also have the potential to trickle out, therefore affecting how platforms handle moderation decisions in other U.S. states (and perhaps beyond).

To be sure, these policies are evolving due in part to the aforementioned shifts in practices and platforms, but many will also come about due to the sharp rise in *positions* being represented in the public sphere. That is, the opening up of the political and journalistic fields has helped increase (or at least diversify) participation in the public sphere, and some legislative efforts may be read as attempts to control or counteract such influence. These increases in access and diversity might be viewed as a double-edged sword. We have seen boosts in various forms of capital for those positioned on the political margins: Black Lives Matter, but also Stop the Steal. At the same time, the gates of our public sphere are being crashed by outsiders—infamously, foreign actors who (should) have little to no role to play in a sovereign nation's political exchanges. Members of democratically aligned *professions*—most notably, journalists—are also integral to the maintenance and governance of our society's information ecosystem. At the same time, there is little doubt that many traditional journalistic structures and practices have contributed to the problems of the contemporary media climate in ways that go beyond their own tendencies to distribute ill-informed or otherwise incomplete accounts. The everyday forms misinformation and disinformation generated and amplified by professional gatekeepers, some more numerous and egregious than others, not only alienate portions of the public but also provide ammunition to those looking to grow their own influence by waging an assault on the journalism profession as well as other democratic forms of communication. Indeed, countless political communication campaigns, including many examined in previous chapters, as well as the Russian sock puppets mentioned in the book's preface, took advantage of *political opportunities*—such as journalistic norms and structures, racial conflict, political polarization, and the public's waning trust in institutions—in service of their broader goals. Although many such opportunities will inevitably wax and wane as the political and professional tides turn, others are likely to remain features of American political culture.

Now that we have considered some of the factors likely to shape contests for (media) power in the years ahead, we can grapple with more pragmatic questions about how democratic societies might respond. Put another way, if the aforementioned exchanges of power are indeed forming a dialectical relationship where democratic and manipulative information leads to a post-truth environment (see Figure 7.1), then the question remains: What might be done about it? In these final pages I offer several potential responses.

There are clear reasons why increases in media literacy and the availability of accurate, trustworthy information would have a net-positive impact. Nevertheless, as discussed earlier in the chapter, such approaches may be seen as necessary but insufficient conditions to address the enduring threats to our public sphere that have emerged in the era of hybrid media. If we accept the premise that the dynamics of media power and deliberative democracy are growing increasingly unsettled thanks in part to the ever-evolving tools of media manipulation and the rise of networked media capital, then it stands to reason that we might benefit from thinking broadly about the nature of the problem as well as about potential solutions.

As arbiters of truth and "custodians of conscience" (Ettema & Glasser, 1998), those in the news profession have an essential role to play in paving the way to a more democratically oriented future. While many reporters have changed how they respond to Trumpism, the erosive discourse of fake news continues to undermine newsmakers' ability to reach substantial portions of the public. A seemingly logical (and all-too-common) response to charges of liberal bias has been to lean into the discourse of objectivity, relying on "he said, she said" frames (Rosen, 2009) while asserting a "view from nowhere" (Rosen, 2003). Given the inevitability of (accusations of) bias, journalists and the public would be better served by a more honest accounting of bias that explicates journalistic decisions and blind spots as well as their structural and cultural underpinnings and gives the public the information necessary to make informed decisions about where to place their trust (cf. Jensen, 2015). Indeed, as many have suggested, transparency should be the new objectivity.

Alongside renewed attempts to give the public a more accurate picture of journalistic norms and practices—strategies which themselves could bolster trust from portions of the public and provide them better tools to differentiate between more and less problematic forms of information—news professionals should also continue to devote reportorial resources where they are most needed. Beyond a broad focus on issues of power and inequality at all levels of society, news media professionals should place greater emphasis on the structures and practices of the hybrid media system. Greater awareness of political and economic incentives as well as of cutting-edge manipulation strategies may help journalism professionals prepare for the inevitable onslaught of deceptive information produced and amplified with help from AI, thus limiting its flow through their channels. Such efforts could also enable them to educate the public about deceptive communication practices, to clarify how journalism professionals and platforms respond to such efforts, and to demonstrate how more trustworthy forms of communication are different. While these initiatives can address information that is professionally produced, there is a particular need for messaging that helps uncover efforts at systematic manipulation while breaking the cycle of sensationalistic "flak wars" that so often occur between left- and right-leaning media outlets. Although providing quality metacoverage can be challenging, helping the public better understand how media can be used to manipulate could foster greater media literacy, and perhaps even boost critical awareness and collective discussions of social, economic, and technological features that are (not) democratically aligned. Facilitating these conversations, like so many other aspects of journalists' work, will require concerted efforts to include and accurately represent a diversity of perspectives and to break out of the hegemonic ideologies that have limited mainstream reporting for many decades (Herman & Chomsky 1988/2002; Jensen, 2015). And despite the cost, news companies should also continue to invest in critical, investigative work on a wide array of issues of social import.

Many of these suggestions may be deemed impractical due to the current state of American political culture, and of the news business. But rather than fall back on excuses and justifications that will continue to reproduce the status quo, a more effective response would be to honestly consider the barriers keeping our society from realizing a more democratically oriented media system, and then to reflect on ways to mitigate or circumvent them. Two fundamental barriers may be the governance structures and business models that dominate the media business. In the post–Fairness Doctrine era, when so much of the news we receive is shaped by shallow or misleading information, we see constant (though often taken-for-granted) reminders that media companies have little incentive to break out of their niche market for fear of alienating their base audience. Such disincentives are fundamental limitations of the advertising-supported and fee-based funding models that drive the American mass media market (Lindner & Barnard, 2020). By contrast, the United States funds public media endeavors at much lower rates per capita than most other developed *and* developing nations. Given the strong association between funding public media and democratic health (Neff & Pickard, 2021), such little public investment is cause for concern and correction. Diversifying the economic models that undergird the news business could provide the opportunity necessary to reshape the norms around political communication in the journalism profession as well as the broader public.

Of course, in the era of hybrid media, the factors that drive legacy media are interwoven with those that govern and sustain digital media platforms. In that vein, the public will invariably need to grapple with the limitations of Section 230 of the CDA, and perhaps with the democratic costs (and benefits) associated with America's radical free speech laws. We should also update data privacy laws to reflect the realities of daily life in a mediatized society (Couldry & Mejias, 2019; Zuboff, 2019). Discussions of such issues should include a reckoning with the logics and incentives inherent in the data capture and advertising-driven models that fund most major platforms. In addition to experimenting with new funding models, we might consider implementing public interest mandates, whereby companies are tasked with democratizing their business models or are taxed to support other democratically aligned initiatives, like the production of news.

Other opportunities for improvement can be found in the gatekeeping process. Journalism professionals have themselves made headway in recent years by heightening their awareness of media manipulation practices and avoiding unnecessary amplification of problematic information. Yet there is still significant work to be done (Donovan & boyd, 2021). For their part, platforms have even more room to improve in the areas of gatekeeping and moderation. While U.S.-based companies will likely remain relatively lax about content moderation given the country's cultural norms surrounding free speech, we are witnessing what appears to be the formation of two tiers of ICTs. On the one hand, there are those that take (some) responsibility for moderation of highly problematic content and thus remain popular platforms for mainstream public discourse. On the other hand, there are platforms that abdicate this responsibility in hopes of gaining favor with populations that find themselves restricted by popular platforms due to patterns of violation. There is substantial variation within and across these tiers, and even the most celebrated platforms have considerable room for improvement. Whether that happens through company-led efforts, user-driven initiatives, governmental regulations, or some combination of these, escaping the cycle of disinformation will require progress on multiple fronts.

As actors from across the political field have made apparent, additional governmental regulation may be one viable avenue to compel platforms and publishers to take greater responsibility for the way their channels are used to spread egregiously problematic information that stands to erode the public sphere and undermine democratic processes (Tworek, 2021). For example, regulators could require platforms to spend a minimum percentage of annual earnings on content moderation efforts. They could also establish and compel participation in moderation consortiums that facilitate collaboration across platforms. Such a regulatory body might also implement reward systems for curtailing manipulation attempts, or penalties for failing to restrict egregious violators or for systematically profiting from them (Braun & Eklund, 2019). Yet no matter how forward-thinking such regulations may be, the cat-and-mouse game that exists between (manipulative) political communicators and gatekeepers will almost certainly continue. This fact was made abundantly clear following Musk's takeover of Twitter, which resulted in a cascade of new manipulation efforts that achieved varying levels of success (Harwell, 2022; Newton & Schiffer, 2022).

While updating legal precedents could spark improvements in the way platforms and publishers handle problematic information, we must also better prepare members of the public for the inevitable onslaught of manipulation they are likely to be subjected to throughout their lifetime. Indeed, such practices are becoming increasingly professionalized and are being used widely by public relations firms (Edwards, 2021) and politicians (Kusche, 2020; McGregor, 2020a), among others. Given the inevitable diffusion of innovations (Rogers, 2003) and the ever-increasing quality of manipulation operations, it may be worth considering the combined potential of supply- *and* demand-side efforts. For example, if improvements in journalistic communication can help repair the public's trust in establishment media (Pingree et al., 2021), then members of the public may be less likely to create or consume problematic information, and when they do, many will have built up more resistance to the manipulative strategies such content typically displays. Although optimism may be unwarranted given that partisan doxa often takes precedence over honesty and facticity (Benkler et al., 2018), such efforts are likely a necessary step in the longer journey toward a healthier public sphere rooted in more rational and inclusive forms of communicative action (Habermas, 1985). If we are to redirect ourselves on a better path, we must not only prepare to resist and collectively root out manipulation, but we must also inspire more democratically attuned forms of communication.

This realization serves to remind us that as much as the hybrid media system has led to disruptions in our communicative structures and pathologies in many practices, it also contains the keys to a healthier, more sensible future.

Despite the threat posed by emergent forms of problematic information, there is a tendency to place undue emphasis on the new and remarkable over the more traditional and mundane aspects of social and political life (Brekhus, 1998). It is not that mediatization has not brought about new challenges for journalism and democracy, just that it does not pose the only—and perhaps not even the greatest—threat (cf. Carlson, 2020). Therefore, although journalism and scholarship alike should continue to investigate the implications of new forms of disinformation and fake news for democracy, it should also maintain a focus on more common and less remarkable forms of propaganda and manipulation, as well as their many hybrid iterations.

Overall, the decline in trust in news institutions may be seen as both cause and effect of mediatization, insofar as the hybridities of form (news and opinion) and gatekeepers (journalist and citizen, platform and publisher) have radically altered the information landscape—and this is to say nothing of the content itself. Notwithstanding the potential for journalism to serve as a vehicle of propaganda, whether directly through their own channels or indirectly through impersonation by purveyors of fake news, the profession has an integral role to play in fostering well-reasoned, fact-based discourse. The catch, of course, is that the power to shape public perceptions lies not just in the hands of those privileged enough to reach mass audiences, but in the public's ability to place their own trust, and to increase or undermine others'. This is yet another reminder of the recursive and ever-evolving interactions that make up the press-public relationship (Barnard, 2018a; Ettema & Glasser, 1998; Kovach & Rosenstiel, 2007).

Like it or not, networked media capital is growing more ubiquitous by the day. Thanks to the deepening of mediatization (Couldry & Hepp, 2017), actors from an array of social fields are developing digitally oriented dispositions that make new kinds of networked practices possible, even likely. As more actors discover this power, we are likely to see greater innovation in media-related practices. One result of this may be more, and more sophisticated, efforts to manipulate public discourse and, by extension, public perception. Indeed, such an outcome may be inevitable given the ongoing intermixing of media logics that is characteristic of the hybrid media system (Chadwick, 2017). At the same time, we should expect networked publics to form new alliances and develop new practices that leverage their capital in novel ways to detect, dissect, and disarm deceptive or otherwise problematic forms of information. However lofty they may seem, such opportunities for radical reform are not unprecedented in the United States (or abroad), though they would inevitably require a resurgence of the movement for media reform (Pickard, 2014). Whichever path we take, media's power will undoubtedly remain contested in the political and journalistic fields, as it will in (and beyond) academe.

The primary aim of this book has been to bring the landscape surrounding media, power, and problematic information into clearer focus. I hope it has also helped to elucidate the challenges that lie ahead, both in theory as well as in practice. If we have learned anything through this work it is that power and practice are deeply linked to one another and to the structures and cultures from which they emerge. Sharing this knowledge may enable us to build better sociotechnical systems, to repair journalistic and political cultures, to resist attempts at manipulation, and to reshape practices around shared, democratic norms. This is the antidote to manipulative media power, and the "reality-based community" (Danner, 2009, p. 555) needs it now more than ever.

Notes

Chapter 1

1. As an extreme but telling illustration, one attendee took a photo of the press, which he called a "fake news panorama" (Blake, 2019).
2. Nearly a third of these stories were published by international news outlets.
3. A more detailed discussion of these concepts can be found in chapter 2.

Chapter 2

1. Certainly, the current political moment, which many have somewhat problematically referred to as "post-truth" (McIntyre, 2018) is broadly attributable to an array of political, economic, journalistic, cultural, and technological factors.
2. This conception is similar to my own prior theorizing about a "networked habitus" (Barnard, 2018a).
3. Here, the focus is on *communicative* practices, although this focus does not negate the possibility of other forms of manipulation.

Chapter 3

1. After leaving Fox News, O'Reilly moved back into talk radio through his short program, *The O'Reilly Update*. He rebuilt an audience for his *No Spin News* program, which aired on his website, BillOReilly.com. That program was later aired under the same name by the conservative digital network The First (Concha 2020; Wemple 2019).
2. It is only when media and practices are hybridized, and when participating actors are less well positioned, that media capital emerges in a truly networked form.

Chapter 4

1. Trump's Twitter, Facebook, and Instagram accounts were reinstated in early 2023, but as of this writing, Trump had not rejoined these platforms.
2. Although the strategy is logically fraught—that is, using popular media channels to claim that many of those same social media are silencing them—it has nonetheless proven effective in galvanizing public opinion, especially among many of their base supporters (Vogels, 2022).
3. The Trump campaign outspent their rivals on Facebook in both the 2016 and 2020 presidential races.

4. The same ideas underlie the painstaking work, including focus groups and topic modeling, that often go into the development of contemporary political messages (Tufekci, 2017b).
5. These policies seemed custom-built to allow right-wing populists like Trump and Brazil's Jair Bolsonaro to continue using social media to spread sensational or otherwise problematic content, and thus to attract audiences to the platforms. However, the balance shifted slightly in the other direction when Facebook and Twitter announced changes to these policies (Heath, 2021; Robertson, 2020).
6. The inverse is often true of problematic information, which usually circulates initially through social media but can be amplified to greater effect by larger outlets (Marwick & Lewis, 2017).
7. This is precisely the concern I noted in the preface regarding my own (and countless others') distorted perception of American citizens' view of the protests in Ferguson, Missouri, thanks, in all likelihood, to intentional acts of media manipulation.
8. Anecdotally, I have led over a dozen workshops about data privacy with groups of college students, and the overwhelming majority are always shocked by how much information social media companies have about them.
9. While a number of tweaks were suggested by Facebook developers, many were not implemented because they were expected to decrease user engagement on the platform—and therefore, profits (Hagey & Horwitz, 2021).

Chapter 5

1. Watson (2018) contends the video was not intentionally doctored (by him, at least), but rather was a zoomed-in clip of a GIF, which he downloaded from Daily Wire. Nevertheless, it includes numerous elements of manipulated video described by Ajaka et al. (2019), given that the viral video is missing context and was deceptively edited, if not maliciously transformed.
2. Notably, more professionalized news organizations strive for greater accuracy than audiences typically associate with highly misleading "clickbait" headlines.
3. The Boolean search terms for the query were as follows: ("Jim Acosta") AND assault* OR "press pass" OR microphone OR "hard pass."
4. Influence was determined based on the number of Facebook shares a publisher's articles received. The most influential sites for each category were: left = (1) HuffPost, (2) Bipartisan Report, (3) Raw Story, (4) Shareblue, and (5) ThinkProgress; center = (1) CNN, (2) *Washington Post*, (3) ABC, (4) NBC, (5) CNBC; right = (1) Fox News, (2) Daily Wire, (3) Daily Caller, (4) Breitbart, and (5) *New York Post*.
5. Four of these sites had no Alexa ranking.
6. While there is no clear linkage between the number of shares a story receives on Facebook and the ranking of the publisher's website on Alexa.com beyond the fact that click-throughs from social media will inevitably boost the latter, the ranking is a widely recognized measure of a publisher's popularity and perceived legitimacy.
7. Center sites had 2 of the top 10 (5 of the top 30); left sites had 1 of the top 10 (5 of the top 30); and center-right sites had none in the top 30.
8. As of this writing, Ben Shapiro has over 9 million followers on Facebook.
9. CrowdTangle did not have data on the distribution of stories by HuffPost.
10. Although paid promotion on social media has long been a clandestine act, the events of the 2016 election spurred platforms like Facebook to improve transparency in political advertising.

Chapter 6

1. See the preface of this book for a brief reflection on this temptation.

2. The connections between TD and some QAnon forums are so strong that users often float back and forth between them, using similar terminology and cross-posting links. This will be clear later in the chapter when examining the group's approach to boosting networked media capital among its ranks.
3. The Internet Archive was also used as a supplementary source to review trends and threads when necessary.
4. This information has no known author but has been circulating in online forums for years.
5. According to many ardent believers of the "big lie" that the 2020 U.S. presidential election was illegally stolen from Trump, the vice president had the power to stop the certification of electoral college votes, and his failure to do so meant that he needed to be brought to justice. Hence the slogan chanted by many who attacked the Capitol: "Hang Mike Pence."
6. It is possible that some portion of this dysfunction is due to intentional disruption by those who oppose TD. Nevertheless, the ambient culture established in this online community (and many others like it) suggests that trolling and "shitposting"—practices that inevitably dilute and disrupt rational, organized conversation—are generally considered an accepted part of alt-right doxa.
7. "Beta" is a term commonly used by technologists to describe features that are in a late stage of development but have not yet been made standard for all users.
8. This is likely because the technological affordances of Instagram discourage users from sharing unoriginal content.
9. The same could be said for the distribution of other forms of capital, including networked media capital.
10. As prior research has shown, memes are seen as an important tactic in some repertoires of communication, mostly because their visual and humorous nature can help activists make extremist ideology seem more palatable to a broad audience (McSwiney et al., 2021).
11. Although they are not mutually exclusive, internal forms of communication are integral for ideation, collaboration, and mobilization, whereas external communication—the public-facing side of political communication campaigns—is where practices of manipulation are most often brought to life.

Chapter 7

1. Criticism of Twitter from those on the political right appeared to subside following Elon Musk's purchase of the company in October 2022.
2. It is worth noting that Holiday uses "bloggers" to describe virtually all online content producers, whether they write voluntarily for a self-hosted website with minimal traffic or professionally for a popular digital media site run by savvy journalists.

References

Abernathy, P. M. (2018). *The loss of local news*. The Expanding News Desert. https://www.usnewsdeserts.com/reports/expanding-news-desert/loss-of-local-news/

About. (n.d.). Media Cloud. Retrieved July 29, 2019, from https://mediacloud.org/about

Ajaka, N., Samuels, E., & Kessler, G. (2019, July 1). The Washington Post's guide to manipulated video. *Washington Post*. https://www.washingtonpost.com/graphics/2019/politics/fact-checker/manipulated-video-guide/

Altheide, D. L., & Schneider, C. J. (2012). *Qualitative media analysis*. SAGE.

American views: Trust, media and democracy. (2018, January 16). Knight Foundation. https://knightfoundation.org/reports/american-views-trust-media-and-democracy.

Angwin, J., & Grassegger, H. (2017, June 28). Facebook's secret censorship rules protect White men from hate speech but not Black children. *ProPublica*. https://www.propublica.org/article/facebook-hate-speech-censorship-internal-documents-algorithms?token=EnKCO7S5tur0EVV_U9AOlNE-b5icIEOw

Ants in a web: Deconstructing Guo Wengui's online "whistleblower movement." (2021). Graphika. https://graphika.com/reports/ants-in-a-web/

Arceneaux, K., & Johnson, M. (2013). *Changing minds or changing channels? Partisan news in an age of choice*. University of Chicago Press.

Auter, Z. J., & Fine, J. A. (2018). Social media campaigning: Mobilization and fundraising on Facebook. *Social Science Quarterly, 99*(1), 185–200. https://doi.org/10.1111/ssqu.12391

Bagdikian, B. H. (2014). *The new media monopoly: A completely revised and updated edition with seven new chapters*. Beacon Press.

Bakir, V. (2020). Psychological operations in digital political campaigns: Assessing Cambridge Analytica's psychographic profiling and targeting. *Frontiers in Communication, 5*, 1-16. https://doi.org/10.3389/fcomm.2020.00067

Bakir, V., Herring, E., Miller, D., & Robinson, P. (2019). Organized persuasive communication: A new conceptual framework for research on public relations, propaganda and promotional culture. *Critical Sociology, 45*(3), 311–328. https://doi.org/10.1177/0896920518764586

Ball, P., & Maxmen, A. (2020). The epic battle against coronavirus misinformation and conspiracy theories. *Nature, 581*(7809), Article 7809. https://doi.org/10.1038/d41586-020-01452-z

Banaji, S., Bhat, R., Agarwal, A., Passanha, N., & Sadhana Pravin, M. (2019). *WhatsApp vigilantes: An exploration of citizen reception and circulation of WhatsApp misinformation linked to mob violence in India* [Monograph]. London School of Economics and Political Science. http://www.lse.ac.uk/media-and-communications/research/research-projects/whatsapp-vigilantes

Bard, M. T. (2017). Propaganda, persuasion, or journalism? Fox News' prime-time coverage of health-care reform in 2009 and 2014. *Electronic News, 11*(2), 100–118. https://doi.org/10.1177/1931243117710278

Barker, D. C. (1999). Rushed decisions: Political talk radio and vote choice, 1994–1996. *The Journal of Politics, 61*(2), 527–539. JSTOR. https://doi.org/10.2307/2647515

Barnard, S. R. (2016). "Tweet or be sacked": Twitter and the new elements of journalistic practice. *Journalism, 17*(2), 190–207. https://doi.org/10.1177/1464884914553079

Barnard, S. R. (2018a). *Citizens at the gates: Twitter, networked publics, and the transformation of American journalism.* Palgrave Macmillan.

Barnard, S. R. (2018b). Tweeting #Ferguson: Mediatized fields and the new activist journalist. *New Media & Society, 20*(7), 2252–2271. https://doi.org/10.1177/1461444817712723

Barnard, S. R. (2021). Fake news. In J. Collins & S. Sen (Eds.), *Globalizing collateral language: From 9/11 to endless war* (pp. 83–92). University of Georgia Press.

Bashyakarla, V. (2019). Towards a holistic perspective on personal data and the data-driven election paradigm. *Internet Policy Review.* 8(4). https://policyreview.info/articles/news/towards-holistic-perspective-personal-data-and-data-driven-election-paradigm/1445

Benjamin, R. (2019). *Race after technology: Abolitionist tools for the New Jim Code.* Polity.

Benkler, Y., Faris, R., & Roberts, H. (2018). *Network propaganda: Manipulation, disinformation, and radicalization in American politics.* Oxford University Press.

Bennett, S. E. (2016). Predicting Americans' exposure to political talk radio in 1996, 1998, and 2000. *Harvard International Journal of Press/Politics, 7*(1), 9–22. https://doi.org/10.1177/1081180X0200700102

Bennett, W. L., Lawrence, R. G., & Livingston, S. (2008). *When the press fails: Political power and the news media from Iraq to Katrina.* University of Chicago Press.

Benson, R. (2014). Strategy follows structure: A media sociology manifesto. In S. Waisbord (Ed.), *Media sociology: A reappraisal* (pp. 26–44). Polity Press.

Berger, J. M. (2013, August 14). Zero degrees of al Qaeda. *Foreign Policy.* https://foreignpolicy.com/2013/08/14/zero-degrees-of-al-qaeda/

Berkowitz, D. (2018). Interpretive community. In T. P. Vos, F. Hanusch, D. Dimitrakopoulou, M. Geertsema-Sligh, & A. Sehl (Eds.), *The international encyclopedia of journalism studies* (pp. 1–7). John Wiley & Sons, Inc. https://doi.org/10.1002/9781118841570.iejs0024

Berry, J. M., & Sobieraj, S. (2011). Understanding the rise of talk radio. *PS: Political Science & Politics, 44*(4), 762–767. https://doi.org/10.1017/S1049096511001223

Berry, J. M., & Sobieraj, S. (2014). *The outrage industry: Political opinion media and the new incivility.* Oxford University Press.

Blake, A. (2019, September 4). Analysis: An embarrassing scene in the White House Rose Garden. *Washington Post.* https://www.washingtonpost.com/politics/2019/09/04/an-embarrassing-scene-white-house-rose-garden/

Blodgett, B. M. (2020). Media in the post #GamerGate era: Coverage of reactionary fan anger and the terrorism of the privileged. *Television & New Media, 21*(2), 184–200. https://doi.org/10.1177/1527476419879918

Bodó, B., Helberger, N., & Vreese, C. H. de. (2017). Political micro-targeting: A Manchurian candidate or just a dark horse? *Internet Policy Review, 6*(4), 1–13. https://policyreview.info/articles/analysis/political-micro-targeting-manchurian-candidate-or-just-dark-horse

Bolin, J. L., & Hamilton, L. C. (2018). The News You Choose: News media preferences amplify views on climate change. *Environmental Politics, 27*(3), 455–476. https://doi.org/10.1080/09644016.2018.1423909

Boorstin, D. J. (2012). *The image: A guide to pseudo-events in America.* Knopf Doubleday. (Original work published 1962)

Bossetta, M. (n.d.). Pro-Trump social networks: The Donald on Reddit and TheDonald.win. No. 96. Retrieved July 12, 2022, from https://player.fm/episodes/247444519

Bouko, C., Ostaeyen, P. V., & Voué, P. (2021). Facebook's policies against extremism: Ten years of struggle for more transparency. *First Monday, 26*(9). https://doi.org/10.5210/fm.v26i9.11705

Bourdieu, P. (1977). *Outline of a theory of practice*. Cambridge University Press.
Bourdieu, P. (1986). The forms of capital. In J. F. Richardson (Ed.), *Handbook of research for the sociology of education* (pp. 46–58). Greenwood Press.
Bourdieu, P. (1990). *The logic of practice*. Stanford University Press.
Bourdieu, P. (1991). *Language and symbolic power*. Harvard University Press.
Bourdieu, P. (1993). *The field of cultural production: Essays on art and literature*. Columbia University Press.
boyd, d. (2018, March 16). Did media literacy backfire? Medium. https://points.datasociety.net/did-media-literacy-backfire-7418c084d88d
Bradshaw, S., & Howard, P. N. (2017). *Troops, trolls and troublemakers: A global inventory of organized social media manipulation*. Oxford Internet Institute.
Bradshaw, S., & Howard, P. N. (2018). *Why does junk news spread so quickly across social media? Algorithms, advertising and exposure in public life*. Knight Foundation. https://www.oii.ox.ac.uk/news-events/news/why-does-junk-news-spread-so-quickly-across-social-media-2
Braun, J. A., & Eklund, J. L. (2019). Fake news, real money: Ad tech platforms, profit-driven hoaxes, and the business of journalism. *Digital Journalism, 7*(1), 1–21. https://doi.org/10.1080/21670811.2018.1556314
Brekhus, W. (1998). A sociology of the unmarked: Redirecting our focus. *Sociological Theory, 16*(1), 34–51. https://doi.org/10.1111/0735-2751.00041
Brenan, M. (2019, September 26). *Americans' trust in mass media edges down to 41%*. Gallup. https://news.gallup.com/poll/267047/americans-trust-mass-media-edges-down.aspx
Brenan, M. (2022, July 18). *Media confidence ratings at record lows*. Gallup. https://news.gallup.com/poll/394817/media-confidence-ratings-record-lows.aspx
Brown, B. (n.d.). *Search on Trump Twitter archive*. Retrieved February 9, 2023, from www.thetrumparchive.com
Brown, M. A., Bisbee, J., Lai, A., Bonneau, R., Nagler, J., & Tucker, J. A. (2022). Echo chambers, rabbit holes, and algorithmic bias: How YouTube recommends content to real users. SSRN Scholarly Paper No. 4114905. https://doi.org/10.2139/ssrn.4114905
Bruns, A. (2014). Gatekeeping, gatewatching, real-time feedback: New challenges for journalism. *Brazilian Journalism Research, 10*(2 EN), 224–237.
Bruns, A., & Burgess, J. (2015). Twitter hashtags from ad hoc to calculated publics. In N. Rambukkana (Ed.), *Hashtag publics: The power and politics of discursive networks* (pp. 13–28). Peter Lang.
Bump, P. (2021a, February 11). Analysis: A year of election misinformation from Trump, visualized. *Washington Post*. https://www.washingtonpost.com/politics/2021/02/11/year-election-misinformation-trump-visualized/
Bump, P. (2021b, November 8). Analysis: The unique role of Fox News in the misinformation universe. *Washington Post*. https://www.washingtonpost.com/politics/2021/11/08/unique-role-fox-news-misinformation-universe/
Bursztyn, L., Rao, A., Roth, C. P., & Yanagizawa-Drott, D. H. (2020). *Misinformation during a pandemic* (Working Paper No. 27417). National Bureau of Economic Research. https://doi.org/10.3386/w27417
Carey, A. (1996). *Taking the risk out of democracy: Corporate propaganda versus freedom and liberty*. University of Illinois Press.
Carlson, M. (2016). Metajournalistic discourse and the meanings of journalism: Definitional control, boundary work, and legitimation. *Communication Theory, 26*(4), 349–368. https://doi.org/10.1111/comt.12088
Carlson, M. (2018). The information politics of journalism in a post-truth age. *Journalism Studies, 19*(13), 1879–1888. https://doi.org/10.1080/1461670X.2018.1494513
Carlson, M. (2020). Fake news as an informational moral panic: The symbolic deviancy of social media during the 2016 US presidential election. *Information, Communication & Society, 23*(3), 374–388. https://doi.org/10.1080/1369118X.2018.1505934
Carter, C., & Allan, S. (2000). "If it bleeds, it leads": Ethical questions about popular journalism. In D. Berry (Ed.), *Ethics and media culture: Practices and representations* (pp. 132–153). Routledge.

Castelli Gattinara, P., & Bouron, S. (2020). Extreme-right communication in Italy and France: Political culture and media practices in CasaPound Italia and Les Identitaires. *Information, Communication & Society, 23*(12), 1805–1819. https://doi.org/10.1080/1369118X.2019.1631370

Castells, M. (2015). *Networks of outrage and hope: Social movements in the internet age* (2nd ed.). Polity.

Chadwick, A. (2017). *The hybrid media system: Politics and power* (2nd ed.). Oxford University Press.

Chadwick, A., & Stanyer, J. (2022). Deception as a bridging concept in the study of disinformation, misinformation, and misperceptions: Toward a holistic framework. *Communication Theory, 32*(1), 1–24. https://doi.org/10.1093/ct/qtab019

Chang, A. (2018, May 30). The stories Fox News covers obsessively—and those it ignores—in charts. *Vox*. https://www.vox.com/2018/5/30/17380096/fox-news-alternate-reality-charts

Chaplin, H., & Bell, E. (2018). *Episode 10: What are journalists for?* Journalism Design.

Chappell, B. (2015, December 29). Number of police officers killed by gunfire fell 14 percent in 2015, study says. NPR. https://www.npr.org/sections/thetwo-way/2015/12/29/461402091/number-of-police-officers-killed-by-gunfire-fell-14-percent-in-2015-study-says

Chayko, M. (2016). *Superconnected: The internet, digital media, and techno-social life*. SAGE.

Chen, S. X. (2022). The elitist public sphere in China: A case study of online contestation by former critical journalists during the coronavirus outbreak. *Javnost—The Public, 29*(2), 179–196. https://doi.org/10.1080/13183222.2022.2042790

Chernobrov, D., & Briant, E. L. (2022). Competing propagandas: How the United States and Russia represent mutual propaganda activities. *Politics, 42*(3), 393–409. https://doi.org/10.1177/0263395720966171

Chester, J., & Montgomery, K. C. (2017). The role of digital marketing in political campaigns. *Internet Policy Review, 6*(4), 1–20. https://policyreview.info/articles/analysis/role-digital-marketing-political-campaigns

Christin, A. (2018). Counting clicks: Quantification and variation in web journalism in the United States and France. *American Journal of Sociology, 123*(5), 1382–1415. https://doi.org/10.1086/696137

Clark, B. (2018, April 4). Facebook confirms: Donald trumped Hillary on the social network during 2016 election. *The Next Web*. https://thenextweb.com/facebook/2018/04/04/facebook-confirms-trumps-ads-bested-clintons-during-presidential-bid/

Cleveland, A. S. (1947). *Some political aspects of organized industry* [Doctoral dissertation]. Harvard University Thesis Collection, Harvard College Library.

Cohen, B. C. (1963). *The press and foreign policy*. Princeton University Press.

Cohen, N. S. (2019). At work in the digital newsroom. *Digital Journalism, 7*(5), 571–591. https://doi.org/10.1080/21670811.2017.1419821

Collins, G. R., Ben. (2016, September 23). Palmer Luckey: The Facebook near-billionaire secretly funding Trump's meme machine. *The Daily Beast*. https://www.thedailybeast.com/articles/2016/09/22/palmer-luckey-the-facebook-billionaire-secretly-funding-trump-s-meme-machine

Concha, J. (2020, June 1). O'Reilly's "No Spin News" to air on conservative digital network The First [Text]. *The Hill*. https://thehill.com/homenews/media/500562-oreillys-no-spin-news-to-air-on-conservative-digital-network-the-first

Confessore, N., & Yourish, K. (2016, March 15). $2 billion worth of free media for Donald Trump. *The New York Times*. https://www.nytimes.com/2016/03/16/upshot/measuring-donald-trumps-mammoth-advantage-in-free-media.html

Conger, K. (2019, November 15). What ads are political? Twitter struggles with a definition. *The New York Times*. https://www.nytimes.com/2019/11/15/technology/twitter-political-ad-policy.html

Conner, C. T., & MacMurray, N. (2022). The Perfect Storm: A Subcultural Analysis of the QAnon Movement. *Critical Sociology, 48*(6), 1049–1071. https://doi.org/10.1177/08969205211055863

Conway, B. A., Kenski, K., & Wang, D. (2015). The rise of Twitter in the political campaign: Searching for intermedia agenda-setting effects in the presidential primary. *Journal of Computer-Mediated Communication, 20*(4), 363–380. https://doi.org/10.1111/jcc4.12124

Conway, M. (2020). Routing the extreme right. *The RUSI Journal, 165*(1), 108–113. https://doi.org/10.1080/03071847.2020.1727157

Conway-Silva, B. A., Filer, C. R., Kenski, K., & Tsetsi, E. (2018). Reassessing Twitter's agenda-building power: An analysis of intermedia agenda-setting effects during the 2016 presidential primary season. *Social Science Computer Review, 36*(4), 469–483. https://doi.org/10.1177/0894439317715430

Couldry, N. (2003). Media meta-capital: Extending the range of Bourdieu's field theory. *Theory and Society, 32*(5/6), 653–677.

Couldry, N. (2004). Theorising media as practice. *Social Semiotics, 14*(2), 115–132. https://doi.org/10.1080/1035033042000238295

Couldry, N. (2012). *Media, society, world: Social theory and digital media practice*. Polity.

Couldry, N. (2014a). Mediatization and the future of field theory. In K. Lundby (Ed.), *Mediatization of communication* (pp. 227–245). Walter de Gruyter.

Couldry, N. (2014b). When mediatization hits the ground. In A. Hepp & F. Krotz (Eds.), *Mediatized worlds: Culture and society in a media age* (pp. 54–71). Palgrave Macmillan.

Couldry, N. (2016). Celebrity, convergence, and the fate of media institutions. In P. D. Marshall & S. Redmond (Eds.), *A companion to celebrity* (pp. 98–113). John Wiley & Sons. https://doi.org/10.1002/9781118475089.ch6

Couldry, N., & Curran, J. (2003). The paradox of media power. In. N. Couldry & J. Curran (Eds.), *Contesting media power: Alternative media in a networked world* (pp. 3–15). Rowman & Littlefield.

Couldry, N., & Hepp, A. (2017). *The mediated construction of reality*. Polity.

Couldry, N., & Mejias, U. A. (2019). *The costs of connection: How data is colonizing human life and appropriating it for capitalism*. Stanford University Press.

Cox, K. (2019, November 22). Google bans microtargeting and "false claims" in political ads. Ars Technica. https://arstechnica.com/tech-policy/2019/11/google-bans-microtargeting-and-false-claims-in-political-ads/

Crain, M., & Nadler, A. (2019). Political manipulation and internet advertising infrastructure. *Journal of Information Policy, 9*, 370–410. doi:10.5325/jinfopoli.9.2019.0370

Curran, D. (2018, March 30). Are you ready? This is all the data Facebook and Google have on you. *The Guardian*. https://www.theguardian.com/commentisfree/2018/mar/28/all-the-data-facebook-google-has-on-you-privacy

Daniels, J. (2018). The algorithmic rise of the "alt-right." *Contexts, 17*(1), 60–65. https://doi.org/10.1177/1536504218766547

Danner, M. (2009). *Stripping bare the body: Politics violence war*. PublicAffairs.

Davey, J., & Ebner, J. (2017). *The fringe insurgency: Connectivity, convergence and mainstreaming of the extreme right*. Institute for Strategic Dialogue. https://www.isdglobal.org/wp-content/uploads/2017/10/The-Fringe-Insurgency-221017.pdf

Davis, J. L. (2020). *How artifacts afford: The power and politics of everyday things*. MIT Press.

Davis, J. L., & Chouinard, J. B. (2016). Theorizing affordances: From request to refuse. *Bulletin of Science, Technology & Society, 36*(4), 241–248. doi:10.1177/0270467617714944

Denisova, A. (2022). Viral journalism. Strategy, tactics and limitations of the fast spread of content on social media: Case study of the United Kingdom quality publications. *Journalism, 24*(9), 1919–1937. https://doi.org/10.1177/14648849221077749

Dewey, C. (2014, October 20). Inside Gamergate's (successful) attack on the media. *Washington Post*. https://www.washingtonpost.com/news/the-intersect/wp/2014/10/20/inside-gamergates-successful-attack-on-the-media/

Diakopoulos, N. (2019). *Automating the news: How algorithms are rewriting the media*. Harvard University Press.

DiBranco, A. (2020). Conservative news and movement infrastructure. In A. Nadler & A. J. Bauer (Eds.), *News on the right: Studying conservative news cultures* (pp. 123–140). Oxford University Press.

Dobber, T., Metoui, N., Trilling, D., Helberger, N., & de Vreese, C. (2021). Do (microtargeted) deepfakes have real effects on political attitudes? *The International Journal of Press/Politics, 26*(1), 69–91. https://doi.org/10.1177/1940161220944364

Domhoff, G. W. (2001). *Who rules America? Power and politics* (4th ed.). McGraw-Hill Humanities/Social Sciences/Languages.

Donovan, J. (n.d.). *The lifecycle of media manipulation*. DataJournalism. Retrieved February 4, 2022, from https://datajournalism.com/read/handbook/verification-3/investigating-disinformation-and-media-manipulation/the-lifecycle-of-media-manipulation

Donovan, J., & boyd, d. (2021). Stop the presses? Moving from strategic silence to strategic amplification in a networked media ecosystem. *American Behavioral Scientist, 65*(2), 333–350. https://doi.org/10.1177/0002764219878229

Donovan, J., & Friedberg, B. (2019). Source hacking: Media manipulation in practice. *Data & Society*. https://datasociety.net/output/source-hacking-media-manipulation-in-practice/

Douek, E. (2020). *The rise of content cartels (The tech giants, monopoly power, and public discourse)*. Knight First Amendment Institute at Columbia University. http://knightcolumbia.org/content/the-rise-of-content-cartels

Driessens, O. (2013). Celebrity capital: Redefining celebrity using field theory. *Theory and Society, 42*(5), 543–560. https://doi.org/10.1007/s11186-013-9202-3

Dumenco, S., & Brown, K. (2020, October 30). Here's what Trump and Biden have spent on Facebook and Google ads. *Ad Age*. https://adage.com/article/campaign-trail/heres-what-trump-and-biden-have-spent-facebook-and-google-ads/2291531

Dwoskin, E., Tiku, N., & Timberg, C. (2021, November 21). Facebook's race-blind practices around hate speech came at the expense of Black users, new documents show. *Washington Post*. https://www.washingtonpost.com/technology/2021/11/21/facebook-algorithm-biased-race/

Dwoskin, E., Timberg, C., & Romm, T. (2020, June 28). Zuckerberg once wanted to sanction Trump. Then Facebook wrote rules that accommodated him. *Washington Post*. https://www.washingtonpost.com/technology/2020/06/28/facebook-zuckerberg-trump-hate/

Earl, J., Hurwitz, H. M., Mesinas, A. M., Tolan, M., & Arlotti, A. (2013). This protest will be tweeted. *Information, Communication & Society, 16*(4), 459–478. https://doi.org/10.1080/1369118X.2013.777756

Earl, J., & Kimport, K. (2011). *Digitally enabled social change: Activism in the internet age*. MIT Press.

Edwards, L. (2021). Organised lying and professional legitimacy: Public relations' accountability in the disinformation debate. *European Journal of Communication, 36*(2), 168–182. https://doi.org/10.1177/0267323120966851

Egelhofer, J. L., & Lecheler, S. (2019). Fake news as a two-dimensional phenomenon: A framework and research agenda. *Annals of the International Communication Association, 43*(2), 97–116. https://doi.org/10.1080/23808985.2019.1602782

Ehrett, C., Linvill, D. L., Smith, H., Warren, P. L., Bellamy, L., Moawad, M., Moran, O., & Moody, M. (2021). Inauthentic newsfeeds and agenda setting in a coordinated inauthentic information operation. *Social Science Computer Review, 40*(6), 1595–1613. https://doi.org/10.1177/08944393211019951

Eisenberg, B., & Eisenberg, J. (2006, October 9). *Creating persuasion architecture online*. User Interface Engineering. https://www.uie.com/events/uiconf/2006/sessions/eisenberg/

Ellick, A. B., & Westbrook, A. (2018, November 12). Opinion: Operation Infektion: A three-part video series on Russian disinformation. *The New York Times*. https://www.nytimes.com/2018/11/12/opinion/russia-meddling-disinformation-fake-news-elections.html

Ellis, G. (2014). *Trust ownership and the future of news: Media moguls and white knights*. Springer.

Entman, R. M. (1993). Framing: Toward clarification of a fractured paradigm. *Journal of Communication, 43*(4), 51–58. https://doi.org/10.1111/j.1460-2466.1993.tb01304.x

Ettema, J. S., & Glasser, T. L. (1998). *Custodians of conscience: Investigative journalism and public virtue.* Columbia University Press.

Etter, M., & Albu, O. B. (2021). Activists in the dark: Social media algorithms and collective action in two social movement organizations. *Organization, 28*(1), 68–91. https://doi.org/10.1177/1350508420961532

"Facebook: From Election to Insurrection." (2021, March 18). Avaaz. https://secure.avaaz.org/campaign/en/facebook_election_insurrection/

Fayard, A.-L., & Weeks, J. (2014). Affordances for practice. *Information and Organization, 24*(4), 236–249. https://doi.org/10.1016/j.infoandorg.2014.10.001

Fedorov, A., & Levitskaya, A. (2020). Typology and mechanisms of media manipulation. *International Journal of Media and Information Literacy, 5*(1), 69–78. https://doi.org/10.13187/ijmil.2020.1.69

Ferrara, E., Chang, H., Chen, E., Muric, G., & Patel, J. (2020). Characterizing social media manipulation in the 2020 U.S. presidential election. *First Monday, 11*(2). https://doi.org/10.5210/fm.v25i11.11431

Fiorini, S. (2022, May 19). *Local news most trusted in keeping Americans informed about their communities.* Knight Foundation. https://knightfoundation.org/articles/local-news-most-trusted-in-keeping-americans-informed-about-their-communities/

Fish, S. E. (1980). *Is there a text in this class? The authority of interpretive communities.* Harvard University Press.

Fisher, M., Flynn, M., Contrera, J., & Leonnig, C. D. (2021, January 7). *The four-hour insurrection.* Washington Post. https://www.washingtonpost.com/graphics/2021/politics/trump-insurrection-capitol/

Fisher, S., & Gold, A. (2021, January 11). All the platforms that have banned or restricted Trump so far. *Axios.* https://www.axios.com/platforms-social-media-ban-restrict-trump-d9e44f3c-8366-4ba9-a8a1-7f3114f920f1.html

Fletcher, R., & Nielsen, R. K. (2017). Are news audiences increasingly fragmented? A cross-national comparative analysis of cross-platform news audience fragmentation and duplication. *Journal of Communication, 67*(4), 476–498. https://doi.org/10.1111/jcom.12315

Foucault, M. (1995). *Discipline and punish: The birth of the prison.* Knopf Doubleday.

Foxnews.com traffic, demographics and competitors (n.d.). Alexa. Retrieved November 17, 2019. https://web.archive.org/web/20191029093226/https://www.alexa.com/siteinfo/foxnews.com

Freedman, D. (2014). *The contradictions of media power.* Bloomsbury Academic.

Freelon, D., Marwick, A., & Kreiss, D. (2020). False equivalencies: Online activism from left to right. *Science, 369*(6508), 1197–1201. https://doi.org/10.1126/science.abb2428

Fuchs, C. (2018). Propaganda 2.0: Herman and Chomsky's propaganda model in the age of the internet, big data and social media. In J. Pedro-Carañana, D. Broudy, and J. Klaehn (Eds.), *The propaganda model today: Filtering perception and awareness* (pp. 71–92). University of Westminster Press. doi:10.16997/book27.f

Full transcript: Trump's 2020 State of the Union address. (2020, February 5). *The New York Times.* https://www.nytimes.com/2020/02/05/us/politics/state-of-union-transcript.html

Gallup, & Knight Foundation. (2020, November 9). *American Views 2020: Trust, Media and Democracy.* https://knightfoundation.org/reports/american-views-2020-trust-media-and-democracy/

Garrett, R. K., & Bond, R. M. (2021). Conservatives' susceptibility to political misperceptions. *Science Advances, 7*(23), eabf1234. https://doi.org/10.1126/sciadv.abf1234

Gaudette, T., Scrivens, R., Davies, G., & Frank, R. (2021). Upvoting extremism: Collective identity formation and the extreme right on Reddit. *New Media & Society, 23*(12), 3491–3508. https://doi.org/10.1177/1461444820958123

The gentleperson's guide to forum spies. (n.d.). Retrieved June 27, 2022, from https://cryptome.org/2012/07/gent-forum-spies.htm

Gerbaudo, P. (2017). Social media teams as digital vanguards: The question of leadership in the management of key Facebook and Twitter accounts of Occupy Wall Street, Indignados and UK Uncut. *Information, Communication & Society, 20*(2), 185–202. https://doi.org/10.1080/1369118X.2016.1161817

Gerbaudo, P. (2022). Theorizing reactive democracy: The social media public sphere, online crowds, and the plebiscitary logic of online reactions. *Democratic Theory, 9*(2), 120–138. https://doi.org/10.3167/dt.2022.090207

Ghaffary, S. (2022, November 4). A comprehensive guide to how Elon Musk is changing Twitter. *Vox.* https://www.vox.com/recode/23440075/elon-musk-twitter-layoffs-check-mark-verification

Giglietto, F., Righetti, N., Rossi, L., & Marino, G. (2020). It takes a village to manipulate the media: Coordinated link sharing behavior during 2018 and 2019 Italian elections. *Information, Communication & Society, 23*(6), 867–891. https://doi.org/10.1080/1369118X.2020.1739732

Gil de Zúñiga, H, Correa, T., & Valenzuela, S. (2012). Selective exposure to cable news and immigration in the U.S.: The relationship between FOX News, CNN, and attitudes toward Mexican immigrants. *Journal of Broadcasting & Electronic Media, 56*(4), 597–615. https://doi.org/10.1080/08838151.2012.732138

Gil de Zúñiga, H., Koc Michalska, K., & Römmele, A. (2020). Populism in the era of Twitter: How social media contextualized new insights into an old phenomenon. *New Media & Society, 22*(4), 585–594. https://doi.org/10.1177/1461444819893978

Gillespie, T. (2014). The relevance of algorithms. In T. Gillespie, P. J. Boczkowski, & K. A. Foot (Eds.), *Media technologies* (pp. 167–194). MIT Press.

Gillespie, T. (2018). *Custodians of the Internet: Platforms, Content Moderation, and the Hidden Decisions That Shape Social Media*. Yale University Press.

Gillmor, D. (2006). *We the media: Grassroots journalism by the people, for the people*. O'Reilly Media.

Gitlin, T. (1980). *The whole world is watching: Mass media in the making and unmaking of the New Left*. University of California Press.

Gladwell, M., & Shirky, C. (2011, March 15). From innovation to revolution. *Foreign Affairs.* https://www.foreignaffairs.com/articles/2011-01-19/innovation-revolution

Goffman, E. (1974). *Frame analysis: An essay on the organization of experience*. Harvard University Press.

Golebiewski, M., & boyd, d. (2019). Data voids. *Data & Society.* https://datasociety.net/library/data-voids/

Gorwa, R., & Guilbeault, D. (2020). Unpacking the social media bot: A typology to guide research and policy. *Policy & Internet, 12*(2), 225–248. https://doi.org/10.1002/poi3.184

Gottfried, J. (2021, July 1). *Republicans less likely to trust their main news source if they see it as "mainstream"; Democrats more likely*. Pew Research Center. https://www.pewresearch.org/fact-tank/2021/07/01/republicans-less-likely-to-trust-their-main-news-source-if-they-see-it-as-mainstream-democrats-more-likely/

Gottfried, J., & Liedke, J. (2021, August 30). *Partisan divides in media trust widen, driven by a decline among Republicans*. Pew Research Center. https://www.pewresearch.org/fact-tank/2021/08/30/partisan-divides-in-media-trust-widen-driven-by-a-decline-among-republicans/

Gramlich, J. (2020, April 8). *5 facts about Fox News*. Pew Research Center. https://www.pewresearch.org/fact-tank/2020/04/08/five-facts-about-fox-news/

Gregorian, D., Collins, B., & Hillyard, V. (2022, August 30). *Trump shares barrage of QAnon content and other conspiracy theories on his social media platform*. NBC News. https://www.nbcnews.com/politics/donald-trump/trump-shares-barrage-qanon-content-conspiracy-theories-social-media-pl-rcna45465

Guess, A., Nyhan, B., & Reifler, J. (2018). *Selective exposure to misinformation: Evidence from the consumption of fake news during the 2016 US presidential campaign*. European Research Council.

Guo, L., & Vargo, C. (2020). "Fake news" and emerging online media ecosystem: An integrated intermedia agenda-setting analysis of the 2016 U.S. presidential election. *Communication Research, 47*(2), 178–200. https://doi.org/10.1177/0093650218777177

Habermas, J. (1985). *The theory of communicative action: Vol. 1. Reason and the rationalization of society*. Beacon Press.

Habermas, J. (1989). *The structural transformation of the public sphere: An inquiry into a category of bourgeois society*. MIT Press.

Haenschen, K., & Jennings, J. (2019). Mobilizing millennial voters with targeted internet advertisements: A field experiment. *Political Communication, 36*(3), 357–375. https://doi.org/10.1080/10584609.2018.1548530

Hagey, K., & Horwitz, J. (2021, September 15). Facebook tried to make its platform a healthier place. It got angrier instead. *Wall Street Journal*. https://www.wsj.com/articles/facebook-algorithm-change-zuckerberg-11631654215

Haggin, P., & Glazer, E. (2020, June 4). Facebook, Twitter and Google write their own rules for political ads—and what you see. *Wall Street Journal*. https://www.wsj.com/graphics/how-google-facebook-and-twitter-patrol-political-ads/

Haigh, M., Haigh, T., & Kozak, N. I. (2017). Stopping fake news. *Journalism Studies, 19*(4), 2062–2087. https://doi.org/10.1080/1461670X.2017.1316681

Halliday, J. (2012, March 22). Twitter's Tony Wang: "We are the free speech wing of the free speech party." *The Guardian*. http://www.theguardian.com/media/2012/mar/22/twitter-tony-wang-free-speech

Halpin, J., Heidbreder, J., Lloyd, M., Woodhull, P., Scott, B., Silver, J., & Turner, S. D. (2007, June 21). *The structural imbalance of political talk radio*. Center for American Progress. https://www.americanprogress.org/issues/general/reports/2007/06/20/3087/the-structural-imbalance-of-political-talk-radio/

Hameleers, M. (2022). "I don't believe anything they say anymore!" Explaining unanticipated media effects among distrusting citizens. *Media and Communication, 10*(3), 158–168. https://doi.org/10.17645/mac.v10i3.5307

Hampton, M. (2009). The Fourth Estate ideal in journalism history. In S. Allan (Ed.), *The Routledge companion to news and journalism* (pp. 3–12). Routledge.

Hao, K. (2021, March 11). He got Facebook hooked on AI. Now he can't fix its misinformation addiction. *MIT Technology Review*. https://www.technologyreview.com/2021/03/11/1020600/facebook-responsible-ai-misinformation/

Harwell, D. (2022, November 14). A fake tweet sparked panic at Eli Lilly and may have cost Twitter millions. *Washington Post*. https://www.washingtonpost.com/technology/2022/11/14/twitter-fake-eli-lilly/

Harwell, D., & Timberg, C. (2019, June 26). Pro-Trump message board "quarantined" by Reddit following violent threats. *Washington Post*. https://www.washingtonpost.com/technology/2019/06/26/pro-trump-message-board-quarantined-by-reddit-following-violent-threats/

Hawkins, I., & Saleem, M. (2021). Rise UP! A content analytic study of how collective action is discussed within White nationalist videos on YouTube. *New Media & Society, 25*(12), 3308–3327. https://doi.org/10.1177/14614448211040520

H.B. 20. (2021, August). Reg. Sess. (Tex. 2021). https://capitol.texas.gov/tlodocs/872/billtext/html/HB00020S.htm

Heath, A. (2021, June 3). Facebook to end special treatment for politicians after Trump ban. *The Verge*. https://www.theverge.com/2021/6/3/22474738/facebook-ending-political-figure-exemption-moderation-policy

Heilweil, R., & Ghaffary, S. (2021, January 8). How Trump's internet built and broadcast the Capitol insurrection. *Vox*. https://www.vox.com/recode/22221285/trump-online-capitol-riot-far-right-parler-twitter-facebook

Hemmer, N. (2016). *Messengers of the right: Conservative media and the transformation of American politics*. University of Pennsylvania Press.

Herman, E. S., & Chomsky, N. (2002). *Manufacturing consent: The political economy of the mass media*. Pantheon. (Original work published 1988)

Hersh, E. (2015). *Hacking the electorate: How campaigns perceive voters*. Cambridge University Press.

Hiaeshutter-Rice, D., & Weeks, B. (2021). Understanding audience engagement with mainstream and alternative news posts on Facebook. *Digital Journalism, 9*(5), 519–548. https://doi.org/10.1080/21670811.2021.1924068

Hiar, C. (2010, October 28). How the Tea Party Utilized Digital Media to Gain Power. *MediaShift.* http://mediashift.org/2010/10/how-the-tea-party-utilized-digital-media-to-gain-power301/

Hmielowski, J. D., Feldman, L., Myers, T. A., Leiserowitz, A., & Maibach, E. (2014). An attack on science? Media use, trust in scientists, and perceptions of global warming. *Public Understanding of Science, 23*(7), 866–883. https://doi.org/10.1177/0963662513480091

Holiday, R. (2013). *Trust me, I'm lying: Confessions of a media manipulator* (unabridged ed.). Portfolio.

Holiday, R. (2016, October 27). Exclusive interview: How this right-wing "troll" reaches 100M people a month. *Observer.* https://observer.com/2016/10/exclusive-interview-how-this-right-wing-troll-reaches-100m-people-a-month/

Holt, J. (2022). *After the insurrection: How domestic extremists adapted and evolved after the January 6 US Capitol attack.* Atlantic Council. https://www.atlanticcouncil.org/in-depth-research-reports/report/after-the-insurrection-how-domestic-extremists-adapted-and-evolved-after-the-january-6-us-capitol-attack/

Huppke, R. (2018, November 8). Absurd Acosta story shows how disinformation bubbles from bots to the White House. *Chicago Tribune.*https://www.chicagotribune.com/columns/rex-huppke/ct-met-acosta-video-white-house-chop-intern-huppke-20181108-story.html

Isaac, M. (2020, June 29). Reddit, acting against hate speech, bans "The_Donald" subreddit. *The New York Times.* https://www.nytimes.com/2020/06/29/technology/reddit-hate-speech.html

Jack, C. (2017.) Lexicon of lies: Terms for problematic information. *Data & Society.* https://datasociety.net/output/lexicon-of-lies/.

Jackson, D. (2017, October 17). *Issue brief: Distinguishing disinformation from propaganda, misinformation, and "fake news."* National Endowment for Democracy. https://www.ned.org/issue-brief-distinguishing-disinformation-from-propaganda-misinformation-and-fake-news/

Jacoby, J. (2018a, May 18). The Frontline interview: Andrew Anker. *Frontline.* https://www.pbs.org/wgbh/frontline/interview/andrew-anker/

Jacoby, J. (2018b, August 8). The Frontline interview: Brad Parscale. *Frontline.* https://www.pbs.org/wgbh/frontline/interview/brad-parscale/

Jamieson, A. (2018, November 2). Ilana Glazer had to shut down an event at a Brooklyn synagogue because someone scrawled "Die Jew rat" on the wall. *BuzzFeed News.* https://www.buzzfeednews.com/article/amberjamieson/ilana-glazer-racist-graffii-union-temple

Jamieson, K. H. (1996). *Packaging the presidency: A history and criticism of presidential campaign advertising* (3rd ed.). Oxford University Press.

Jamieson, K. H., & Albarracín, D. (2020). The relation between media consumption and misinformation at the outset of the SARS-CoV-2 pandemic in the US. *Harvard Kennedy School Misinformation Review, 1*(3). https://doi.org/10.37016/mr-2020-012

Jamieson, K. H., & Cappella, J. N. (2008). *Echo chamber: Rush Limbaugh and the conservative media establishment.* Oxford University Press.

Jansen, S. C. (2013). Semantic tyranny: How Edward L. Bernays stole Walter Lippmann's mojo and got away with it and why it still matters. *International Journal of Communication, 7,* 18.

Jensen, R. (2013). *Arguing for our lives: A user's guide to constructive dialog.* City Lights Books.

Jensen, R. (2015, June 11). American journalism's ideology: Why the "liberal" media is fundamentalist. *Resilience.* https://www.resilience.org/stories/2015-06-11/american-journalisms-ideology-why-the-liberal-media-is-fundamentalist/

Jowett, G. S., & O'Donnell, V. (2014). *Propaganda and persuasion.* SAGE Publications.

Juarez Miro, C., & Toff, B. (2022). How right-wing populists engage with cross-cutting news on online message boards: The case of ForoCoches and Vox in Spain. *The International Journal of Press/Politics, 28*(4), 770–790. https://doi.org/10.1177/19401612211072696

Jukes, S. (2019). Crossing the line between news and the business of news: Exploring journalists' use of Twitter. *Media and Communication*, 7(1), 248–258. https://doi.org/10.17645/mac.v7i1.1772

Jurkowitz, M. (2014, March 26). *The growth of digital reporting*. Pew Research Center. http://www.journalism.org/2014/03/26/the-growth-in-digital-reporting/

Kaplan, R. L. (2002). *Politics and the American press: The rise of objectivity, 1865–1920*. Cambridge University Press.

Kaplan, R. L. (2008). Yellow journalism. In W. Donbash & J.H. Lipshultz (Eds.), *The international encyclopedia of communication* (pp. 5369–5371). John Wiley & Sons. https://doi.org/10.1002/9781405186407.wbiecy001

Kappel, K. (2018, October 15). There is no middle ground if we have deep disagreements about facts. *Fast Company*. https://www.fastcompany.com/90251513/there-is-no-middle-ground-if-we-have-a-deep-disagreements-about-facts

Karlova, N. A., & Fisher, K. E. (2013). Plz RT: A social diffusion model of misinformation and disinformation for understanding human information behaviour. *Information Research*, 18(1), 1–17.

Karpf, D. (2016). *Analytic activism: Digital listening and the new political strategy*. Oxford University Press.

Karpf, D. (2018). Analytic activism and its limitations. *Social Media + Society*, 4(1), 1–10. https://doi.org/10.1177/2056305117750718

Katz, A. J. (2022, June 29). June 2022 cable network ranker: Fox News remains most-watched in total day and prime; MSNBC's ratings growth driven by Jan. 6 hearings. *Adweek*. https://www.adweek.com/tvnewser/june-2022-cable-network-ranker-fox-news-remains-most-watched-in-total-day-and-prime-msnbcs-ratings-growth-driven-by-jan-6-hearings/510124/

Katz, E., & Lazarsfeld, P. F. (1955). *Personal influence: The part played by people in the flow of mass communications*. Free Press.

Keegan, J., Lecher, C., & Faife, C. (2021, February 16). Trump's false posts were treated with kid gloves by Facebook. *The Markup*. https://themarkup.org/citizen-browser/2021/02/16/trumps-false-posts-were-treated-with-kid-gloves-by-facebook

Kellner, D. (2009). Media spectacle and media events: Some critical reflections. In N. Couldry, A. Hepp, & F. Krotz (Eds.), *Media events in a global age* (pp. 76–91). Routledge.

Kelly, C. (2020, February 4). Watch Trump give the 2020 State of the Union. *Wired*. https://www.wired.com/story/how-to-watch-the-state-of-the-union-2020/

Kessler, G., Rizzo, S., & Kelly, M. (2021, January 24). Analysis: Trump's false or misleading claims total 30,573 over 4 years. *Washington Post*. https://www.washingtonpost.com/politics/2021/01/24/trumps-false-or-misleading-claims-total-30573-over-four-years/

Khaldarova, I., & Pantti, M. (2016). Fake news: The narrative battle over the Ukrainian conflict. *Journalism Practice*, 10(7), 891–901. https://doi.org/10.1080/17512786.2016.1163237

King, G., Schneer, B., & White, A. (2017). How the news media activate public expression and influence national agendas. *Science*, 358(6364), 776–780. https://doi.org/10.1126/science.aao1100

Klonick, K. (2019, April 25). Inside the team at Facebook that dealt with the Christchurch shooting. *The New Yorker*. https://www.newyorker.com/news/news-desk/inside-the-team-at-facebook-that-dealt-with-the-christchurch-shooting

Köhler, D., & Ebner, J. (2019). Strategies and tactics: Communication strategies of jihadists and right-wing extremists. In J. Baldauf, J. Ebner, & J. Guhl (Eds.), *Hate speech and radicalisation online: The OCCI research report* (pp. 1–65). Institute for Strategic Dialogue. https://www.isdglobal.org/wp-content/uploads/2019/06/ISD-Hate-Speech-and-Radicalisation-Online-English-Draft-2.pdf#page=18

Kovach, B., & Rosenstiel, T. (2007). *The elements of journalism: What newspeople should know and the public should expect* (revised, updated ed.). Three Rivers Press.

Krafft, P. M., & Donovan, J. (2020). Disinformation by design: The use of evidence collages and platform filtering in a media manipulation campaign. *Political Communication*, 37(2), 194–214. https://doi.org/10.1080/10584609.2019.1686094

Kreiss, D., Lawrence, R. G., & McGregor, S. C. (2018). In their own words: Political practitioner accounts of candidates, audiences, affordances, genres, and timing in strategic social media use. *Political Communication, 35*(1), 8–31. https://doi.org/10.1080/10584609.2017.1334727

Kreiss, D., & McGregor, S. (2021, April 5). Polarization isn't America's biggest problem—or Facebook's. *Wired.* https://www.wired.com/story/polarization-isnt-americas-biggest-problem-or-facebooks

Kristensen, N. N., & From, U. (2015). From Ivory Tower to cross-media personas. *Journalism Practice, 9*(6), 853–871. https://doi.org/10.1080/17512786.2015.1051370

Kruikemeier, S., Sezgin, M., & Boerman, S. C. (2016). Political microtargeting: Relationship between personalized advertising on Facebook and voters' responses. *Cyberpsychology, Behavior, and Social Networking, 19*(6), 367–372. https://doi.org/10.1089/cyber.2015.0652

Kull, S., Ramsay, C., & Lewis, E. (2003). Misperceptions, the media, and the Iraq War. *Political Science Quarterly, 118*(4), 569–598. https://doi.org/10.1002/j.1538-165X.2003.tb00406.x

Kusche, I. (2020). The old in the new: Voter surveillance in political clientelism and datafied campaigning. *Big Data & Society, 7*(1), 2053951720908290. https://doi.org/10.1177/2053951720908290

Ladd, J. M. (2011). *Why Americans hate the media and how it matters.* Princeton University Press.

LaCorte News. (n.d.). Retrieved November 27, 2019.: https://www.lacortenews.com

Lane, J. B. (2020). Cultivating distrust of the mainstream media: Propagandists for a liberal machine and the American establishment. In A. Nadler & A. J. Bauer (Eds.), *News on the right: Studying conservative news cultures* (pp. 157–173). Oxford University Press.

Larson, K. R., & McHendry, G. F. (2019). Parasitic publics. *Rhetoric Society Quarterly, 49*(5), 517.

Lavigne, M. (2021). Strengthening ties: The influence of microtargeting on partisan attitudes and the vote. *Party Politics, 27*(5), 965–976. https://doi.org/10.1177/1354068820918387

Lazarsfeld, P. F., Berelson, B., & Gaudet, H. (1948). *The people's choice: How the voter makes up his mind in a presidential campaign.* Columbia University Press.

Legum, J. (2019a, July 24). Trump using Facebook ads to lie about his Democratic opponents. *Popular Information.* https://popular.info/p/trump-using-facebook-ads-to-lie-about

Legum, J. (2019b, October 28). Facebook allows prominent right-wing website to break the rules. *Popular Information.* https://popular.info/p/facebook-allows-prominent-right-wing

Levendusky, M. (2013). *How partisan media polarize America.* University of Chicago Press.

Levy, A., Rodriguez, S., & Graham, M. (2020, October 8). *Why political campaigns are flooding Facebook with ad dollars.* CNBC. https://www.cnbc.com/2020/10/08/trump-biden-pacs-spend-big-on-facebook-as-election-nears.html

Lewis, J., Williams, A., & Franklin, B. (2008). A compromised Fourth Estate? *Journalism Studies, 9*(1), 1–20. https://doi.org/10.1080/14616700701767974

Lewis, M. (2018, February 9). Has anyone seen the president? *Bloomberg.* https://www.bloomberg.com/opinion/articles/2018-02-09/has-anyone-seen-the-president

Lievrouw, L. (2011). *Alternative and activist new media.* Polity.

Lindner, A. M., & Barnard, S. R. (2020). *All media are social: Sociological perspectives on mass media.* Routledge.

Lipsky, M. (2019, June 4). Radio's top talkers for 2019. *The Radio Agency.* https://www.radiodirect.com/radios-top-talkers-for-2019/

Littau, J. (2019, January 26). The crisis facing American journalism did not start with the internet. *Slate.* https://slate.com/technology/2019/01/layoffs-at-media-organizations-the-roots-of-this-crisis-go-back-decades.html

Liu, J. (2020). *Shifting dynamics of contention in the digital age: Mobile communication and politics in China.* Oxford University Press.

Loucaides, D. (2022, February 8). How Telegram became the anti-Facebook. *Wired.* https://www.wired.com/story/how-telegram-became-anti-facebook/

Lowery, W. (2016, July 11). Analysis: Aren't more White people than Black people killed by police? Yes, but no. *Washington Post.* https://www.washingtonpost.com/news/post-nation/wp/2016/07/11/arent-more-white-people-than-black-people-killed-by-police-yes-but-no/

Lukes, S. (2005). *Power: A radical view* (2nd ed.). Palgrave Macmillan.
Lukito, J., Suk, J., Zhang, Y., Doroshenko, L., Kim, S. J., Su, M.-H., Xia, Y., Freelon, D., & Wells, C. (2020). The wolves in sheep's clothing: How Russia's Internet Research Agency tweets appeared in U.S. news as vox populi. *The International Journal of Press/Politics, 25*(2), 196–216. https://doi.org/10.1177/1940161219895215
Luo, M., Hancock, J. T., & Markowitz, D. M. (2022). Credibility perceptions and detection accuracy of fake news headlines on social media: Effects of truth-bias and endorsement cues. *Communication Research, 49*(2), 171–195. https://doi.org/10.1177/0093650220921321
Lyons, K. (2020, May 23). President Trump is reportedly considering creating a panel to examine bias online. *The Verge*. https://www.theverge.com/2020/5/23/21268433/president-trump-conservative-bias-social-media-twitter-facebook-google
Maares, P., & Hanusch, F. (2020). Interpretations of the journalistic field: A systematic analysis of how journalism scholarship appropriates Bourdieusian thought. *Journalism, 23*(4), 736–754. https://doi.org/10.1177/1464884920959552
Mac, R., & Silverman, C. (2021, February 21). "Mark changed the rules": How Facebook went easy on Alex Jones and other right-wing figures. *BuzzFeed News*. https://www.buzzfeednews.com/article/ryanmac/mark-zuckerberg-joel-kaplan-facebook-alex-jones
MacKinnon, R. (2013). *Consent of the networked: The worldwide struggle for internet freedom*. Basic Books.
Maloy, S. (2012, March 5). *Rush Limbaugh's decades of sexism and misogyny*. Media Matters for America. https://www.mediamatters.org/sean-hannity/rush-limbaughs-decades-sexism-and-misogyny
Martin, G. J., & Yurukoglu, A. (2017). Bias in cable news: Persuasion and polarization. *American Economic Review, 107*(9), 2565–2599. https://doi.org/10.1257/aer.20160812
Martin, K. (2019, July 13). White House social media summit recap. *All Things Considered*. https://www.npr.org/2019/07/13/741485104/white-house-social-media-summit-recap
Marwick, A. (2018). Why do people share fake news? A sociotechnical model of media effects. *Georgetown Law Technology Review, 2*(2), 474–512.
Marwick, A. E. (2021). Morally motivated networked harassment as normative reinforcement. *Social Media + Society, 7*(2), 1–13. https://doi.org/10.1177/20563051211021378
Marwick, A., & Lewis, R. (2017). *Media manipulation and disinformation online*. Data and Society Research Institute. https://datasociety.net/output/media-manipulation-and-disinfo-online/
Mattoni, A. (2013). Repertoires of communication in social movement processes. In B. Cammaerts, A. Mattoni & P. McCurdy (Eds.), *Mediation and protest movements* (pp. 39–56). Intellect.
Mattoni, A. (2020). Practicing media—mediating practice: A media-in-practices approach to investigate the nexus between digital media and activists' daily political engagement. *International Journal of Communication, 14*, 18.
Mattoni, A., & Treré, E. (2014). Media practices, mediation processes, and mediatization in the study of social movements. *Communication Theory, 24*(3), 252–271. https://doi.org/10.1111/comt.12038
Mayer, J. (2017). *Dark money: The hidden history of the billionaires behind the rise of the radical right* (illustrated ed.). Anchor.
Mayer, J. (2019, March 4). The making of the Fox News White House. *The New Yorker*. https://www.newyorker.com/magazine/2019/03/11/the-making-of-the-fox-news-white-house
Mayer, J. (2021, July 31). The big money behind the big lie. *The New Yorker*. https://www.newyorker.com/magazine/2021/08/09/the-big-money-behind-the-big-lie
McCarthy, N. (2021, May 27). Infographic: Russia and Iran are Facebook's top sources of disinformation. *Statista Infographics*. https://www.statista.com/chart/24930/coordinated-inauthentic-behavior-networks-removed-by-facebook/
McChesney, R. W. (2000). *Rich media, poor democracy: Communication politics in dubious times*. The New Press.

McChesney, R. W. (2004). *The problem of the media: U.S. communication politics in the twenty-first century*. Monthly Review Press.

McChesney, R. W. (2013). *Digital disconnect: How capitalism is turning the internet against democracy*. The New Press.

McCombs, M. E., & Shaw, D. L. (1972). The agenda-setting function of mass media. *Public Opinion Quarterly, 36*(2), 176–187. https://doi.org/10.1086/267990

McGregor, S. C. (2019). Social media as public opinion: How journalists use social media to represent public opinion. *Journalism, 20*(8), 1070–1086. https://doi.org/10.1177/1464884919845458

McGregor, S. C. (2020a). "Taking the temperature of the room": How political campaigns use social media to understand and represent public opinion. *Public Opinion Quarterly, 84*(S1), 236–256. https://doi.org/10.1093/poq/nfaa012

McGregor, S. C. (2020b, September 17). What even is "coordinated inauthentic behavior" on platforms? *Wired*. https://www.wired.com/story/what-even-is-coordinated-inauthentic-behavior-on-platforms

McGregor, S. C., Barrett, B., & Kreiss, D. (2021). Questionably legal: Digital politics and foreign propaganda. *Journal of Information Technology & Politics, 19*(1), 1–17. https://www.tandfonline.com/doi/abs/10.1080/19331681.2021.1902854

McIntyre, L. (2018). *Post-truth*. MIT Press.

McLuhan, M. (1964). *Understanding media: The extensions of man*. Signet Books.

McNair, B. (2011). *An introduction to political communication* (5th ed.). Routledge.

McSwiney, J., Vaughan, M., Heft, A., & Hoffmann, M. (2021). Sharing the hate? Memes and transnationality in the far right's digital visual culture. *Information, Communication & Society, 24*(16), 2502–2521. https://doi.org/10.1080/1369118X.2021.1961006

Meeks, L. (2020). Defining the enemy: How Donald Trump frames the news media. *Journalism & Mass Communication Quarterly, 97*(1), 211–234. https://doi.org/10.1177/1077699019857676

Mejias, U. A., & Vokuev, N. E. (2017). Disinformation and the media: The case of Russia and Ukraine. *Media, Culture & Society, 39*(7), 1027–1042. https://doi.org/10.1177/0163443716686672

Meraz, S. (2009). Is there an elite hold? Traditional media to social media agenda setting influence in blog networks. *Journal of Computer-Mediated Communication, 14*(3), 682–707. https://doi.org/10.1111/j.1083-6101.2009.01458.x

Metz, R. (2021, October 27). *Likes, anger emojis and RSVPs: The math behind Facebook's News Feed—and how it backfired*. CNN Business. https://www.cnn.com/2021/10/27/tech/facebook-papers-meaningful-social-interaction-news-feed-math/index.html

Michailidou, A., & Trenz, H.-J. (2021). Rethinking journalism standards in the era of post-truth politics: From truth keepers to truth mediators. *Media, Culture & Society, 43*(7), 1340–1349. https://doi.org/10.1177/01634437211040669

Mihailidis, P., & Viotty, S. (2017). Spreadable spectacle in digital culture: Civic expression, fake news, and the role of media literacies in "post-fact" society. *American Behavioral Scientist, 61*(4), 441–454. https://doi.org/10.1177/0002764217701217

Miller-Idriss, C. (2020). *Hate in the homeland: The new global far right*. Princeton University Press.

Mills, C. W. (1956). *The power elite*. Oxford University Press.

Mitchell, A., Gottfried, J., Kiley, J., & Matsa, K. E. (2014, October 21). *Political polarization and media habits*. Pew Research Center's Journalism Project. https://www.pewresearch.org/journalism/2014/10/21/political-polarization-media-habits/

Mitchell, A., Jurkowitz, M., Oliphant, J. B., & Shearer, E. (2021a, February 22). *Americans who mainly got news via social media knew less about politics and current events, heard more about some unproven stories*. Pew Research Center's Journalism Project. https://www.journalism.org/2021/02/22/americans-who-mainly-got-news-via-social-media-knew-less-about-politics-and-current-events-heard-more-about-some-unproven-stories/

Mitchell, A., Jurkowitz, M., Oliphant, J. B., & Shearer, E. (2021b, February 22). *How Americans navigated the news in 2020: A tumultuous year in review*. Pew Research Center's Journalism

Project. https://www.pewresearch.org/journalism/2021/02/22/how-americans-navigated-the-news-in-2020-a-tumultuous-year-in-review/

Morris, J. S. (2007). Slanted objectivity? Perceived media bias, cable news exposure, and political attitudes. *Social Science Quarterly*, *88*(3), 707–728. https://doi.org/10.1111/j.1540-6237.2007.00479.x

Most visited websites—Top websites ranking for May 2022. (2022, May). Similarweb. https://www.similarweb.com/top-websites/

Motta, M., Stecula, D., & Farhart, C. (2020, May 1). How right-leaning media coverage of COVID-19 facilitated the spread of misinformation in the early stages of the pandemic in the U.S. *Canadian Journal of Political Science/Revue Canadienne de Science Politique*, 1–8. https://doi.org/10.1017/S0008423920000396

Mukerjee, S., Majó-Vázquez, S., & González-Bailón, S. (2018). Networks of audience overlap in the consumption of digital news. *Journal of Communication*, *68*(1), 26–50. https://doi.org/10.1093/joc/jqx007

Muto, J. (2013). *An atheist in the FOXhole: A liberal's eight-year odyssey inside the heart of the right-wing media*. Dutton.

Nadler, A., Crain, M., & Donovan, J. (2018, October 17). Weaponizing the digital influence machine. *Data & Society*. https://datasociety.net/output/weaponizing-the-digital-influence-machine/

Nagy, P., & Neff, G. (2015). Imagined affordance: Reconstructing a keyword for communication theory. *Social Media + Society*, *1*(2), 1–9. https://doi.org/10.1177/2056305115603385

NAM propaganda. (1951, March 5). *New Republic*.

Naylor, B. (2021, February 10). *Read Trump's Jan. 6 speech, a key part of impeachment trial*. NPR. https://www.npr.org/2021/02/10/966396848/read-trumps-jan-6-speech-a-key-part-of-impeachment-trial

Neff, T., & Pickard, V. (2021). Funding democracy: Public media and democratic health in 33 countries. *The International Journal of Press/Politics*, 1–27. https://doi.org/10.1177/19401612211060255

Nelson, J. L., & Taneja, H. (2018). The small, disloyal fake news audience: The role of audience availability in fake news consumption. *New Media & Society*, *20*(10), 3720–3737. https://doi.org/10.1177/1461444818758715

Nelson, J. L., & Webster, J. G. (2017). The myth of partisan selective exposure: A portrait of the online political news audience. *Social Media + Society*, *3*(3), 2056305117729314. https://doi.org/10.1177/2056305117729314

Newman, N., Fletcher, R., Robertson, C. T., Eddy, K., & Nielsen, R. K. (2022). *Digital news report 2022*. Reuters Institute for the Study of Journalism. https://www.digitalnewsreport.org/

Newman, N., Fletcher, R., Schulz, A., Andı, S., Robertson, C. T., & Nielsen, R. K. (2021.) *Reuters Institute digital news report 2021*. Reuters Institute for the Study of Journalism. https://www.digitalnewsreport.org/

Newton, C. (2019a, February 25). The secret lives of Facebook moderators in America. *The Verge*. https://www.theverge.com/2019/2/25/18229714/cognizant-facebook-content-moderator-interviews-trauma-working-conditions-arizona

Newton, C. (2019b, April 26). Why Twitter has been slow to ban White nationalists. *The Verge*. https://www.theverge.com/interface/2019/4/26/18516997/why-doesnt-twitter-ban-nazis-white-nationalism

Newton, C., & Schiffer, Z. (2022, November 10). Inside the Twitter meltdown. *Platformer*. https://www.platformer.news/p/inside-the-twitter-meltdown

Nguyen, C. T. (2018, April 9). Why it's as hard to escape an echo chamber as it is to flee a cult. *Aeon*. https://aeon.co/essays/why-its-as-hard-to-escape-an-echo-chamber-as-it-is-to-flee-a-cult

Nielsen, R. K., & Ganter, S. A. (2022). *The power of platforms: Shaping media and society*. Oxford University Press.

Nissenbaum, A., & Shifman, L. (2017). Internet memes as contested cultural capital: The case of 4chan's /b/ board. *New Media & Society*, *19*(4), 483–501. https://doi.org/10.1177/1461444815609313

Noam, E. M. (2009). *Media ownership and concentration in America*. Oxford University Press.

Noble, S. U. (2018). *Algorithms of oppression: How search engines reinforce racism* (illustrated ed.). NYU Press.

Norteño, C. (2018, November 8). *A few minutes after the incident shown in this video (which doesn't show @Acosta laying hands on anyone, contrary to @PressSec's claims), tweets containing anti-Acosta hashtags such #AcostaAccosts and #AcostaAssaults started appearing. Let's take a look. Cc: @ZellaQuixote https://twitter.com/AltUSPressSec/status/1060380457567694848 ...* [Tweet]. Retrieved November 19, 2018, from @conspirator0. https://twitter.com/conspirator0/status/1060401654086811650?s=11

Notopoulos, K., & Mac, R. (2018, November 2). Twitter is sorry for listing "Kill all Jews" as a trending topic. *BuzzFeed News*. https://www.buzzfeednews.com/article/katienotopoulos/twitter-is-sorry-for-listing-kill-all-jews-as-a-trending

Nyhan, B. (2019, October 31). Americans trust local news. That belief is being exploited. *The New York Times*. https://www.nytimes.com/2019/10/31/upshot/fake-local-news.html

O'Callaghan, D., Greene, D., Conway, M., Carthy, J., & Cunningham, P. (2015). Down the (white) rabbit hole: The extreme right and online recommender systems. *Social Science Computer Review*, 33(4), 459–478. https://doi.org/10.1177/0894439314555329

O'Connell, M. (2014, June 30). Fox News hits 50-quarter ratings streak with Megyn Kelly on the rise, Benghazi still a hot topic. *The Hollywood Reporter*. https://www.hollywoodreporter.com/news/fox-news-exec-talks-50-715660

O'Neil, C. (2017). *Weapons of math destruction: How big data increases inequality and threatens democracy* (reprint ed.). Crown.

Orwell, G. (1982). *Nineteen eighty-four*. Penguin Books.

Papakyriakopoulos, O., Hegelich, S., Shahrezaye, M., & Serrano, J. C. M. (2018). Social media and microtargeting: Political data processing and the consequences for Germany. *Big Data & Society*, 5(2), 1–15. https://doi.org/10.1177/2053951718811844

Pariser, E. (2012). *The filter bubble: How the new personalized web is changing what we read and how we think* (reprint ed.). London: Penguin Books.

Parmelee, J. H. (2014). The agenda-building function of political tweets. *New Media & Society*, 16(3), 434–450.

Peck, R. (2019). *Fox populism: Branding conservatism as working class*. Cambridge University Press.

Peck, R. (2020, August 3). The hate-fueled rise of r/The_Donald—and its epic takedown. *Wired*. https://www.wired.com/story/the-hate-fueled-rise-of-rthe-donald-and-its-epic-takedown/

Penney, J. (2017). *The citizen marketer: Promoting political opinion in the social media age*. Oxford University Press.

Perlman, A. (2012). Rush Limbaugh and the problem of the color line. *Cinema Journal*, 51(4), 198–204. JSTOR.

Perlroth, N. (2019, November 21). A former Fox News executive divides Americans using Russian tactics. *The New York Times*. https://www.nytimes.com/2019/11/21/technology/LaCorte-edition-news.html

Peters, C. (2010). No-spin zones. *Journalism Studies*, 11(6), 832–851. https://doi.org/10.1080/14616701003658390

Peters, J. W. (2022, February 5). Where Fox News and Donald Trump took us. *The New York Times*. https://www.nytimes.com/2022/02/05/business/media/trump-fox-news.html

Petre, C. (2015, May 7). The traffic factories: Metrics at Chartbeat, Gawker Media, and The New York Times. *Columbia Journalism Review*. https://www.cjr.org/tow_center_reports/the_traffic_factories_metrics_at_chartbeat_gawker_media_and_the_new_york_times.php

Pew Research Center. 2010. *State of the news media 2010: An annual report on American journalism*. Pew Project for Excellence in Journalism. https://assets.pewresearch.org/files/journalism/State-of-the-News-Media-Report-2010-FINAL.pdf

Phillips, W. (2018). *The oxygen of amplification*. Data and Society Research Institute. https://datasociety.net/library/oxygen-of-amplification/

Pickard, V. (2014). *America's battle for media democracy: The triumph of corporate libertarianism and the future of media reform*. Cambridge University Press.

Pingree, R. J., Santia, M., Bryanov, K., & Watson, B. K. (2021). Restoring trust in truth-seekers: Effects of op/eds defending journalism and justice. *PLOS ONE, 16*(5), 1–15. https://doi.org/10.1371/journal.pone.0251284

Pomerantsev, P. (2019). *This is not propaganda: Adventures in the war against reality*. PublicAffairs.

Poulsen, K. (2018, December 10). Cambridge Analytica's real role in Trump's dark Facebook campaign. *The Daily Beast*. https://www.thedailybeast.com/cambridge-analyticas-real-role-in-trumps-dark-facebook-campaign

Project for Excellence in Journalism. 2004. *State of the news media 2004*. Pew Research. https://www.pewresearch.org/wp-content/uploads/sites/8/2017/05/State-of-the-News-Media-Report-2004-FINAL.pdf

Rainie, L., & Wellman, B. (2012). *Networked: The new social operating system*. MIT Press.

Red Lion Broadcasting Co. v. FCC, 395 U.S. 367 (1969).

Reed, A., Whittaker, J., Votta, F., & Looney, S. (2019). *Radical filter bubbles: Social media personalisation algorithms and extremist content*. Paper No. 8. Global Research Network on Terrorism and Technology. https://www.academia.edu/42832341/Radical_Filter_Bubbles_Social_Media_Personalisation_Algorithms_and_Extremist_Content

Reid, S. E., & Valasik, M. (2020). *Alt-right gangs: A hazy shade of White*. University of California Press.

Reiman, J., & Leighton, P. (2016). *The rich get richer and the poor get prison: Ideology, class, and criminal justice* (11th ed.). Routledge.

Rhodes, S. C. (2022). Filter bubbles, echo chambers, and fake news: How social media conditions individuals to be less critical of political misinformation. *Political Communication, 39*(1), 1–22. https://doi.org/10.1080/10584609.2021.1910887

Richardson, A. V. (2020). *Bearing witness while Black: African Americans, smartphones, and the new protest #Journalism*. Oxford University Press.

Roberts, S. T. (2019). *Behind the screen: Content moderation in the shadows of social media* (illustrated ed.). Yale University Press.

Robertson, A. (2019, October 25). Mark Zuckerberg is struggling to explain why Breitbart belongs on Facebook News. *The Verge*. https://www.theverge.com/2019/10/25/20932653/facebook-news-breitbart-mark-zuckerberg-statement-bias

Robertson, A. (2020, November 7). Trump will lose his Twitter "public interest" protections in January. *The Verge*. https://www.theverge.com/2020/11/7/21552606/trump-twitter-world-leader-public-interest-exception-ends-january-loss

Robinson, P. (2019). Expanding the field of political communication: Making the case for a fresh perspective through "propaganda studies." *Frontiers in Communication, 4*, Article 26. https://doi.org/10.3389/fcomm.2019.00026

Rodriguez, C. (2001). *Fissures in the mediascape: An international study of citizens' media* (B. Dervin, Ed.; new ed.). Hampton Press.

Rogers, E. M. (2003). *Diffusion of innovations* (5th ed.). Free Press.

Rogers, K. (2019, July 11). Trump uses Twitter to govern. I used it to cover his social media summit. *The New York Times*. https://www.nytimes.com/2019/07/11/us/politics/trump-social-media-summit.html

Rohlinger, D. A., & Bunnage, L. (2017). Did the Tea Party movement fuel the Trump-train? The role of social media in activist persistence and political change in the 21st century. *Social Media + Society, 3*(2), 1–11. https://doi.org/10.1177/2056305117706786

Romm, T. (2019, July 12). White House social media summit not a "one-and-done," Trump's allies say. *Washington Post*. https://www.washingtonpost.com/technology/2019/07/12/white-house-social-media-summit-not-one-and-done-trumps-allies-say/

Rondeaux, C. (2021, June 27). How Trump ally Michael Flynn nurtured—and profited from—the QAnon conspiracy theory. *The Intercept*. https://theintercept.com/2021/06/27/qanon-michael-flynn-digital-soldiers/

Rønlev, R., & Bengtsson, M. (2022). The media provocateur: A rhetorical framework for studying an emerging persona in journalism. *Journalism*, 23(6), 1233–1249. https://doi.org/10.1177/1464884920957166

Roozenbeek, J., van der Linden, S., Goldberg, B., Rathje, S., & Lewandowsky, S. (2022). Psychological inoculation improves resilience against misinformation on social media. *Science Advances*, 8(34), 1–11. https://doi.org/10.1126/sciadv.abo6254

Rosalsky, G. (2020, August 4). *Are conspiracy theories good for Facebook?* NPR. https://www.npr.org/sections/money/2020/08/04/898596655/are-conspiracy-theories-good-for-facebook

Rosen, J. (2003, September 18). The view from nowhere. *PressThink*. http://archive.pressthink.org/2003/09/18/jennings.html

Rosen, J. (2006, June 27). The people formerly known as the audience. *PressThink*. http://archive.pressthink.org/2006/06/27/ppl_frmr.html

Rosen, J. (2009, April 12). He said, she said journalism: Lame formula in the land of the active user. *PressThink*. http://archive.pressthink.org/2009/04/12/hesaid_shesaid.html.

Rosenberg, S. (2019, October 20). How social media rules give politicians a free pass to lie. *Axios*. https://www.axios.com/facebook-twitter-social-media-politicans-misinformation-54703286-a674-4277-92c9-600bf28142f0.html

Rosenwald, B. (2019). *Talk radio's America: How an industry took over a political party that took over the United States.* Harvard University Press.

Rossman, G. (2012). *Climbing the charts: What radio airplay tells us about the diffusion of innovation.* Princeton University Press.

Rothman, J. (2018, November 8). The White House's video of Jim Acosta shows how crude political manipulation can be. *The New Yorker.* https://www.newyorker.com/news/current/the-white-houses-video-of-jim-acosta-shows-how-crude-political-manipulation-can-be

Russell, A. (2016). *Journalism as activism: Recoding media power.* Polity.

Russell, A. (2018). Climate justice, hacktivist sensibilities, prototypes of change. In G Meikle (Ed.), *The Routledge companion to media and activism* (pp. 271-279). Routledge.

Russell, A. (2020). Coming to terms with dysfunctional hybridity: A conversation with Andrew Chadwick on the challenges to liberal democracy in the second-wave networked era. *Studies in Communication Sciences*, 20(2), Article 2. https://doi.org/10.24434/j.scoms.2020.02.005

Sanderson, Z., Brown, M. A., Bonneau, R., Nagler, J., & Tucker, J. A. (2021). Twitter flagged Donald Trump's tweets with election misinformation: They continued to spread both on and off the platform. *Harvard Kennedy School Misinformation Review*, 2(4), 1–19. https://doi.org/10.37016/mr-2020-77

Saslow, E. (2018, November 17). "Nothing on this page is real": How lies become truth in online America. *Washington Post.* https://www.washingtonpost.com/national/nothing-on-this-page-is-real-how-lies-become-truth-in-online-america/2018/11/17/edd44cc8-e85a-11e8-bbdb-72fdbf9d4fed_story.html

Schatzki, T. R., Cetina, K. K., & von Savigny, E. (2001). *The practice turn in contemporary theory.* Routledge.

Scheufele, D. A. (1999). Framing as a theory of media effects. *Journal of Communication*, 49(1), 103–122.

Schill, D., & Hendricks, J. A. (2016). Media, message, and mobilization: Political communication in the 2014 election campaigns. In J. A. Hendricks & D. Schill (Eds.), *Communication and midterm elections: Media, message, and mobilization* (pp. 3–23). Palgrave Macmillan. https://doi.org/10.1057/9781137488015_1

Schleifer, T. (2019, September 26). Facebook and YouTube will keep letting politicians say what they want if it's "newsworthy." *Vox.* https://www.vox.com/recode/2019/9/26/20885783/facebook-twitter-youtube-policies-political-content

Schradie, J. (2019). *The revolution that wasn't: How digital activism favors conservatives.* Harvard University Press.

Schroeder, E., & Stone, D. F. (2015). Fox News and political knowledge. *Journal of Public Economics*, *126*, 52–63. https://doi.org/10.1016/j.jpubeco.2015.03.009

Schroeder, R. (2018). Rethinking digital media and political change. *Convergence*, *24*(2), 168–183. https://doi.org/10.1177/1354856516660666

Schudson, M. (1978). *Discovering the news: A social history of American newspapers*. Basic Books.

Schwartz, I. (2019, July 11). Sebastian Gorka confronts Playboy's WH reporter taunting Trump social media guests: "You're a punk." *Real Clear Politics*. https://www.realclearpolitics.com/video/2019/07/11/sebastian_gorka_confronts_playboys_wh_reporter_taunting_trump_social_media_guests_youre_a_punk.html

Schwartz, O. (2018, November 12). You thought fake news was bad? Deep fakes are where truth goes to die. *The Guardian*. https://www.theguardian.com/technology/2018/nov/12/deep-fakes-fake-news-truth

Searles, K., & Banda, K. K. (2019). But her emails! How journalistic preferences shaped election coverage in 2016. *Journalism*, *20*(8), 1052–1069. https://doi.org/10.1177/1464884919845459

Shane, S., & Blinder, A. (2019, January 7). Democrats faked online push to outlaw alcohol in Alabama race. *The New York Times*. https://www.nytimes.com/2019/01/07/us/politics/alabama-senate-facebook-roy-moore.html

Shearer, E. (2018, December 10). *Social media outpaces print newspapers in the U.S. as a news source*. Pew Research Center. https://www.pewresearch.org/fact-tank/2018/12/10/social-media-outpaces-print-newspapers-in-the-u-s-as-a-news-source/

Shearer, E. (2021, January 12). *86% of Americans get news online from smartphone, computer or tablet*. Pew Research Center. https://www.pewresearch.org/fact-tank/2021/01/12/more-than-eight-in-ten-americans-get-news-from-digital-devices/

Shehata, A., & Strömbäck, J. (2013). Not (yet) a new era of minimal effects: A study of agenda setting at the aggregate and individual levels. *The International Journal of Press/Politics*, *18*(2), 234–255. https://doi.org/10.1177/1940161212473831

Sherman, G. (2014). *The loudest voice in the room: How the brilliant, bombastic Roger Ailes built Fox News—and divided a country*. Random House.

Shirky, C. (2009). *Here comes everybody: The power of organizing without organizations* (reprint ed.). Penguin Books.

Shoemaker, P. J., & Vos, T. (2009). *Gatekeeping theory*. Routledge.

Shove, E., Pantzar, M., & Watson, M. (2012). *The dynamics of social practice: Everyday life and how it changes*. Sage.

Siapera, E. (2022). AI content moderation, racism and (de)coloniality. *International Journal of Bullying Prevention*, *4*(1), 55–65. https://doi.org/10.1007/s42380-021-00105-7

Simonov, A., Sacher, S. K., Dubé, J.-P. H., & Biswas, S. (2020). *The persuasive effect of Fox News: Non-compliance with social distancing during the Covid-19 pandemic*. Working Paper No. 27237. National Bureau of Economic Research. https://doi.org/10.3386/w27237

Sink, J., & Jacobs, J. (2018, November 7). White House suspends CNN reporter Jim Acosta's press ass. *Bloomberg*. https://www.bloomberg.com/news/articles/2018-11-07/defiant-trump-knew-sessions-was-gone-as-he-ducked-blame-for-loss

Sobieraj, S. (2020). *Credible Threat: Attacks Against Women Online and the Future of Democracy*. Oxford University Press.

Soules, M. (2015). *Media, persuasion and propaganda*. Edinburgh University Press.

Stanley, J. (2016). *How propaganda works* (reprint ed.). Princeton University Press.

Starr, P. (2004). *The creation of the media: Political origins of modern communications*. Basic Books.

Statista. (2022, February 18). *Facebook: Annual revenue*. https://www.statista.com/statistics/268604/annual-revenue-of-facebook/

Stephansen, H. C., & Treré, E. (2019). Practice what you preach? Currents, connections and challenges in theorizing citizen media and practice (pp. 1–34). In H. C. Stephansen & E. Treré (Eds.), *Citizen media and practice: Currents, connections, challenges*. Routledge. http://orca.cf.ac.uk/124359/

Stoddard, E., & Collins, J. (2016). *Social and cultural foundations in global studies*. Taylor & Francis.
Strömbäck, J. (2005). In search of a standard: Four models of democracy and their normative implications for journalism. *Journalism Studies*, 6(3), 331–345. https://doi.org/10.1080/14616700500131950
Subramanian, S. (2017, February 15). Meet the Macedonian teens who mastered fake news and corrupted the US election. *Wired*. https://www.wired.com/2017/02/veles-macedonia-fake-news/
Susser, D., Roessler, B., & Nissenbaum, H. (2019). Technology, autonomy, and manipulation. *Internet Policy Review*, 8(2), 1–22. https://policyreview.info/articles/analysis/technology-autonomy-and-manipulation
Swartz, D. (1997). *Culture and power: The sociology of Pierre Bourdieu*. University of Chicago Press.
Talbot, P. (2019, September 20). Twitter removes thousands of accounts for manipulating its platform. NPR. https://www.npr.org/2019/09/20/762799187/twitter-removes-thousands-of-accounts-for-manipulating-their-platform
Tandoc Jr., E. C. (2019). The facts of fake news: A research review. *Sociology Compass*, 13(9), 1–9. https://doi.org/10.1111/soc4.12724
Tandoc Jr., E. C., Lim, Z. W., & Ling, R. (2018). Defining "fake news." *Digital Journalism*, 6(2), 137–153. https://doi.org/10.1080/21670811.2017.1360143
Tandoc, E. C., & Vos, T. P. (2016). The journalist is marketing the news. *Journalism Practice*, 10(8), 950–966. https://doi.org/10.1080/17512786.2015.1087811
Tarrow, S. (2008). Charles Tilly and the practice of contentious politics. *Social Movement Studies*, 7(3), 225–246. https://doi.org/10.1080/14742830802485601
Telecommunications Act of 1996. (2013, June 20). Federal Communications Commission. https://www.fcc.gov/general/telecommunications-act-1996
Terkildsen, N., & Schnell, F. (1997). How media frames move public opinion: An analysis of the women's movement. *Political Research Quarterly*, 50(4), 879–900. https://doi.org/10.2307/448991
Thompson, J. (1995). *The media and modernity: A social theory of the media*. Stanford University Press.
Tilly, C. (2008). *Contentious performances*. Cambridge University Press. https://doi.org/10.1017/CBO9780511804366
Tilly, C., & Tarrow, S. (2006). *Contentious politics*. Oxford University Press.
Timberg, C. (2020, February 20). How conservatives learned to wield power inside Facebook. *Washington Post*. https://www.washingtonpost.com/technology/2020/02/20/facebook-republican-shift/
Timberg, C., & Dwoskin, E. (2020, June 29). Reddit closes long-running forum supporting President Trump after years of policy violations. *Washington Post*. https://www.washingtonpost.com/technology/2020/06/29/reddit-closes-long-running-forum-supporting-president-trump-after-years-policy-violations/
Tobin, A., Varner, M., & Angwin, J. (2017, December 28). Facebook's uneven enforcement of hate speech rules allows vile posts to stay up. *ProPublica*. https://www.propublica.org/article/facebook-enforcement-hate-speech-rules-mistakes?token=lJNvxxuh75EINCaEK1u64Xa0hzhPQaml
Treré, E. (2015). Reclaiming, proclaiming, and maintaining collective identity in the #YoSoy132 movement in Mexico: An examination of digital frontstage and backstage activism through social media and instant messaging platforms. *Information, Communication & Society*, 18(8), 901–915. https://doi.org/10.1080/1369118X.2015.1043744
Tripodi, F. (2018, May 16). Searching for alternative facts. *Data & Society*. https://datasociety.net/output/searching-for-alternative-facts/
Tripodi, F., & Ma, Y. (2022). You've got mail: How the Trump administration used legislative communication to frame his last year in office. *Information, Communication & Society*, 25(5), 669–689. https://doi.org/10.1080/1369118X.2021.2020873

Trump, D. (2019). *Remarks by President Trump at the presidential social media summit* [Transcript]. https://www.whitehouse.gov/briefings-statements/remarks-president-trump-presidential-social-media-summit/

Tsfati, Y., Boomgaarden, H. G., Strömbäck, J., Vliegenthart, R., Damstra, A., & Lindgren, E. (2020). Causes and consequences of mainstream media dissemination of fake news: Literature review and synthesis. *Annals of the International Communication Association*, 44(2), 157–173. https://doi.org/10.1080/23808985.2020.1759443

Tucker, J. A., Guess, A., Barberá, P., Vaccari, C., Siegel, A., Sanovich, S., Stukal, D., & Nyhan, B. (2018). Social media, political polarization, and political disinformation: A review of the scientific literature. Hewlett Foundation. https://hewlett.org/library/social-media-political-polarization-political-disinformation-review-scientific-literature/

Tufekci, Z. (2017a). *Twitter and tear gas: The power and fragility of networked protest*. Yale University Press.

Tufekci, Z. (2017b). *We're building a dystopia just to make people click on ads*. TED Talks. https://www.ted.com/talks/zeynep_tufekci_we_re_building_a_dystopia_just_to_make_people_click_on_ads

Tufekci, Z. (2018, March 11). Opinion: YouTube, the great radicalizer. *The New York Times*. https://www.nytimes.com/2018/03/10/opinion/sunday/youtube-politics-radical.html

Turcotte, J., York, C., Irving, J., Scholl, R. M., & Pingree, R. J. (2015). News recommendations from social media opinion leaders: Effects on media trust and information seeking. *Journal of Computer-Mediated Communication*, 20(5), 520–535. https://doi.org/10.1111/jcc4.12127

Tworek, H. J. S. (2021). Fighting hate with speech law: Media and German visions of democracy. *The Journal of Holocaust Research*, 35(2), 106–122. https://doi.org/10.1080/25785648.2021.1899510

Tyko, K. (2020, October 26). Trump tweet about problems with mail-in ballots quickly labeled by Twitter as misleading. *USA TODAY*. https://www.usatoday.com/story/tech/2020/10/26/donald-trump-twitter-mail-ballots-election-tweet-misleading/6049734002/

U.S. Census Bureau. (2015). *American FactFinder—results*. Retrieved November 29, 2017, from https://factfinder.census.gov/faces/tableservices/jsf/pages/productview.xhtml?src=bkmk

Vailshery, L. S. (2022, November 22). *IoT connected devices worldwide 2019-2030*. Statista. https://www.statista.com/statistics/1183457/iot-connected-devices-worldwide/

Van Duyn, E., & Collier, J. (2019). Priming and fake news: The effects of elite discourse on evaluations of news media. *Mass Communication and Society*, 22(1), 29–48. https://doi.org/10.1080/15205436.2018.1511807

Van Sant, S. (2018, October 27). What's known about Robert Bowers, the suspect in the Pittsburgh synagogue shooting. NPR. website: https://www.npr.org/2018/10/27/661409410/whats-known-about-robert-bowers-the-suspect-in-the-pittsburgh-synagogue-shooting

Vargo, C. J., Guo, L., & Amazeen, M. A. (2018). The agenda-setting power of fake news: A big data analysis of the online media landscape from 2014 to 2016. *New Media & Society*, 20(5), 2028–2049. https://doi.org/10.1177/1461444817712086

Villi, M., Grönlund, M., Linden, C.-G., Lehtisaari, K., Mierzejewska, B., Picard, R. G., & Röpnack, A. (2019). "They're a little bit squeezed in the middle": Strategic challenges for innovation in US Metropolitan newspaper organisations. *Journal of Media Business Studies*, 17(1), 33–50. https://doi.org/10.1080/16522354.2019.1630099

Vogels, E. A. (2022, May 13). *Support for more regulation of tech companies has declined in U.S., especially among Republicans*. Pew Research Center. https://www.pewresearch.org/short-reads/2022/05/13/support-for-more-regulation-of-tech-companies-has-declined-in-u-s-especially-among-republicans/

Vos, T. P., & Craft, S. (2016). The discursive construction of journalistic transparency. *Journalism Studies*, 18(12), 1505–1522. http://www.tandfonline.com/doi/abs/10.1080/1461670X.2015.1135754

Vos, T. P., Thomas, R. J., & Tandoc Jr., E. C. (2023). Constructing the legitimacy of journalists' marketing role. *Journalism Studies*, 24(6), 763–782. https://doi.org/10.1080/1461670X.2023.2187650

Vosoughi, S., Roy, D., & Aral, S. (2018). The spread of true and false news online. *Science*, 359(6380), 1146–1151. https://doi.org/10.1126/science.aap9559

Wagner, K. (2021, September 21). Facebook says it has spent $13 billion on safety and security efforts since 2016. *Fortune*. https://fortune.com/2021/09/21/facebook-says-it-has-spent-13-billion-on-safety-and-security-efforts-since-2016/

Waisbord, S. (2016). Media sociology. In E. W. Rothenbuhler, J. D. Pooley, K. B. Jensen, & R. T. Craig (Eds.), *The international encyclopedia of communication theory and philosophy* (vol. 3, pp. 1167–1185). John Wiley & Sons. https://doi.org/10.1002/9781118766804.wbiect161

Wardle, C. (2017, February 16). Fake news. It's complicated. *First Draft*. https://medium.com/1st-draft/fake-news-its-complicated-d0f773766c79

Wardle, C., & Derakshan, H. (2017). *Information disorder: Toward an interdisciplinary framework for research and policy making*. Council of Europe. https://www.coe.int/en/web/freedom-expression/information-disorder#{%2235128646%22:[0]}

Warner, B. R., & Neville-Shepard, R. (2014). Echoes of a conspiracy: Birthers, truthers, and the cultivation of extremism. *Communication Quarterly*, 62(1), 1–17. https://doi.org/10.1080/01463373.2013.822407

Waters, G., & Postings, R. (2018). *Spiders of the caliphate: Mapping the Islamic State's global support network on Facebook*. Counter Extremism Project. https://www.counterextremism.com/sites/default/files/Spiders%20of%20the%20Caliphate%20%28May%202018%29.pdf

Watson, P. J. (2018, November 8). 1) The video was not "doctored" by me—All I did was zoom in on the original from the Daily Wire. I did not "speed up" anything. The screenshot from Sony Vegas Pro here proves that. 2) I am not a "White supremacist." 3) Retract these lies.pic.twitter.com/XHghtziCMo [Tweet]. Retrieved January 18, 2019, from @PrisonPlanet. https://twitter.com/PrisonPlanet/status/1060521980615634944

Weber, M. (1958). *From Max Weber: Essays in sociology* (H. H. Gerth & C. W. Mills, Eds.). Oxford University Press.

Weeks, B. E., Ksiazek, T. B., & Holbert, R. L. (2016). Partisan enclaves or shared media experiences? A network approach to understanding citizens' political news environments. *Journal of Broadcasting & Electronic Media*, 60(2), 248–268. https://doi.org/10.1080/08838151.2016.1164170

Weeks, B. E., Lane, D. S., Kim, D. H., Lee, S. S., & Kwak, N. (2017). Incidental exposure, selective exposure, and political information sharing: Integrating online exposure patterns and expression on social media. *Journal of Computer-Mediated Communication*, 22(6), 363–379. https://doi.org/10.1111/jcc4.12199

Weiss, Philip, P. (2006, January 6). The rise of Craigslist and how it's killing your newspaper. *New York Magazine*. http://nymag.com/nymetro/news/media/internet/15500/

Wemple, E. (2019, March 26). Opinion: Bill O'Reilly heading back to radio. *Washington Post*. https://www.washingtonpost.com/opinions/2019/03/26/bill-oreilly-heading-back-radio/

White House hosting social media summit following fresh allegations of anti-conservative bias. (2019, July 11). *Fox News*. http://video.foxnews.com/v/6057828722001/

Winner, L. (2013). Propaganda and dissociation from truth. In H. M. Jerónimo, J. L. Garcia, & C. Mitcham (Eds.), *Jacques Ellul and the technological society in the 21st century* (pp. 99–113). Springer Netherlands. https://doi.org/10.1007/978-94-007-6658-7_8

Winston, J. (2016, November 18). How the Trump campaign built an identity database and used Facebook ads to win the election. *Medium*. https://medium.com/startup-grind/how-the-trump-campaign-built-an-identity-database-and-used-facebook-ads-to-win-the-election-4ff7d24269ac#.xpwe08w8b

Woolley, S. C., & Howard, P. N. (Eds.). (2018). *Computational propaganda: Political parties, politicians, and political manipulation on social media*. Oxford University Press.

Wu, T. (2017). *The attention merchants: The epic scramble to get inside our heads*. Atlantic Books.

Yglesias, M. (2018, October 23). The hack gap: How and why conservative nonsense dominates American politics. *Vox.* https://www.vox.com/2018/10/23/18004478/hack-gap-explained

York, J. C. (2014, September 29). Facebook's "real names" policy is legal, but it's also problematic for free speech. *The Guardian.* http://www.theguardian.com/commentisfree/2014/sep/29/facebooks-real-names-policy-is-legal-but-its-also-problematic-for-free-speech

Young America's Foundation (Director). (2016, November 14). *Lieutenant General Michael T. Flynn.* https://www.youtube.com/watch?v=W0CThXL37Jk

Zaller, J. (2003). A new standard of news quality: Burglar alarms for the monitorial citizen. *Political Communication, 20*(2), 109–130. https://doi.org/10.1080/10584600390211136

Zarouali, B., Dobber, T., De Pauw, G., & de Vreese, C. (2020). Using a personality-profiling algorithm to investigate political microtargeting: Assessing the persuasion effects of personality-tailored ads on social media. *Communication Research, 49*(8), 1066–1091. https://doi.org/10.1177/0093650220961965

Zeeuw, D. de, Hagen, S., Peeters, S., & Jokubauskaite, E. (2020). Tracing normiefication: A cross-platform analysis of the QAnon conspiracy theory. *First Monday, 25*(11). https://doi.org/10.5210/fm.v25i11.10643

Zelizer, B. (1993). Journalists as interpretive communities. *Critical Studies in Mass Communication, 10*(3), 219–237. https://doi.org/10.1080/15295039309366865

Zollmann, F. (2017). Bringing propaganda back into news media studies. *Critical Sociology, 45*(3), 329–345.. https://doi.org/10.1177/0896920517731134

Zuboff, S. (2019). *The age of surveillance capitalism: The fight for a human future at the new frontier of power.* PublicAffairs.

Index

For the benefit of digital users, indexed terms that span two pages (e.g., 52–53) may, on occasion, appear on only one of those pages.

Note: Figures are indicated by an italic *f* following the page number.

Acosta, Jim, 12, 68, 77, 78–79, 83–97, 142–43
activist media
  ad-hoc activists, 142
  digital activists, 10, 63, 98–100, 105, 120*f*, 120–22, 121*f*, 126
  media power and, 138
  political activists, 28, 42, 73–74, 138
  practice-oriented approach to, 24
  social movements and, 28
  volunteer activists, 75–76
ad-hoc activists, 142
affordances
  The_Donald (TD) platform and, 108–9
  of ICTs, 135–36, 137–38
  media power, 20–22, 66
affordance theory, 10–11, 136
agenda-building, 67–68, 143
agenda-setting, 4–5, 6–7, 13, 24–25, 39–40, 47, 67–68, 80–81, 100, 103–6, 128–30, 141
Ailes, Roger, 24–25, 44
algorithm, 27–28, 29–30, 37–38, 56, 66, 68–69, 71–73, 89–90, 99, 109, 122, 137–38
algorithmic amplification, 27–28, 29–30, 53–54, 63–64, 71–72, 90, 113–14, 135–36
alternative media (alt-tech), 13, 37, 66–67, 99–100, 106–8
alt-right, 13, 77, 102–4, 106, 112, 115–16, 117–22, 130–31, 145
alt-tech. *See* alternative media
artificial intelligence (AI), 152–53
attention-hacking. *See* persuasion and attention-hacking
attention merchants, 95
audience segmentation, 68–71

Bagdikian, Ben, 40
Bannon, Steve, 141
Benkler, Yochai, 4
Bernays, Edward, 66
Berry, Jeffrey, 7
bigotry on The_Donald (TD) platform, 113, 114, 130–31
Big Tech, 62–75
Boorstin, Daniel, 3
bots, 6, 27–28, 80–81, 122–23, 152–53
broadcast media, 10, 33–34, 48, 49–50, 63, 136–37
Bush, George H. W., 44

cable news, 4, 5, 33, 37, 43, 54
Cambridge Analytica, 57–58
Capella, Joseph, 42
capital
  Bourdieusian conception of, 8
  celebrity, 22–23
  economic, 17, 22, 125–26
  formation of, 11
  media manipulation and, 28–30
  media meta-capital, 9–10, 22–23, 127–28
  media-related capital, 11, 16, 22–25, 34, 40–41, 44, 143–44
  networked media capital, 9–10, 23–24, 100–6
  Nguyen, C. Thi, 39
  political field and, 144–46
  potential for, 24
  social, 17, 22, 48, 74–75, 125
  symbolic, 17, 22, 48–49, 86–91, 96, 126
  theorizing on, 10–11
  See also networked media capital

189

Index

capital-building, 75, 100, 112, 115–16, 119–26, 128, 129, 131
capitalism, 52–53, 57–58, 62, 137
celebrity capital, 22–23
Chadwick, Andrew, 2–3, 18–19, 25
Chomsky, Noam, 10–11, 15, 128
citizen journalists, 5, 135
clickbait, 47, 73, 81–82, 94, 162n.2
Clinton, Bill, 44
CNN, 12, 44–45, 68, 77–78, 85, 91, 93, 95–96, 142–43
collective identity, 63, 73–74, 98, 99–103, 113
Communications Decency Act (1966), 54, 156
conservative talk radio, 39–43
conspiracy theories, 47, 51–52, 82, 112–13, 114–16, 118, 130–31
coordinated inauthentic behavior, 27–28, 59–60, 96–97, 139
Couldry, Nick, 9–10, 19–20, 22–25
COVID-19 pandemic, 45, 100–1
cultural capital, 17, 22, 48, 126
custodians of conscience, 36, 154–55

Daily Wire, 77, 86, 89, 90*f*, 92, 96–97, 162n.1
dark ads, 57–58, 70–71
data voids, 73
deception, 8–9, 16, 26–28, 31–32, 94, 139–40, 144–45
deep disagreements, 38, 147–48
deliberative democracy, 10, 16, 36, 39, 66, 135, 154
democratic communication, 135–36, 138, 146–47, 150
democratization of news, 35–36
dialectics of (dis)information, 146–50, 148*f*
digital activists, 10, 13, 63, 98–100, 105, 120–22, 120*f*, 121*f*, 126
digital army of Trump Donald. *See* The_Donald (TD) platform
digital ethnographic content analysis (DECA), 107
(dis)information
  defined, 26–27
  dialectics of, 146–50, 148*f*
  false information, 4, 26–27, 53–54, 71, 95
  introduction to, 10, 13, 77–79
  as problematic information, 135–36, 147–48, 148*f*, 150–51, 152
  social media and, 1–3, 51–62
  Trump, Donald and, 112, 126
  See also social media (dis)information
(dis)trust, 42–43, 147–49. *See also* trustworthiness
The_Donald (TD) platform
  agenda-setting and, 100, 103–6, 128–30
  bigotry and hatred on, 113, 114, 130–31
  communication and affordances, 108–9
  conspiracy theories by, 112–13, 114–16, 118, 130–31
  digital activists and, 13, 98–100, 105, 120–22, 120*f*, 121*f*, 126
  divisions of labor and, 116–28, 117*f*
  hypermasculinity on, 113, 114, 130–31
  introduction to, 8, 13, 98–100
  meaning and audience, 109–12, 110*f*, 111*f*
  media manipulation on, 100, 102–5, 106–28, 130–33
  media practice and, 128–33
  misinformation on, 99
  networked media capital and, 100–6
  themes and practices, 112–28
Dorsey, Jack, 3
doxa, 130, 131, 135, 140–41, 145–46, 157

echo chambers, 34, 37–39, 44–45
economic capital, 17, 22, 125–26
epistemic bubbles, 37–38, 98, 109

Facebook News, 3
Fairness Doctrine (1987), 37, 39, 54, 155–56
fake news, 16, 26–27, 34–36, 80
false information, 4, 26–27, 53–54, 71, 95. *See also* (dis)information
Farris, Robert, 4
Federal Communications Commission (FCC), 39
flak wars, 155
Flynn, Michael, 118
Fox News
  birth of, 43–45
  establishment media skepticism, 37–38
  influence of, 4
  O'Reilly, Bill, 33–34
  problematic information and, 97
  propaganda broadcasting and, 24–25
  social media and, 4
framing, 3, 6–7, 39, 42–43, 61, 67–68, 86, 92, 104–5

GamerGate, 105–6, 129–30
gatecrashing, 21, 63, 104, 138, 147
gatekeepers/gatekeeping, 21, 38–39, 40–41, 48–49, 56, 61, 63, 66–68, 71, 80, 135–38, 141, 149–50, 153–54, 156–58
gatewatching, 42–43, 94–95
Global Data Protection Regulation (GDPR), 153
Google, 1–2, 4, 21, 30, 41, 46, 55, 56–58, 152–53
Gorka, Sebastian, 5

habitus, 22–23, 100–1, 107, 131, 140–42, 145–46
hack gap, 24–25, 152
Hannity, Sean, 41
hashtags, 74, 77, 105, 119, 123

hash-targeting, 106, 123, 130, 145
hatred on The_Donald (TD) platform, 113, 114, 130–31
Herman, Edward, 10–11, 15, 128
Holiday, Ryan, 144–46
hypermasculinity on The_Donald (TD) platform, 113, 114, 130–31

identity, collective, 63, 73–74, 98, 99–103, 113
information and communication technologies (ICTs), 135–36, 137–38, 142
information disorder, 79
information sharing, 114–15
information warfare, 4, 98, 115–19, 122, 124
informative communication, 25–26
Internet of Things (IoT), 57
interpretive communities, 45–47

Jamieson, Kathleen Hall, 42
Johnson, Benny, 1–2
Journalism as Activism (Russell), 24

Kaplan, Joel, 53–54
Kaplan, Richard, 35
Karem, Brian, 5
Kirk, Charlie, 4

LaCorte News, 82–83
legacy media, 11, 56–57, 62–64, 104, 114, 136–37, 142, 144, 147, 156
Lexis Nexis, 5
liberal bias, 2, 3, 42, 43, 81, 142, 154–55
Limbaugh, Rush, 33–34, 39–40, 41–42, 43

manipulation. *See* media manipulation
Manufacturing Consent (Herman, Chomsky), 15, 128
Marwick, Alice, 79–80
mass communication, 21
mass media, 9–11, 21, 31, 34, 39, 48–50, 101, 155–56
media attention, 3, 6–7, 47, 85, 105, 129, 144–45
media capital, , 24, 48–49, 127–28. *See also* capital; networked media capital
Media Cloud, 83–93
media manipulation
 capital and, 28–30
 defined, 26–27
 on The_Donald (TD) platform, 100, 102–5, 106–28, 130–33
 practices of, 139–46
 problematic information and, 25–28
 resources for, 8–9
 social media (dis)information and, 65–68
media meta-capital, 9–10, 22–23, 127–28
media monopolies, 40

media power
 affordances and, 20–22, 66
 debates over, 18–19
 in democratically oriented societies, 15
 future of, 150–59
 hybrid media systems and, 16–18
 introduction to, 11, 15–16, 134–36
 overview, 136–39
 practice theory, 20–22, 30–32, 139–46
 problematic information and, 16, 30–32
 social media (dis)information and, 62–75
 structured practice and, 19–20
media-related capital, 11, 16, 22–25, 34, 40–41, 44, 143–44
media spectacle, 4–5, 7
mediated public sphere, 11, 141. *See also* public awareness
mediatization
 defined, 7
 media capital and, 144
 media power and, 11, 30–32
 of political communication, 6–9, 66–67
mediatized superstructure, 75, 132–33, 138
metadiscourse, 100, 107–8, 114–15, 132–33, 152
microtargeting, 65, 68–71, 80–81
misinformation, 26–27, 53–54, 61, 66, 77–78, 99, 149–50, 153–54
misogyny, 41, 59, 113
moderation of social media (dis)information, 58–62
moral panic, 16, 69, 150
Murdoch, Rupert, 44
Musk, Elon, xi, 3, 152–53, 157

networked habitus, 22–23, 131, 141–42
networked media capital, 9–10, 23–24, 49–50, 96, 100–6
Nguyen, C. Thi, 39
Nixon, Richard, 44

O'Keefe, James, 1–2
O'Reilly, Bill, 33–34
organized persuasive communication (OPC), 10–11, 17–18, 26–28, 30
outrage discourse, 7
Overton window, 130

partisan press/news media
 brief history, 34–37
 conservative talk radio, 39–43
 (dis)trust and, 42–43, 147–49
 interpretive communities and, 45–47
 introduction to, 11, 33–34
 mass media manipulation, 48–50
 media ecosystem changes, 37–39
persuasion architecture, 56–57, 58

persuasive communication. *See* organized persuasive communication
Pew Research Center, 62–63
polarization, 37–38, 61–62, 79–80, 94, 134–35, 153–54
political action committees (PACs), 89
political activists, 28, 42, 73–74, 138
political communication
  digital activists and, 101–3, 104, 118–19, 131, 132–33
  mediatization of, 6–10, 66–67
  problematic information and, 16, 17–18, 23, 26–27, 31
  social media (dis)information, 57–58, 63–64, 66–67, 71, 75–76
  understanding of, 139–43, 150, 153–54, 155–56
political participation, 17–18, 150
political right, 2, 4, 8, 24–25, 31, 49, 55, 77, 113, 138, 149, 151–52
populists/populism, 33, 41, 49, 89–90, 98–99, 129, 162n.5
practices of manipulation, 139–46
practice theory, 20–22, 30–32, 139–46
pre-bunking, 149–50
problematic information
  case study on, 77, 78–79, 83–97, 85f, 87f, 88f
  critical examination of, 146–50, 148f
  deception, 8–9, 16, 26–28, 31–32, 94, 139–40, 144–45
  defined, 26–27
  (dis)information as, 135–36, 147–48, 148f, 150–51, 152
  interpretive approach to, 79–80
  introduction to, 15–16, 77–79
  meaning and visibility in, 80–83
  media manipulation and, 25–30
  media power and, 16, 30–32
  misinformation as, 26–27, 53–54, 61, 66, 77–78, 149–50, 153–54
propaganda
  advancements in, 57–58
  broadcasters of, 24–25
  defined, 25–26
  evolution of, 11
  feed-back loops, 4, 46–47, 104–5
  problematic information and, 25–28
  undemocratic, 26
pseudo-events, 3, 5, 80–81, 144–45
pseudo-journalism, 4, 41, 49
public awareness, 3, 4, 23–24, 60–61, 70–71, 106, 142–43, 149–50
public relations (PR), 66, 80–81, 144–45, 157

QAnon, 77, 89–91, 100, 103, 112–13, 116–19, 117f, 129, 163n.2

racism, 41, 48–49, 59, 98, 103, 113
rational-critical debate, 35
Raw Story, 90, 93
repertoires of communication, 28, 130, 139–40, 163n.10
repertoires of manipulation, 16, 28–30, 29f, 52–53, 65, 71–72, 139–40
Roberts, Hal, 4
Rogers, Katie, 2
Russell, Adrienne, 24
Russia's Internet Research Agency, 64–65

Sanders, Sarah, 77
Schradie, Jen, 101–2
Schudson, Michael, 36–37
search engine optimization (SEO), 6, 49, 73, 152–53
sensationalism, 7, 36–37, 39, 47, 49, 80–81, 82, 89–90, 93–96, 106, 130, 155
September 11, 2001, terrorist attacks, 44
set spaces, 99–100, 105, 106, 111–12, 131, 135–36
shadow-banning, 2
Shapiro, Ben, 89
Sobieraj, Sarah, 7
social action, 8, 20, 23, 125–26, 128
social capital, 17, 22, 48, 74–75, 125
social media (dis)information
  audience segmentation, 68–71
  Big Tech and, 62–75
  coordination and mobilization, 73–75
  dark ads, 57–58, 70–71
  introduction to, 10, 13, 51–62
  manipulative practices, 65–68
  media power and, 62–75
  microtargeting in, 65, 68–71, 80–81
  moderation of, 58–62
  persuasion and, 55–58
  political communication and, 57–58, 63–64, 66–67, 71, 75–76
  reach and amplification of, 71–73
social movements, 10–11, 16, 17–18, 28, 73–74, 101–3, 131
social theory, 18, 19–20
sock puppets, 6, 81, 123, 153–54
structured practice, 19–20
surveillance and persuasion, 55–58
surveillance capitalism, 52–53, 57–58, 62, 137
symbolic capital, 17, 22, 48–49, 86–91, 96, 126

talk radio. *See* conservative talk radio
Tea Party, 100, 101–3
Telecommunications Act (1996), 40
trading up the chain, 27–28, 68, 144–45

Tripodi, Francesca, 46
trolls/trolling, 1–2, 12, 60–61, 64–65, 102, 103–4, 106, 115–17, 118–19, 122, 123, 130, 131–32, 163n.6
Trump, Donald
   election campaign strategy, 57–58
   Limbaugh, Rush and, 41
   media coverage manipulation by, 47
   social media summit and, 1–3, 4–6
   U.S. Capitol riots/storming, 12, 51–52
   voter fraud claims, 60–61
   See also The_Donald platform
trustworthiness, 21, 42–43, 64, 73, 138–39, 142, 147–48, 149–50, 154–55. *See also* (dis)trust

undemocratic propaganda, 26
U.S. Capitol riots/storming (2021), 12, 51–52, 99, 103
U.S. hybrid media, 30–32

volunteer activists, 75–76

Watson, Paul Joseph, 77
White supremacism, 74, 102–3

xenophobia, 59, 89–90, 98, 113

Yglesias, Matthew, 24–25

Zuckerberg, Mark, 3, 53–54